C000139163

Devi's Emerald

Ruzbeh Nari Bharucha

Credits

Edited by:
Cher Commissariat, Absa Bapunhi

Front & Back Cover:
Hanoze F Boga, Niranjan M Railkar

Inside Covers:
Satya Banerji

Page Layout:
Ramadevi R Kutty, Rohan S Somnath

Desktop publishing:
Meena Exports (Digital Publication & Software)

First Edition 2002

Copyright © **Shree Mookambika Bhakta Mandali**
No. 840, 13th Cross Road
Mahalakshmi Layout, Bangalore 560 086
Ph: (080) 3491861/3490912

ISBN 81-87111-56-9

Price: Rs. 250

Published by:
Bimal A. Mehta
for Vakils, Feffer & Simons Ltd.
Hague Building, 9 Sprott Road
Ballard Estate, Mumbai 400 001, India

Printed by:
Arun K. Mehta
Vakil & Sons Pvt. Ltd.
Industry Manor
Appasaheb Marathe Marg,
Worli, Mumbai 400 025, India

To Ma Mookambika,

Sai Baba of Shirdi

&

All the Perfect Masters

Khshnaothra Ahura Mazdao
Panamé Yazdan
Jasamé Avangahé Mazdao

Sai Baba of Shirdi

"Sai Baba of Shirdi has sent you to me!" It was not a question. Swamiji leaned on the bed and looked deep into my eyes. "Isn't it?"

"Yes..."

"You have a birth mark near the right shoulder!" Once again it was not a query, but stated as matter of fact. Well, the birthmark was certainly present. In fact, its presence hurt like the dickens as my daughter, just a few days ago, to express her deep love, regard and solidarity with me, had sunk her teeth into my flesh and had tried real hard to bite away the damned birthmark from my body. "In fact between your shoulders."

I was rather confounded. I looked at my publisher, friend and well wisher, Sunit Banerji for some explanation.

"You see, Sunit, this boy has always wondered and doubted as to whether Sai Baba of Shirdi communicates through him. He wonders why? He does not realise that it is because Sai Baba has been his Guru since many lifetimes. Yes! Sai Baba has been his Guru and Guide since ages. That is why in this present life, he has become a 'medium' to Sai Baba. Of course, he has a long way to go to mature into a ripe fruit but the journey has begun."

"Now you and Baba can take care of him." Spoke Meena, Sunit's wife, who according to me is one of the firmest followers of Shirdi Sai Baba. Swamiji smiled and breathed in deep. He was at the moment in a hospital, recovering from a really severe heart attack. The doctors insisted that he get operated immediately but Swamiji wanted to go back to Ma Mookambika's temple.

He would, then, phone them his intention. Logically and medically, the doctors were right to insist on an operation, but with Swamiji there is not much place for either logic or conventional medical treatment. Also, there are not many people who can force Him to do something He has set His mind against. So, not only was He exasperating the entire medical staff and His devotees by refusing to be operated, but also insisted on cracking jokes and talking to all and sundry, much to the worry of His family and the medical fraternity.

DEVI AND SWAMIJI

"You know Meena, these Gods and Goddesses living above are very dangerous and have a strange sense of humour. Before I became a Swamiji I was a really carefree person. No bloody tensions and no problems and no heart attacks. I was very fond of eating fish and drinking beer. MA MOOKAMBIKA kept giving me messages not to eat fish or beer. But I am not the type to listen and as you know I was virtually dragged into this spiritual field. I was never keen to become a Swamiji. In fact I would always tell people going to the temple, that instead of spending money buying flowers and coconuts for God, if they would give me the money I would do their work." Swamiji has a loud laughter and that is exactly what followed. I saw His family members wince with worry. "So Devi warned me a few times. Then one night, whilst returning home, after enjoying my fish and beer, I met with an accident and the hot exhaust pipe of the bike burnt into my skin. Next morning when we removed the bandage what do we see? The burnt mark on my leg was in the exact shape of a fish. So you see these Gods and Goddesses are dangerous and have a strange sense of humour." He once again smiled and took a deep breath. Even when so ill, one could not fail to feel Swamiji's powerful aura. It was virtually physical. He had long hair pushed back, and a handsome beard. He was, as usual, dressed in a kurta and lungi. He looked powerful yet very gentle.

"You want to write a book on me? You can write it, but not now. Wait for a few months and after your birthday you can start. Your Guru (Saturn), the planet, is not very powerful, at the moment. After your birthday it will settle in your house and you can begin to work on the book. And yes, remember don't try to rush your growth. It will happen when it has to happen. I know circumstances are preventing you from really moving fast up the spiritual path. I know that. It is not your fault…"

"You tell him now what he should do Swamiji?" Meena inquired.

"Arey Meena, these people have given me so many medicines that there is a great chance of a cross connection. It will be like trying to get Radio India and getting Radio Pakistan." Lots of laughter. Then somebody spoke something anti-Pakistan.

"The first donation for constructing Devi's temple was given to me by a Muslim lady from Pakistan. In fact it was only after her donation that the temple work began. It is another thing that Devi changed her life for the better but I can never forget that lady's generous contribution. Now you all better go or you will miss the plane..."

"You are there to take care that the plane will not take off without us Swamiji."

"Sunit, at the moment instead of stopping your plane from flying, with all this cross connection going on in my head, some other plane might be grounded for no reason. Go. Devi's blessings and My blessings are with you all." Saying this He blessed us. All of a sudden I found myself alone with Swamiji.

"Swamiji, I can write the book, right?" I touched His feet.

"Yes, but wait till your birthday. And yes, I have to talk to you but when we are alone. Worry not, Our blessings are with you and the book." He looked deep into my eyes and smiled.

On our way to the airport, the topic of discussion was the family's concern towards Swamiji's health. On one hand you have Swamiji, the Sage and Medium to Ma Mookambika. On the other hand you have Swamiji, the family man. This has led to a lot of tension and conflict for not only Swamiji but also for His family and devotees.

That eventful day in Bangalore, before my first meeting with Swamiji, Sunit, Meena and I had halted at Ma Mookambika's Temple, the complex in which Swamiji resides, to pay our obeisance to Devi. There we met His family and they were naturally worried. Of course, if one looks at it from the family's point of view, they are justified in their concern over His health. Amma, Swamiji's wife, was sick with worry and really upset that Swamiji insisted on living alone in the massive building complex that housed... a mandir, a feeding hall, a guest room and living quarters. Before the heart attack, at night, Swamiji lived all alone. Thus, when He suffered the heart attack there was nobody to take care of Him. Although in excruciating pain, He walked down two floors, opened the massive gate, got out, shut the gate behind Him, got into the car and then informed His family that He had suffered a heart attack, which would have for sure been fatal for a normal human being.

MA MOOKAMBIKA' S TEMPLE

The temple is on the ground floor of the same complex in which Swamiji resides. You enter through a massive gate. The moment you enter you realise that you are in the midst of something divine, and Devi's powerful vibrations encompass you completely. To the right is a statue of Lord Ganesh and next to Him, are numerous *Naga* (Snake) statues. Then you come to a small mandir that is made completely of silver in which reside various Deities. Like all of Swamiji's projects, this silver mandir, too, began with humble origins and then the costing went completely berserk and instead of a small silver statue, virtually by default a huge silver mandir was made.

Next to the silver temple, is Ma Mookambika's abode. The moment you enter this small spiritual powerhouse you are overcome with Devi's presence. Bowing to Ma Mookambika, you cannot help but be overwhelmed with Her grandeur, Her gentleness, Her maternal love and Her power. You really need to be made of some different material if in Her presence you remain unmoved. I have spoken to devotees belonging to different faiths (Christians, Muslims, Gujaratis) and they have all felt Her presence and also mentioned the need to return and keeping returning to meet and pay their respects to Ma.

Thus after paying my darshan to Devi, I was shown around the building by Sunit and Meena. On the first floor is the kitchen and a hall where people are fed all through the day. I was amazed to see the Dining Hall. Swamiji insists on feeding all those who come to Devi for help and predictions. In fact once during my stay with Swamiji, nearly a year after meeting Him in the hospital, one morning seeing Amma adorn Devi with flowers, he mentioned: "Ruzbeh, according to me Devi…She is not in that statue. Where I am concerned I am serving my God when I am serving those who come seeking help. My devotees are my God. They can come anytime; be it day or night and they know that Devi and I, are there for them. When I help those in need then I am serving my Goddess. And I know what it is to be hungry. Devi tested me for nine years. There were times when I did not even have rice in the house to feed my family. So, I know what it is to be needy and hungry. That is why nobody comes to this mandir and goes without eating. If you come for predictions, then you have to eat before you go. People come from afar. They are tired and tensed. Their problems are killing them. They are completely bent with worry. They have travelled from far and in all probability have not even eaten properly as they are in a hurry to get their problems solved. I have to make sure they are fed properly." That is why food, fruits and coffee are served all through the day and after the predictions, whether it be an individual or the entire family, one has to go to the first floor and have a hearty meal. Swamiji has time and again mentioned to me the need to feed people. So, on the first floor is the dining hall. The second floor houses Swamiji and His family. On the third floor is the terrace that houses a small guest room.

A year after that meeting in Bangalore, and also through messages from Sai Baba, I have come to the conclusion that Swamiji is one of the most spiritually powerful men on the globe. Though He disguises His power through humour and an absolutely normal lifestyle, the fact remains that He is a spiritual Giant. Even in this age of cellular phones and cyber war, it amazes one and all that there is a man who has the same powers that one only reads about in ancient religious texts. There is no doubt regarding Devi's presence in Swamiji.

That day after meeting Swamiji, we all hurried into the Ambassador car. We were rather late and the traffic in Bangalore is not only bad, but the rickshaw drivers have an agenda of trying their damn all to reduce the booming population. In the plane, after having eaten the meal, I spent sometime looking at the sky. It was pregnant with clouds. I thought back as to the genesis of the book.

A number of people, especially from the healing and psychic fraternity have inquired as to the purpose of writing this book. They are aware that Sai Baba of Shirdi is my eternal Guru and thus they cannot comprehend a book on another Master. So, before I begin enfolding the mystical and enchanting life story of an extremely powerful but unassuming Master, let me narrate as to how Swamiji entered my life.

(The reason why I am going into personal details is because Swamiji insisted that the book be written through my eyes and thus should have details about my interaction and initiation into His world.)

"Write the book through your eyes. You lead the reader through your journey with Devi and Me. First write your experiences. Write about yourself and your growth after meeting Devi. Then you write about other people's experiences. Most important, the book is on Devi and not on Me."

Often I tried to dissuade Swamiji regarding focusing the book through me. But He remained firm. I even mentioned how cruel it is to subject the reader by enforcing the poor chap to bear with my company, but that only brought about a hearty laugh. I write about myself through default. Please bear with me.

SAINATH AND SWAMIJI

During my healing and auto writing sessions with Sainath of Shirdi, Baba has often referred to Swamiji as 'My Brother'. The first time I heard about Swamiji was through Sunit Banerji; my dear friend, philosopher, guide and publisher. God's very own man, Sunit was aware that Sai Baba of Shirdi (for a reason that baffled and astounded all those who were acquainted with me),

11

used me as one of His mediums for 'communication'. In those days I was not very confident about being a psychic medium. Sainath used to communicate through the medium of the pen. This is called automatic writing. The medium holds the pen from its base (furthest distance from the nib) and after chanting prayers, goes into a state of meditation. In this state, known popularly as the alpha state or as Baba calls it, the state of nothingness, the medium detaches the self from all thoughts and emotions and lets his or her guide give messages through the writing instrument. Virtually vacating one's consciousness from one's body, the medium allows the words from the Master to flow through. The writing instrument is held very lightly to make it difficult for the medium to pen his/her own thoughts. Messages flow through the pen, onto the paper and guidance is given to those who seek it.

When I met Sunit, my confidence level as a medium was amazingly low. In his small but very charged cabin, Sunit began to speak about Swamiji. A Master, who till the age of forty odd years, lived a very normal householder life, but who now possessed the powers of Saints, only read about in books and seen in mythological serials. For some reason I never doubted this Master, as Sunit is a man who knows the difference between the grain and the chaff. He is an extremely well read man, who has spent a large part of his life travelling all over the globe. He also comes from a family who have been graced with the presence of real Masters and thus if Sunit called a person 'evolved', you could rest assured that the person was really evolved.

Till then I was merely a listener. Of course my interest to see and meet Swamiji was immense. But being so close to Sainath, I was content just hearing about Swamiji. Then it so happened that Sunit's mother fell seriously ill. I still remember the day. It was a Sunday morning. It was one of those days when you seriously wonder if going to heaven is worth all the fuss; what with all religious books proclaiming that heaven is full of children. My hyperactive children were driving me up the wall and were giving me serious second thoughts about ever wanting to enter heaven. I mean if Heaven was bursting with children then God could keep His heaven. I wanted no place in it.

Around ten thirty in the morning the phone rang. It was Sunit on the other end and he informed, that his mother was in the hospital and she was really seriously ill and could a few questions be put forth to Sainath. I jotted down the questions and promised to call back in a few minutes.

It was during this auto-writing session with Sainath, that Baba for the first time referred to Swamiji as 'My Brother'. I still remember what was penned. "All is as planned. Tell my son (Sunit) not to worry. His mother's time has still not come to leave the physical plane. She will be all right but it will take many weeks for her to be normal. Tell him that My Brother, who he knows as Swamiji, is there to take care of his mother. He should put all faith in My Brother and worry not. God is Great. Saibaba."

I read the note to Sunit and he was ecstatic. For two reasons. His mother was going to be all right and also that Sainath had referred to Swamiji as His brother. I put the phone down and ducked, just in time to prevent a rubber ball from relocating and redesigning my left eye. Two hours later, a worried Sunit was once again on the line. This time the panic was rather palpable in his voice.

"Mummy is sinking. The doctors are worried that she is slipping into coma. Please ask Baba what to do? "

"Give me ten minutes and I will call you back." I washed my hands, face and feet and then alone in the room, lit a few incense sticks and sat near my altar and called on Sainath to help out in this crisis. The message I got was clear. "Do not worry. I am with her. Also tell my son that Swamiji is with his mother so not to worry. Immediately tell my daughter (Sunit's wife, Meena, who Baba refers to as His child) to find the necklace the mother was wearing. It has a picture of Ram Thakur. (Ram Thakur is another extremely enlightened Master, very popular in Calcutta. Sunit had spoken at length about this Saint but he had not once mentioned about any necklace.) Tell my daughter to apply the kumkum (red powder used in prayers to be applied to the forehead of Ma Mookambika) that has been blessed by Ma and

Swamiji. Make sure that the necklace touches the mother's heart. Do not worry. We are taking care. All is as planned. God is Great. Sainath."

I had barely got up from my seat when the phone rang. It was Sunit hoping the message was positive.

"Sunit, did your mother wear a pendant with Ram Thakur's photo on it? "

"Yes, how did you know...oh! Baba is truly great. But Ruzbeh, she does not have it on and I don't know where it has been kept...wait speak to Meena."

"Yes tell me Ruzbeh." That was Meena.

So I read the entire message to Meena who listened and consented that yes there was a pendant; and yes they had the kumkum blessed by Ma Mookambika and Swamiji.

"Meena, please make your mother-in-law wear the pendant. I know the hospital guys will kick up a fuss but I do not know many people who can stop you when you have made up your mind."

"Ruzbeh, any other message from Baba?" Inquired Sunit.

"Yes He mentions that Swamiji is taking care so worry not. Also They all are there to take care of mom..."

"Just pray she does not slip into coma dear. Please. I know Devi, Saibaba, Swamiji, Ram Thakur will take care."

"Yes, especially when Baba has made it clear that her time has not come to leave this physical plane..."

"But she should not be like a vegetable..."

"God forbid. All will be well, He has said so. It will take some time. At least six to nine weeks for all to be well. Just hang in there. See you in the evening."

That evening the moment Sunit saw me, he hugged me and told me that his mother was out of danger and what had transpired was akin to a miracle. He mentioned that as per the message they had found the pendant of Ram Thakur and had applied on it the kumkum blessed by Ma Mookambika and Swamiji. The hospital staff, as expected, created a fuss but then Meena, as also expected convinced the white frocked tribe that the pendant had to be worn by her mother-in-law.

"Mom was virtually sinking Ruzbeh. The doctor told us that at any moment she would slip into a coma and that there was nothing they could do to prevent the inevitable from happening. The moment Meena made her wear the pendant...say half a minute later, mom opened her eyes and her recovery began. I mean she was in a state of coma and in seconds she opened her eyes."

As Baba had informed, it took a few weeks for Sunit's mother to be totally out of danger. Nearly two years after this incident, while publishing this book, Sunit's mother is still very much on planet earth.

Six months after this incident, I got another message through auto-writing, that I must write a book on Devi and Swamiji. Of course, most folks who knew Swamiji were of the opinion that He would refuse. Swamiji is known to shun publicity and tom-toming about His own prowess. When Sunit telephoned and seeked His permission, Swamiji laughed away the suggestion, but mentioned that maybe sometime later He would give His permission. Four months later, Devi and He gave me Their blessings.

The plane landed on a wet August night and with the grounding thud I got out of my reverie. Sunit's car had fortunately arrived and an hour later I was back at home, with the kids all eager to know everything regarding the well-being of Swamiji. In fact, since they had heard that He was ill, the kids, especially Pashaan, my curly haired son, then just five and a half, had been saying prayers for Swamiji's well-being. I found this rather touching, as nobody had taught the kid the need to say prayers for the ailing.

A month after meeting Swamiji, to the surprise of both Sunit and myself, my auto-writing and healing sessions began to pick up amazing momentum. Also my training for 'trance medium-ship', under the able guidance of Mehru Gandhi, too began in all earnest. Earlier, my auto-writing sessions were for family and close friends, but after coming into contact with Swamiji, it was as though Ma Mookambika and He had opened the psychic floodgates. People in need, began to telephone and fix appointments for sittings.

One morning, Sunit telephoned, to inform me that Swamiji had arrived in Mumbai and was staying in G.D. Shah's residence. G.D. Shah, known popularly as GD, is the oldest devotee of Swamiji in Mumbai. In fact he has been responsible for introducing many needy people to Ma Mookambika and Swamiji. The moment my son heard about Swamiji's presence in Mumbai, he began to create a ruckus to meet the Sage. So in the evening we met up with Sunit and his family and together we entered GD's residence.

Swamiji had gone through intensive medical tests and the results all pointed to one thing: He had to get admitted immediately and His heart had to be operated upon. As usual Swamiji smiled and said that He would consider the medical advice and telephone His answer, the moment He reached Ma Mookambika's temple, in Bangalore. This decision was met with the usual response from family and devotees…muffled groans and loud resignations.

The door opened and we were face to face with Swamiji. He did not look like the usual seventy-two year old man who has undergone numerous tests and sedation and whose heart was not only not behaving itself but also exasperating the medical fraternity in two cities. He looked rather like a tranquil lion. We all touched His feet for blessings. My son dived and lay prostrated and touched Swamiji's feet. From where I stood, all I could see was a small head with lots of curly hair. Swamiji blessed him.

"What is your name?"

"Pashaan."

"Pashaan! Very good. "Swamiji turned towards me. "What does it mean?"

"Pashaan was the name of a warrior tribe in Persia. It also means A Rock...."

"Did you know that Pashaan is one of the names of Lord Subramaniya?" Swamiji put His hand on the beaming kid and gave him a lime, blessed by Ma Mookambika and Him.

"How are you feeling, Swamiji?" Inquired Meena.

"Ohhhh, a little tired and drugged. But apart from that, with Devi's blessings everything is alright."

"They want you to be operated upon, Swamiji?"

"These doctors want everybody to be operated upon. That is their job. It seems there are eight blocks in my arteries. You know they performed angioplasty in Bangalore but according to all the doctors, here and there, this is a stop-gap arrangement and I have to be operated within a month..."

"A month is already over, Swamiji?" informed a visibly worried Sunit.

"Yes I know." Saying this he chuckled and looked deep into Sunit's eyes. "I will only do what Ma Mookambika wants me to do. These doctors can say what they want."

Basically, Swamiji's philosophy is very simple. Specialists can go boil their heads, He will obey the final medical Rx of Ma Mookambika.

(And that is exactly what transpired. After this meeting with Him, a few days later, Murli and Lalit, two most intimate devotees of Swamiji, went to Bangalore to implore Swamiji to get Himself operated in Mumbai. They had even purchased the air-tickets and all the medical arrangements had been completed. All Swamiji had to do was consent. Murli and Lalit were made to eat a hearty meal and the issue of going to Mumbai was left in the capable hands of Ma Mookambika. Later, while chatting about various other issues, Swamiji went into a semi trance. He told them to follow Him to the mandir. Once within the womb of the Devi's Temple, Swamiji went into a trance. Murli informed me later as to what transpired that fateful day. When Swamiji goes in a state of trance He has no recollection of what Ma Mookambika speaks through Him. That day Ma was not overjoyed with their intentions of whisking Swamiji away to Mumbai for the operation: "Swamiji lit a camphor and then Devi spoke through Him. She asked us point blank whether we had lost faith in Her. She said that no instrument would dissect the body of Her Patri…messenger's body. That Swamiji need not go through any operation. He was going to be perfectly all right. That was the end of all discussions." It's been over a year now. Swamiji is in perfect health, in spite of a hectic schedule that would exhaust even an iron pumping teenager.)

When we were about to take leave, Swamiji blessed Pashaan and then He once again informed me that He had to talk about certain things with me but the meeting would take place as and when Ma Mookambika desired. Weeks later, once again I realised that every time I met Swamiji, my Master, Shirdi Sai Baba came through with greater intensity and clarity in the auto-writing and healing sessions.

A LIME FOR AN EYE

A few months passed by and one Thursday evening, I returned home, after a hectic healing session. I saw, as usual, my son flat on his back, getting his daily fix of Cartoon Network.

That day Pashaan watched cartoons with just one eye, while the other eye lay concealed under a handkerchief. I was told in great detail how the controversial eye was damaged. He had sharpened both sides of the pencil and was doing his work when some kid tripped and landed on Pashaan. The sharp edge of the pencil entered his eye with force. I insisted that we go and see an ophthalmologist. He insisted that the doctor would inject him in the eye and it did not make sense to be poked twice in the same eye on the same day.

An hour later, after ice therapy and then rose water therapy, only bribe therapy worked. He agreed to come along to the ophthalmologist, if the very next day, he and his sister were taken to McDonald's; an establishment that seems to be created with the sole purpose of driving kids with glee and the harried parents up the wall. The deal was agreed upon and then we left for the doctor. Just before leaving, I checked whether I had the required cash. I had about three hundred and fifty bucks. A small voice within me insisted that I carry a five hundred rupee note. I did.

It was too late to go and meet the family ophthalmologist, Dr. Yasmin Bhagat, and thus we went to this doctor, who treated a wailing and kicking Pashaan with the same kind of finesse a butcher reserves for a disgruntled goat. I kept reminding my shrieking son about McDonald to soothe his nerves. After four seconds he screamed back that McDonald could be burnt down for all he cared but he wanted out of the deal. By then, the doctor and two very able bodied lady co-workers, had managed to pin down Pashaan. The climax of the free for all came when the doctor poured something into my son's eyes, the kid nearly jumped out of his skin. The weary doctor wiped the sweat off his brow and sighed.

"Remind me to put a board outside saying 'Kids Not Allowed'. By the way Mr. Bharucha, somebody really loves you and your son. You know his cornea is scratched. But the cornea is so delicate that usually in such accidents it breaks under impact. It just cracks up even when a little impact meets it head on. The fact that a sharp pencil point went into your violent son's eye and still only managed to just scratch the cornea is nothing less than a miracle. Five hundred rupees please."

The next day we took Pashaan to our ophthalmologist, Yasmin Bhagat, who though just about to leave for Pondicherry to visit her own son, took time off and travelled to the other part of the city only to examine Pashaan's controversial eye under the right equipment.

"A few things you must know and the most important point to be kept in mind is that he is very lucky that he has no need to get his eye operated. It is very common for the cornea to burst due to the pencil nib entering the eye. Very often the child loses the eyesight. So we are talking about your Master's grace in protecting your child. Second thing, which is fascinating, is that he should logically be in real great pain but your son apparently, is bouncing with joy. Thank your God that he does not need surgery."

Next day Pashaan went to school. Exactly a week later, I was rummaging through his school bag. I removed the leather packet, which contained the lime, blessed by Ma Mookambika and Swamiji. Every few days since its arrival, I was in the habit of checking whether the lime still remained and if so under what condition. I removed the lime and simultaneously, both Pashaan and I gasped in disbelief. The lime was still in perfect condition. Expect for one small change....in the middle of the lime, there was a deep hole...as though somebody had poked a sharp instrument within it with great force and the dry lime had cracked with the impact. The lime looked exactly like an eye that had burst. My son looked at me and then smiled.

"Looks like my eye Dhhaddy!" Then he crinkled his eyes and chuckled. "Vahishta see how funnies I would have beens lookings with an eye like theese." In one sentence destroying the Queen's language, he rushed to find his sister and show her the miracle.

Two things still amaze me. First and foremost, the way Ma Mookambika, Swamiji and Sainath protected my son, by letting the blessed lime take the impact that was meant for my son's eye. Secondly, how cool and collected children are about God above and miracles below. They understand the ways of the Divine so coolly, so much quicker, and without fuss; unlike most grown ups.

A number of months elapsed. In that period I met Swamiji's inner circle. First and foremost, I met up with Murlidhar. Called Murli with love (a number of us call him Swamiji Junior), he is really very close to Swamiji. In fact, the love that Swamiji has for Murli is obvious and accepted. While introducing Murli to new devotees, very often Swamiji has referred to Murli as 'just like my son'. In fact without Sunit, Meena and Murli I do not think this book would have progressed beyond a few hundred words. Murli was instrumental in making me meet people and conveying my desires to Swamiji. Most importantly, he was instrumental in convincing Swamiji to gratify a few of my whims and fancies.

I also met up with Lalit and Ranjana. If Shree Ram has Hanuman then Swamiji has Lalit. He is also very possessive about Swamiji and has been known to ruffle many feathers with his direct approach and penchant for calling a spade a spade. There is really not dull moment with Lalit around. He is loud and happy and when in the mood (which he is more than often) he loves to regale one and all with experiences that he and his family have shared with Devi and Swamiji. Lalit is, I think, the only devotee who can virtually emotionally bully Swamiji into doing things by his sheer love and devotion. Of course it is a different matter that Lalit can force Swamiji into doing things only because Swamiji allows him to get away with such forceful love and possessiveness. Whenever Swamiji has needed any sort of assistance to complete a social project, Lalit has without any hesitation entered the arena and bailed the project out. Of course, the fact that it is due to the grace of Ma Mookambika and Swamiji that Lalit has scaled heights that he had never ever even dared to dream of reaching, is something that Lalit and Ranjana are first to admit and acknowledge.

I also met up with G.D. Shah, known simply as GD. He is one of the oldest devotees of Swamiji and another person who has risen to phenomenal heights thanks completely to the grace of Devi and Swamiji. GD is responsible for introducing Swamiji to most of the people from Mumbai and Gujarat. In fact, his association with Swamiji dates back to two and more decades and Swamiji usually spends a large period of his time, when in Mumbai, at GD's residence. GD is involved with numerous social organisations and has often, introduced many Jain Sadhus and Saddvis to Swamiji, for guidance. Just like Lalit and Murli, GD telephones Swamiji everyday at least once to inquire of the latter's health. Of course, the number of acquaintances that have been helped by Devi through Swamiji is something that nobody tries to hide or sideline. They are all openly grateful to Swamiji that Devi has graced their lives and really propelled them to heights never dreamt of.

One day, I received a call from Murli saying that Swamiji wanted us both to travel to Goa and then onwards, we would all proceed to Dandeli, which was a few hours drive away. The trip and the stay would give me an opportunity to spend some quality time together and also give me an insight into Swamiji.

I thanked Murli and then Sunit too. Both of them kept conveying to Swamiji that the book would only really commence when He allowed me to spend sometime with Him. May be Swamiji got tired of their constant reminders and thus had acquiesced to spend two full days with me. Not a very relishing thought to most people who have had any sort of contact with yours truly.

The day Murli and I were to leave for Goa, the Weather Bureau had broad-casted that the coastal region, especially Goa and its surrounding areas were to experience torrential rains and a hot tempered cyclone was just thirsting to lash out all its fury. If left to the track record of the Weather Bureau, such a prediction would automatically be translated by the common man as: "People in Goa and surrounding areas, better stock beer in the deep freezer as the sun would try its dashed all to burn the skins off your backs." But all the national papers and the TV stations kept harping about the cyclone and fishermen all along the Goan coastline were being evacuated. We were to land the very same day when this controversial cyclone was supposed to spit on its hands and get to work.

Murli telephoned Swamiji a day before we were to leave for Goa. Swamiji very casually mentioned that there was no need to worry as Devi would make certain that the cyclone would turn around and fizzle out without causing damage to any body. The next morning on the television, just before leaving for Murli's house, the news broadcaster informed that the cyclone had turned around and fizzled out at sea. No life was taken and no property damaged. This is the most amazing aspect of Swamiji. He very casually informs people that their impending calamities are to be averted or that their huge loan threatening to ruin them shall be taken care of and within the time frame specified it most surely does. As I spoke to many of His devotees, this casual tone of prediction, which always fell true, left even the most ardent followers very nonplussed.

Anyway, I met Murli at his house. His wife, served us breakfast and tea. Murli fed Siddhanth, who was unusually quiet, owing to the fact that his father was to be out of town for a few days. I managed to swallow my food slowly and with great difficulty, as during this time, I was suffering from acute ulcers in the mouth. My body's defense system, had gone stark raving mad. Instead of protecting me, due to some insane and silly reason, my immune system was getting some perverse pleasure in attacking my body.

We caught a cab for the airport and basically talked about our children. We finished with the check-in formalities and parked ourselves in the vacant seats. As mentioned before, Murli is, according to me, the closest devotee of Swamiji and without a doubt Swamiji is extremely fond of the former.

BORN FROM THE ASHES

"Tell me about how you met Swamiji? "I found it difficult to speak, what with the ulcers in my mouth giving me the dickens of a bother.

"Before I tell you about Swamiji I think it is best that you know a little about me. I was born in an Udupi Brahmin family and their vocation was to conduct religious ceremonies, poojas, havans etc. My grandfather was a practising priest, while my dad conducted poojas till he matriculated. He came to Mumbai in 1950. Where I was concerned, as years passed, I slowly began to question the very foundations of religion and rituals. So much so, that I became an atheist and began to question the very existence of God. So when I met Swamiji it was in such circumstances."

"Where did you meet Swamiji?"

"I met Swamiji at Lalit Nagpal's residence."

Lalit Nagpal and his entire family are staunch devotees of Devi and Swamiji.

"Swamiji used to come to Lalit's house regularly and Lalit would always want me to meet his Guru. I did not believe in God and I would tell him that I did not believe in any Swamiji-Wamiji." Murli chuckled and his eyes crinkled with a smile. "One day whilst travelling to my farmhouse on the outskirts of Mumbai, I was passing by Lalit's house and decided to pay him a visit. I knew that Lalit wanted me to meet Swamiji and by not meeting his Guru, I was hurting my friend. So that day, aware that Swamiji too was staying at Lalit's house, I decided to meet Him and thus make Lalit happy. I had no intention of asking any thing to Swamiji, as I did not believe that God existed; so the question of believing a God man did not arise."

"I was introduced to Swamiji and then Lalit forced me to ask Swamiji for a prediction. I was not at all interested, so Lalit informed Swamiji that I wanted a child and the entire medical fraternity was of the opinion that my wife and I would never be able to become parents. So Swamiji asked me my name and date of birth. Then He looked at me and began to describe my ancestral house that is in Udupi, a village in Karnataka, in detail. The way this Man was describing my village was unbelievable. It was as though He was seeing the village and in detail describing everything to me. He not only specified in detail my ancestral house, but also the cowshed, the exact position of our two wells and the location of a rivulet passing beside the house. He informed me that my ancestors were priests of the village temple and then, one by one, he divulged incidents which had occurred in my life and of which no body was privy to." Murli speaks only when he is in the mood. Otherwise he is content to keep his role in the conversation to that of a listener. When he does speak, words come out slowly and softly. I got up and got him a cup of coffee and myself a cold drink.

"Then what happened?"

"You know even after all this description, I was not really impressed. I thought either He had visited Udupi or may be He was just describing a common scene in a small town or village. Every house in a village has a well and cattle and usually the river flows near by, so I concluded that maybe Swamiji was just plain lucky. But then he divulged something that bloody shook me up. My father had expired in May 1991. I was badly affected by his death. He had always wanted to go to the Himalayas; especially he had wanted to visit Gangotri...the source of the Holy Ganga. So when he expired, as a son, I felt, that if he could not physically visit Gangotri, at least I could take his ashes with me and immerse it at Gangotri and thereby merge my father's physical remains within the holy Ganges. About this I had told nobody. Expect for my mother, nobody was aware of the fact that my father's ashes were in my mandir at my house. That day Swamiji looked at me and really angrily told me 'You have kept your father's ashes in your house so that you can visit Gangotri and immerse it. Do it immediately. Till you don't, you will never get a child and also problems of all kinds will keep harassing you.' I tell you, Ruzbeh, I was stunned. Nobody but my mother, was aware that my father's ashes were still at home. No way could this man ever find out about the ashes. The only way possible was that He was really a spiritual giant. I realised that may be, my friend Lalit, was right when he kept saying that Swamiji was not an ordinary soul but a very evolved sage. From that very moment on, slowly my transformation began."

"Tell me some incidents that you feel are really extraordinary."

"Too many Ruzbeh. It boggles the mind. You want to check whether our plane has arrived."

"Bugger the plane. Come on tell me some incidents. I mean I can't go about writing a book on Swamiji when His closest disciple runs out of words."

"The problem is that there are so many incidents that have happened to me and incidents I have witnessed happening to others that I don't know where to start."

"Okay by me. I guess I will tell the readers that as there are so many incidents we have decided not to divulge any." We both chuckled. "Okay, tell me, after you immersed your father's mortal remains what happened?"

"I met Swamiji in September 1995. I went to Gangotri to immerse the ashes of my father sometime later. I kept in constant touch with Swamiji. Of course many people kept ridiculing me that in spite of immersing the ashes of my father, our greatest desire, to be parents was still not fulfilled. But all this never disturbed me, as I knew that only when the time was right would we be blessed with a child. Medical fraternity had virtually given up hope and now only the spiritual fraternity remained and I knew that They took their time. They are never in a hurry. Anyway, after immersing my father's ashes, from Gangotri, I went to Gaumukh and on the way back I stopped to drink tea in a small shack. In a matter of few seconds, a yogi, bare chested, with broad shoulders, big black eyes and jet black hair stood before me and my friend. Remember, in Gaumukh, it gets bloody cold. Thus when everybody was clothed and booted, this guy, virtually half-naked and with no shoes on appears in front of us. He looked around fifty to fifty-five years old. We asked him to share tea with us. We spoke for about twenty minutes and then decided to move on. My friend offered him five hundred rupees and then he touched the yogi's feet. The yogi told him *'Ja bache, sau guna ho gaya'*. Meaning, I bless you that you shall in return get hundred times more money. I then touched His feet but did not give him anything. I mean I did not want him to think that I was offering him money in order to multiply it hundred fold. He said *'Ja tera yatra safal, Hum prasan ho gaya.'* Meaning the purpose for which I undertook the pilgrimage would be successful."

"Now one thing I was certain about and that was that this man was not an ordinary yogi. His face kept haunting me, so the moment we reached Rishikesh, I telephoned Swamiji. All He inquired was whether the yogi had used the word *Prasan*. I said yes, *Prasan* was the very word he had used when talking to me. Swamiji then informed me that *Prasan* was Devi's word and that the person I saw was no ordinary being. Then Swamiji just chuckled and said that if I wanted a word by word recount of all that I had done on the trip I could come over to Bangalore. After that trip it has happened innumerable times, that Swamiji has recounted exactly all that I have seen and done on pilgrimages. I like to travel and He will often narrate an incident from the trip that I have forgotten to narrate to Him. He is really amazing. *Kya bolte hai?* Omnipresent is the right word to describe Devi and Him. Anyway, within six months of immersing the ashes of my father, my wife conceived and gave birth to a baby boy... Siddhanth. The doctors were all baffled that we became parents but by then I was a firm believer of God, Devi and Swamiji. In fact Swamiji had even predicted the time and day of Siddhanth's birth and also how he would look when he grew up..."

"Last call for those flying to Goa..."

"What! When was the first blooming call announced." We got up fast and were the last people to enter the plane, which appeared to be bursting at its seams with passengers.

"Murli we could have missed the flight because of you."

"Extremely funny!"

We located our seats, sat down and got as comfortable as two sardines can, in a sealed tin. After scanning through various newspapers and magazines, we sipped cold lime-water and observed the sky and the floating clouds. Then we observed the air-hostess, who instructed us, with a warm cheerful smile, as to the correct procedure to be adopted, if and when, the damn plane decided to crash in order to justify the laws of gravity.

"Murli, I know you are not sleeping so please continue."

He opened his eyes, looked at me, smiled and refilled his mouth with his favourite tobacco. Under normal conditions I would have eaten the stuff, but with ulcers in my mouth, I might as well have sipped Nitric Acid with a straw.

DEVI IN THE CHURCH

"Sometime later, I received a letter from my best friend, Dr. J.K. Shah, who is settled in Canada. He married a Canadian girl of Indian origin and through the letter I was informed that things were not well between him and his wife. So I went to Bangalore because in my opinion, sitting at the feet of Devi, within the temple, Swamiji's predictions are cent per cent accurate.

"The first thing Swamiji predicted was that my friend's problem was far more serious than what met the eye. Swamiji informed me, that my friend was contemplating suicide and if he was not given help he would in all probability kill himself. Swamiji further divulged that there was a Church very close to where my friend lived and it was the powerful vibrations coming from the Church, which was protecting my friend. Swamiji told me to inform my friend to first and foremost light a candle everyday in the Church and secondly to divorce his wife.

"So I phoned my friend and he sounded very very low and confessed that he was very depressed. He saw no light at the end of the tunnel. When I asked him if there was any Church nearby, he was surprised, as just next to his house, stood a Church. In fact, only a boundary wall separated his house from the Church. He agreed to do all that Swamiji had ordered. A few days later, he confessed that on the day I had telephoned him, he was so depressed and fed up that he was on the verge of committing suicide. As the marriage was already on the rocks, he divorced his wife and is now very happy. By the way, very very rarely does Swamiji advice anybody to go in for a divorce. Unless some tragedy awaits the person, if divorce is not taken, only then does He advise the person to take the drastic step of legal separation. Also though my friend is a Hindu, Swamiji asked him to light a candle in the Church. For Him there are no religious boundaries and restrictions."

We ate our snacks in silence. I decided to give Murli a much needed break. He had already shut his eyes and I looked at the other passengers. Most of them were harried parents with dangerous looking kids, who just could not wait to reach Goa. According to me only a very senile or a very desperate terrorist would ever contemplate on hijacking a plane flying to Goa when the vacation season is in full flow. With a thud the plane landed and Murli opened his eyes. Goa was all sunny and dry. We both smiled. The damn cyclone had really chickened out.

We met Swamiji and Amma outside the airport and took their blessings. There were two Ambassador cars waiting for us but we decided to travel in one car so as to make the best use of the journey. I sat in the front seat, and with Swamiji, Amma and Murli, in the back seat, our journey to Dandeli commenced. The other Ambassador followed our vehicle. For a while, Swamiji and Murli communicated in their native tongue. On and off, both of them would throw in a word or a sentence in English for my benefit. The basic gist of the conversation was regarding a hospital project that Swamiji was keen on constructing in Subramanyia, which for some reason or the other, kept getting postponed.

DEVI SAVES A TOWN

"Murli, with or without anybody, I shall go ahead with the project. You know all my life I have never asked anybody for even a single rupee. This hospital has to be constructed and the moment Devi gives me the signal I shall wait for nobody or no donation. I shall take a loan from a bank and begin the project. By the way, have you both eaten breakfast or should we stop for some food."

Murli and I simultaneously smiled. It is common knowledge amongst those close to Swamiji, that when travelling with Him, a journey's estimated time limit goes for a toss. A four-hour journey might take six hours, as Swamiji loves to halt in quaint restaurants to sip a cold soda or drink piping hot coffee or have tiffin. But more than anything, He loves to feed everybody who is travelling along with Him. Be it a top-notch industrialist or a chauffeur, it does not really matter. Murli assured Swamiji that both of us had eaten enough food to sustain us for a few hours.

"Ruzbeh, I wanted you to come to Dandeli for various reasons. First of all, it is a beautiful and auspicious place to start work on the book. Also, you will get plenty of information regarding how prayers and mainly how Devi helps Her children. Also you have been grumbling that you have not spent anytime with me, so hopefully we will be able to spend sometime together and talk. In Dandeli, there is a paper mill. Around fourteen years ago the mill was in a really bad shape. Accidents, deaths, strikes, were threatening to shut the mill. With the shutting of the mill thousands of workers and their families would have got in real trouble. Many in the management wanted to resign and go away. The company was not able to pay their salary and there were many problems."

"When the company officials met me, I told them to do certain things and also showed them two places where they should build temples. Earlier, every year, not less than twenty-five cases of either accidents or deaths used to take place within the company premises and problems with the management and the union were rampant. The management gave me a place to construct the temples and we performed certain poojas. Of course the workers and the trade union were dead against us. In fact, the first time we were conducting a pooja, the union leaders and the workers came to hit us as they thought we were doing some black magic. They were very unhappy."

"Of course the pooja continued. Devi does not like if Her pooja is disturbed. That year everybody noticed that accidents and deaths at the work place virtually stopped. Apart from this, even between the management and the union there was greater harmony and amicability. In fact in a short period of time, the disputes got sorted out, and now, since a long time, there have been no such problems between them whatsoever. In fact, after two years of the poojas and my coming to this place, the very people who initially opposed us, came to me for predictions and insisted that I perform poojas and construct a temple at the right spot for the welfare of the workers. They themselves came forward and now they support the poojas and the management.

"Another problem with this place was that the morale of the workers was at an all time low. They wanted to leave this place and go elsewhere for employment. But after performing the poojas and the temples being constructed, people are content being associated with this place and in fact, more than eight thousand people work in this factory. Most of them have come for predictions and have benefited with Devi's guidance. Now they have so much of faith that tomorrow they will just be waiting for me. Then after the pooja they will have food and the prasad. I have been visiting this place since fourteen years and they know the positive difference the poojas and the Devi's temples have brought about to their factory and to their lives. So they now have immense faith. In fact, now every Head of the Department comes and requests me to come over to the department, feel the vibrations, and recommend any change to be adopted."

"Remember I come from so far to this place only for one reason. The factory should continue to do well. If the factory closes down the entire town suffers. It is not a question of just the workers. The entire family suffers too. Around forty to fifty thousand people are directly or indirectly connected to this paper factory. My job as a Swamiji is to make sure that the workers and their families are not left on the street with no roof over their heads and no food to feed themselves and their children."

DESTINY & YOU

The car moved on and Swamiji began to inquire about the welfare of the driver and his family. After a while I asked Him regarding the rigidity where destiny is concerned.

"See, in some of the cases, they say that destiny cannot be changed. But there are proofs which state that destiny can be changed. For example, destiny says that you are going to have a major disaster, or a serious accident. All this may be written in your destiny. But if you do certain good things, then I think the catastrophe can be avoided. You may have a fall but instead of falling from the fifth floor, you might fall down from the first step. So you were destined to fall and you have fallen but due to prayers, honest and good living, poojas, penance etc you can cushion the bad effects of your past karmas."

"Of course faith is very important. There is a very good story in our scriptures regarding destiny. Once there was a woman who was a great saint. This saint lost her husband.

Everybody said that the body should be burnt within the stipulated few hours. According to destiny, the lady had to become a widow thus her husband had to die before her. But She said "no my husband will not die". So what does this woman do? She kept her husband's body in a boat and she rowed to the middle of the lake. There she sat with her husband's body and with her determination, faith and yogic powers, legend has it, that she stopped the movement of the sun and the moon etc. Even God realised that this woman was not going to see reason so even HE had no other option but to bring her husband back to life. So though her husband was destined to die, the power of a human being and the power of faith is so much that destiny could be modified. Of course, only if you have tremendous faith, destiny will change. You must have immense faith and complete surrender. There should not be a question in your mind and heart as to whether something is possible or not. Even if for a moment or a second you begin to doubt, then all the meditation and all the penance you have done is wiped out. If faith is lost for even a fraction of a second, then all is lost that very moment; so never ever doubt."

"Always have faith in God, Devi, your Guru, whosoever you worship and believe. There is some Divine Force in this world. Nobody can explain this. Even I cannot explain the Divine Force. You have to experience the unseen power. You cannot experience that Divine Power through somebody else's eyes or through books. It is like five blind people describing an elephant. Each one has a different explanation and experience of the same elephant. One will say God is like this; another chap will say no no no no God is like this only while the third guy will say Nah God is like this."

"The mistakes most people make nowadays is that they read books and try to find and experience God through other people's experiences. You will never know, realise and experience God through another person. It is like the sunrise being described, but till you do not see the sun rise, till you have never seen the sun rays breaking through the darkness and spreading warm light, you will never really know how beautiful a sight it is.

33

Only when you see the sun rising and experience the joy of a new day, will you begin to understand the beauty and glory of God. You have to experience God yourself and not depend upon books and speeches. Yes we can guide you. To get that power I can say 'okay baba, you go that way as I had gone this same way and experienced God'. That is all that can be done. But nowadays, most people rely fully on somebody else's journey. No. You have to travel yourself to find God. Have your own experience. It is million times more valuable. This is my opinion." For a while there was silence.

"Ruzbeh, have you ever sat with Swamiji while He drives the car?"

"It has taken me months just to be able to sit with Him under one roof..."

"He is the oldest teenager when it comes to driving a car. He is faster than all race car drivers put together. Drives like the wind." Then the topic switched to a devotee who was undergoing a major problem financially as well as emotionally.

"One must understand a very important thing, and that is I cannot solve the problems of the devotees. *I cannot*. But I will definitely show them a path as to how they can solve their problems and who can help them solve it. I can guide them that 'this is a very good road and that is a very bad road. You travel by this route as this is a short cut or don't travel on that route as that road is not only very dangerous but will take you more time to reach your destination'. If you listen and have faith and travel as directed then naturally your problems will be sorted out and you will reach your destination, safe and sound and quickly. But remember one thing; each one of us has to travel on the road. You cannot ask me to do your travelling, because your karma necessitates that you experience the journey. Yes, I can help the journey be smoother. Equip you with a road map pointing out which roads to avoid and which to take. I can even give you travelling equipment. But the journey, you have to undertake I am with you but you have to travel on the road to reach a particular destination."

"In fact life is like a journey. Every moment we are travelling; seconds are ticking by and the final destination is drawing closer. Now the road may be good but just a little ahead the roads may be horrible. Even if you are on a good road don't go very fast, drive calmly and slowly. You never know when, on the way, you may all of a sudden get a very uneven road...but by then it might be too late to manage your vehicle and you might either damage it or even meet with an accident. Or ahead some natural calamity might await you like torrential rains, floods etc. So just because, at the moment the road is good, do not take it for granted that all the roads ahead shall be equally good. Depending on the circumstances, travel accordingly. Just because the road is very smooth you should not become careless. There is a chance you might meet with an accident."

"On the other hand, many people try to rush past an uneven or rocky road with the assumption that if they finish this bad stretch fast, then things ahead might be smoother. This is a grave mistake. Don't try to go so fast with the assumption that you will reach a better road ahead. No. Go slow and be more cautious, as on a bad road the chance of your vehicle breaking down is so much greater. Take the advantage of the experience of your Guru and follow the road map given to you by Him or by the God within you. Life is like the road. Sometimes there will be steep ups and at other times there will be steep downs. Ups and downs in life and in a journey will always be there. You cannot only travel up and up. Ups and downs are part and parcel of life and travelling. You move ahead depending upon the circumstances. The best way to get out of these problems is to go slow and have immense faith in the direction showed to you by your Guru or have immense faith in God and leave the rest to Him. Whatever name you give to God, whatever name you call Him, does not matter. Just have faith in Him that He is there with you through the ups and downs of life." Then just to prove the validity of his point, our car broke down. We looked at each other and began to laugh.

"Sometimes even cars have ears."

We all got down and realised that it would take a long time for the car to be repaired. We spotted a small shed and there bought a few bottles of cold water and then boarded the other Ambassador car. Now we were even. There were three of us in the front seat and three at the back. We gulped down the cold water and passed the bottle around.

"Take the example of this water. This water is consumed by animals, humans, friends, enemies…by everybody. Without this water you cannot survive. It is a must. God has not made different water for different religions. No special water for Muslims, Christians, Hindus, Zoroastrians. For all it is the same. And God did not give it any colour. He could have given it different colours. 'Oh this red colour is only for Muslims, this white colour only…'" chuckles and looks around.

"Wild animals and Saints drink the same water. And whichever vessel the water is poured into, water takes the shape of that vessel. I am giving you these simple examples only because the best way to understand God is through simple ways and actions. Don't go deep into trying to understand and experience God for you will not reach anywhere. There is no end to the depth of God and only confusion will arise. Somebody will say one thing, while another will say something else. The best way is to have your own experience and then you will begin to realise God. That is how I have realised my Goddess. In my thirty years of experience, Goddess has done much good. She has protected people. She has saved so many lives. And most important thing, She has done for all of us is that She has given us courage to face life. Apart from faith and total surrender to God and Guru, the most important thing in life is to have courage. Once you lose faith and courage, you are gone. You can't do anything. Your attitude should be ' whatever has to happen let it happen, we will see through it'. That is the trust you should have in God and your Guru. You must tell God 'You can throw me in the water or kill me or put me anywhere I don't bother You are there to take care. You are with me, then why should I bother?"

"Remember, as Swamijis, we don't do anything, we just show the path. If I tell you that as a Swamiji, I can solve your problems, no, that is not possible. We can only guide you to solve your problems. We can only show you the path. I may tell you that if you take a particular road, your problem will be sorted out, but remember the problem is sorted out by the unseen power. There is someone above us who can solve the problem. I can only show you the way. But if I say that 'I am doing this. I did that. I am a great man and I can do anything', then it is completely wrong. That means 'I' comes in and whenever 'I' comes in a person, then we are not giving importance to God/Goddess/Guru and that is really very wrong. Even in the book you plan to write, I want you to concentrate on Devi and Her powers. All I want you to do is to bring out the greatness of the unseen power, which in my case is Devi, Ma Mookambika. We have to prove to the people and the readers that, all one really needs is faith and total surrender. Have faith, that there is a divine power that is taking care of you and is with you all the time. Just have faith and believe in God. Remember lots of people and devotees will tell you experiences and miracles that have taken place in their lives but that is the work of Devi. I am just a medium or an intermediary. That power can go to anybody. It has come to me but it can go to anybody. It can come to you if you try to develop this power."

"But how can one develop it?"

"Well the development can take place through intense desire to serve all living creatures; through prayers and also-mainly through karma. And karma also should be really very good karma."

"But Swamiji the fact that Devi is with you, means you had reached an advanced spiritual level in your past lives? A person can tie himself up in knots or pray the whole day, but I doubt if that person is going to get the grace you have got."

"True, but if one really has the intention and desire to serve mankind then God will give the individual some kind of means to do the needful. It may be through other means but the path will be shown. Remember, once you understand your life you will automatically come to the conclusion that you are nothing. Once you come to that conclusion and realise that you are nothing, that all is zero then you can rest assured that you have already reached a very high stage of evolvement. Then answers come automatically. To reach there you have to just surrender, surrender and surrender. There is no other way. Faith and surrender are the only paths. You must tell God, 'You put me anywhere. You kill me, save me, do whatever You want with me'. You must say, 'it is up to You. Want to kill me go ahead. You want to give me something go ahead. I am not going to ask for anything'. How many things can you ask from God? How many? There are no limitations. If you keep asking, then one day God will say 'listen, you asked so many things, I have given them to you, now get out'. Laughs loudly.

DEVI AND SWAMIJI

"Don't ask anything, let God give you what He wants to give you. When Devi appeared before me and asked me ' what do You want?' the first question that I asked Her was ' Ma please let me know why You have come and what You have decided to give me. You give me what You have decided to give me as I did not call You. You give me what You have in mind.'"

"How did You see Devi? I mean when you say She showed herself to You, did You see Her in Your mind's eye or really see Her?"

"No, no, She comes in front of me in a manner that I cannot explain. All this cannot be explained. It is as though She is transparent. I can see through and through her. And then She asked me 'what do You want?'. I told Her to give me whatever She had decided to give me. I told Her 'Why have You come. To give me no, so You give me what You have decided'. So She once again asked me as to what I wanted and I once again told Her to give me whatever She had decided to hand out. My logic was that 'You have come to give me something so give it to me. Then I shall ask you what I want'.

"So She told me, 'your answer is funny'. I only told Her, 'You give me whatever and when the time comes for me to ask for something, I will ask you." Swamiji chuckled.

"I told Her it will be like a bearer cheque with me. She then asked me why did I not ask Her right away what I wanted and how I was going to cash my so called 'bearer cheque'. So then I gave her my logic. I told her 'Ma suppose You have come to give me money. Say I want ten lakhs, but Ma I don't know whether I can ask for ten lakhs or whether You have ten lakhs or not... so with that fear I might only ask for five lakhs'. Ruzbeh, now all Devis are very smart. You know what They do? They will say 'you have asked for five lakhs, here take it, *tathas tu* (so be it). My five lakhs have got saved'. Laughs loudly.

"They will never say, 'I have come here to give you ten lakhs and more'. No. They will say 'you asked for five lakhs, here take it' and there ends the matter. I said 'I will take whatever You have come to give me and when I want more at that time I shall ask for it'.

"Then Devi smiled and said, 'if I say yes to this condition of yours then tell Me what are you going to ask for?'

"So then I told Her, ' You are the Universal Mother. You know everything going on in this world. You know very well what I am going to ask, but You still want to test me so okay, I shall ask for one thing. Whoever comes to You crying and saying, Ma solve my problems I am in great difficulty, You must solve the person's problem. That time don't tell the person (through me), that *'I cannot do anything, it is karma and you have to undergo your problems.* If that is the answer and if we have to undergo our karma then why should I waste my time as well as five rupees buying flowers and coconut for You and offering them to You. Why should we go on saying Ma, Ma, Ma. If anyway we all are going to undergo the same difficulties then You don't come into the picture. You go. At that time when a devotee comes to you don't tell me to tell that person he or she has to go through all these troubles because of destiny.' I told her this very clearly."

"I told her that 'Ma, we are your children. We might commit mistakes. We are innocent. We don't know anything

39

about life. Knowing that, still You have tested us and shown us many paths including the bad path. Okay, we succumbed to temptations. We did wrong. Okay, we failed but still You are our Mother. As a Mother when a child cries, the Mother's duty is to give milk. Don't say at that time...he is undergoing his karma...if that is the case then I don't want you, Mother'.

"But still Devi insisted that She could not do anything where karma was concerned. She repeated that the person has to undergo difficulties due to the person's karma. So then I said 'Ma, thank you, I don't want to ask any questions. I don't want You. Let us undergo our difficulties and if we have to suffer let us suffer on our own'. Then She said 'I will show you a path'. I inquired as to what the path was? She said 'For every karma, every sin, for every bad thing that a person has done there is a *praschit*...a penance...that has to be undertaken...that has to be performed. I will show them through you, what penance to undertake. You tell them. Tell them the disease and give them the medicine also. You tell them the *praschit* and if they do as told, then their problems will be solved'. I agreed. Today I am asking many people to go to Kuke Subramaniya or to go here and there. I tell them to do whatever Devi asks me to tell the devotees. Those who are following Ma's instructions with faith and patience are realising that their work is being done. Their problems are being solved. Now if you ask me how this works I don't know. I think what is needed is complete faith. Maybe Devi is testing the devotee by asking the person to do certain things. Maybe the *praschit* or penance is nothing but a test of faith. If you have complete faith then automatically the work gets done. I don't think a person should do something told by Ma just to solve the problem. Do it because Devi has asked you to do something. This paper factory that we are visiting is a perfect example. Fourteen years ago, they were in major trouble. I did not do anything. Devi asked them to do certain things that they followed with full faith and the results are for all to see. Faith is needed."

THE SUBRAMANIYA TEMPLE

"But Swamiji, you send so many people to Kuke Subramaniya. What is there in Subramanyia that changes the karmic pattern of the devotee?"

"I do not tell everybody to go to Subramanyia. Devi decides what is best for each person. And even when Ma tells them to go to Subramanyia, different poojas are asked to be performed for different people with varying problems. For some people the *Sudarshan Homa* is prescribed, while for some, the *Nag Prathishta* Pooja is asked to be performed. Different poojas and *praschits* are to be done for different problems. Devi is very well aware that for every illness the same medicine cannot be prescribed. You cannot take the same tablet for a headache and for typhoid. Subramanyia is not the be all and end all of one's problems. Yes, for certain problems to be eradicated, one needs to go to Surbramanyia, but it does not imply that for all problems one has to rush to Subramanyia."

"What is there in Subramanyia that certain types of problems are solved?"

"Actually it is a place of sanctity. There is power in the Subramanyia temple. It is not my temple. I don't earn anything if somebody goes to that temple. The important thing is that there is a supernatural power...what we call as *Naga*...in English they call it Serpent Power...Kundalini Power. That Kundalini Shakti is there in the Nag. A human being's head, from the back of his head and to the spinal chord is like a snake. So there is a link between Nagas and human beings. In fact, there is a Naga called the Vasuki Naga. It can appear and disappear. You might see it on this glass and after a while it just disappears. It has not gone anywhere. So where does it go? Nobody knows. In fact, the Nagas possess certain shaktis or powers that nobody can explain. For instance, when a couple is not being blessed with a child, Devi recommends that a Nag Pooja be performed. In what way does the Naga either benefit or help out, I do not know, but so often the prayers are answered. I mean if you look at it logically, how does the Naga benefit if you pour milk on the statue? And how does pouring milk, chanting certain prayers get you a child? If

41

you tell the Americans that by pouring milk on a stone, a woman shall conceive or you will get a child…they will think us to be really crazy. I mean their logic is proper too. Why have they spent so much time and money becoming doctors if just by pouring milk on a snake, women can get pregnant. I guess there is a deeper significance, but we do not need to dwell on all this. As I told you don't try to go too deep into religion. Just have faith and that will take care of all your needs."

"But Swamiji, what is the significance of putting milk on a statue? How does it help?"

"See, first of all you cannot pour milk on a real cobra. And if a real cobra comes very close the same people, in all probability will kill it. That will add further karma. Of course, remember, all the Nagas are not the same. The real reason why certain prayers are answered by going to Subramanyia are two fold. First of all the place is very vibrationally charged. If you spend time in such places automatically you get strength, peace of mind and wisdom to face life. The second reason could be that Devi wants to test your faith. A great effort is required to go to an out of the place pilgrimage spot, taking time off work, maybe even going through pilgrimage expenses. May be all this is just to test one's faith. Of course, for each problem there is a medicine and for a childless couple, if Devi recommends Nag pooja then cent per cent the prayers are answered. So many couples will testify to the power of the Nag Shakti."

"Kundalini Shakti and Serpent Power are one and the same. Human beings have the power that usually is lying dormant. Through meditation and prayers, we make the *kundalini jagrat* i.e we awaken the kundalini. One by one, we activate the chakras and let the power rise from the base of the spine, through the chakras to the crown chakra. When it reaches the crown chakra, we call it *Bhramagyan* (knowledge of the Gods). When the *Bhramagyan* comes to you (or when the shakti/energy reaches the crown chakra) then you will know the past, present and future. You can make things happen. Even those things that are not possible, one can make them happen. So that is the Kundalini Shakti and that is the powers these Nagas have got. That is why every God, every supernatural power has got a serpent. But there are good serpents and bad serpents. It does not mean all snakes are good shaktis. Just like all Brahmins are not good Brahmins." Once again laughs loudly. "You have good Brahmins and really bad Brahmins."

"Just remember one thing. Whatever you do, you must do it with faith. Full faith and surrender. Another thing that you must be sure of is that there is an unseen power that governs this world and is always there to help and guide you. And to understand this unseen divine force takes time and realisation, meditation, prayers etc. And also the paths differ to get this realisation. Some people get God realisation through meditation and through prayers. While some of the devotees get God realisation through *Bhajans* (singing devotional songs). Some people get it because of their past karma; for whatever they have done in their past lives. You must have done something good so that you have to come to Dandeli with me. Otherwise you would not have come. Why should you come? All these years...fourteen to fifteen years that I have been coming I have never asked anybody to come with me. But I said that Dandeli is the place where you can come with me and begin the book. It is not only a very beautiful and picturesque place, but it is also called Sundharyalahiri. Written by Adi Sankara where He describes the beauty of the world. This place is really beautiful. Also in Dakshin Kanada it is called Pashuram Shetra. Pashuram has created this place and thus all the year through there is never any problem for water and food. There are no problems for water and food in Pashuram's land. In fact, when we do poojas we say in Sanskrit, that 'I am doing my sharda for my so and so in Pashuram's Shetra'. In Delhi we say Ram Shetra."

"In fact legend says that this place was under the sea and called Dev Loka (the abode of the Gods) and Naga Loka (the abode of the Serpent Kingdom). Naturally, there were lots of snakes here and when God decided to get this place out of water onto land, all the snakes asked God what their fate would be, as the human race would surely kill them. So God blessed them by saying, 'You have every right to punish those who harm you, kill you, destroy your house. You have every right to give them punishment and you are the master of your destiny'. Thus came into existence *Nag Dosh*; the penalty of killing Cobras. So you and me and Murli are going to Pashuram Shetra.

COBRA POWER

"You know these so called modern people find it strange that by killing a Cobra either in this life or past lives one suffers so badly. When you interview people you will realise how they have been wiped out because somebody in the family killed a Cobra. In fact, at the factory where we are going, the workers wanted to make a road and there was a big anthill. A bulldozer was brought and the anthill was destroyed. A lot of snakes came out and slithered away. I was informed about this entire incident later on. The next day it seems there were cobras in front of most of the houses. Also, one of those who incited the breaking of the anthill lost a member of the family due to a snake bite. I think his father died. In fact, due to the destruction of the anthill the vibration of the place was very badly affected. It was only after constructing a Devi Temple that things settled down and now there is no problem. So as I said snakes should not be angered or tampered with. In fact generators began to go anti clockwise. After I put the Lime, everything was all right. (A lime blessed by Ma Mookambika Devi. It has immense power as mentioned above in my own personal experience.)

"Of course, sometimes due to either karmic laws or just due to oversight sensible people do things which land them in trouble. For instance, a very successful industrialist wanted to set up a mineral water plant. You know the bottled water found everywhere nowadays. So the entire project was completed but they made one mistake. After completing the entire project and constructing everything, they then went about searching for water." Laughs aloud. "The raw material was water but there was no water. They tried their level best but every day there was a breakdown in the unit. They were not able to do anything. They were able to just fill a few bottles of water everyday, that is if there was no breakdown. Also, the workers complained to the management as well as to me, that in the afternoon between one and two o'clock, the factory used to shake. As though there was an earthquake. So every day, between this time, all the workers used to come out of the unit due to fear. Obviously something was wrong and they got various astrologers and lots of other people to check into the matter, but without success. In the end, somebody must have given them my name. I entered the complex and Devi informed Me that they had constructed a dirty water pit. Oblivious, to them there was a temple of Naga where now they were allowing dirty water to collect. I also told them that when they were digging the pit, a cobra came and they killed it. The management and the workers agreed that a cobra was killed. So we constructed a small temple of Naga, did poojas and after that day there were no problems whatsoever. Water never seems to stop flowing and the unit has not experienced a breakdown since then. That is the power of Nag, so one should be very careful during constructing anything. If there is a cobra around, make certain you are not harming it or destroying its habitat. Otherwise there is big trouble."

"Where was I, yes this place we are travelling through and towards is always green and nature has blessed this place. We have an attachment to this place because of our past connections. Originally, we are from Kashmir. We were staying on the banks of the Saraswati river. Thus we are known as Saraswat Brahmins. There was trouble in Kashmir, similar to what is happening now, so we ran to Calcutta and lived on the banks of the Gowda river. Due to shortage of food, our ancestors began to eat fish, and were hence called *Macha Brahmins* (fish eating brahmins). Again there were problems, so our forefathers came running to Goa. So our ancestors came down here. Thus centuries ago they all were worshippers of Devi. But with the arrival of the Portuguese, conversion began. They had a unique way of converting people to Christianity. What they would do is throw flesh into the well and those who drank water from the well became Christians. So, in a family one brother was a Christian and one brother was a Hindu. But even today, once a year, Christians have to visit a Devi Temple. They call her *Urli Mai*...Big Mother. So even today they have not yet broken off all connections with their Mother roots. So when the Portuguese conversion started, our people started running from there and came down to Mangalore, Kerala, Cochin etc. Thus, though we call ourselves Manglorians we are really Goanese. But in reality we are Kashmiris. But not all Macha Brahmins eat fish. Some of them do and some don't."

DIET AND SPIRITUALITY

"How important is diet, especially a veg diet, where at least realisation of God is concerned?"

"You see spirituality has nothing to do with diet. You can eat what you like. The only difference is that non-vegetarian food has its own effects on the body. You do not get tolerance and patience. You become rude. You become like the animal you eat. There is a saying 'you are what you eat and drink'. Now take me for example. I am a Swamiji. Why should I not drink? I can drink and eat whatever I want. If the body says I want to eat this, then I can eat whatever my body desires. But you know the most important thing, according to me, is the control of sex. Especially if you are a Swamiji and a man of God, you have to control sex. That is most important. There are various reasons for this but take it from Me, control of sex, is most important. But how one can control sex if you drink liquor and eat non-vegetarian food? It is very difficult. In fact, I don't think sex can be controlled if you are a nonvegetarian."

"You might ask why should sex be controlled and what is wrong with sex? The answer is that there is nothing wrong with sex, but if you are a Swamiji it is best to avoid it. The reason is simple. Now I am a Swamiji. A lot of people come to me. A lot of ladies come to me for help and advice. Good people may come and also people with not good intentions may come. Good and bad I mean motive wise. Now if I am consuming liquor and non-vegetarian food I may not be able to restrain myself from baser emotions. So to make sure that Sages do not ruin the lives of women it is important that They curtail and stop sex. It becomes very difficult to get a grip on your emotions and desires if you consume liquor and non-vegetarian food. First thing needed to become a Swamiji is the will power to curtail sex. Sex can create lot of problems. But remember indulging in sex is not a sin. Provided it is in limits, sex is certainly not a sin. But if sex is going to ruin lives then it is very bad."

"Of course, there is another reason to curtail sex. The power of the human beings is based in the Muladhara Chakra, the root chakra. From here the power moves upwards and in the end merges with the crown chakra and ShivShakti is achieved. But if you go on enjoying sex, the power is dissipated. The very word 'discharge' says it all. The spiritual battery is charged and can achieve a lot, but with discharge the progress is very slow. So you have to control sex to get more spiritual power. If you cannot control yourself how will you control others? And you are with a lot of people. You will meet lots of people. Good people, bad people, ladies…good or bad…they may come to ruin you…and if you cannot control your sex then you become a victim of it. In fact, in my horoscope it is said that I am a *Bhrashta Sanyasi* (a Fallen Angel). That is what the astrologers say… that I am a *Bhrashta Sanyasi*. That is, in my last life as a Sanyasi (sage/monk)I should not have done certain things but I indulged in them. So that is why in this life I am neither a Sanyasi nor a complete family man."

"So once again I repeat that sex and non-vegetarian food is not bad but it should not be taken because of the above mentioned things. It should not be taken because the effect it has on the body. For example, long ago, sanyasis used to wear wooden *chappals* and at the top, there was a vertical wooden nail like thing coming out, which was meant to fit between the big toe and the index toe. Even priests in your religion wear something similar. Well, this was compulsory for all sanyasis. This has got something to do with accu-pressure. The point where the wooden nail meets the flesh between the big toe and the other toe is supposed to be the pressure point where by sex control takes place. This point controls the urge to have sex. But now, modern day swamijis have put a belt and thrown the nail out." Once again He laughs loudly and looks at me intently. "Earlier, there was a reason and logic for everything. For instance, ladies should not come in front of Swamijis and Sages. That is to make certain that temptation does not arise. If you can control your body and if you can control your mind, then it does not matter what you are doing and what you are eating and drinking. But for that realisation to come through is very difficult. It is very difficult to control all the desires. Many Saints failed in their attempts because of sex. But within limits I don't think sex is bad. It is nature's law. How can it be bad."

We arrived at the famous Maha Lakshmi temple. We all paid our obeisance and while Amma offered special prayers, we took a stroll through the massive complex.

"I believe that every body, every creature has the right to live. We have no right to take their life just to eat or enjoy ourselves. When God has given us so many different things to eat and live by, why should we take the life of innocent animals. But once again I repeat, spirituality and diet have no connection. Do you know that the Ramakrishna Paramahansa Mission (International Hostel) in Calcutta serves chicken and eggs? In Kerala, liquor is served in some temples. So, as I was saying, if you can digest liquor physically and also control your senses, especially in regards to sex, then I don't think there is any harm in drinking. But how many can control their senses after consuming liquor? Sages and Saints have failed due to sex and liquor." We sat down on the steps under the shade. Murli walked around lost in his own contemplation.

DEVI AND SWAMIJI

"Devi has tested me for nearly nine years. I went through a very bad phase. There were times when there was no food to eat or feed the family. She really tested me very strictly. I remember once She materialized a glass of whisky and a glass of holy water. She asked me to drink from whichever glass I wanted. Now before I became a Swamiji I used to drink and enjoy my drinks. I have bought a bottle for just fifty paisa and also bought a bottle costing two thousand rupees. So, when after months, I was being given a chance to drink liquor, that too by Devi herself, I wanted to make the most out of it. But for an hour or more I contemplated. My hand would reach for the whisky glass but I would pull it back. I could drink the whisky and then if scolded, I could easily say 'But Ma I was only doing what You asked me to do. You gave me an option and I chose one of them'. But I knew that Devi is very shrewd. She always has something up Her sleeve. So in the end, very reluctantly, I chose the glass of holy water. Of course, She still scolded me for taking so much time to decide between nectar and liquor, but then what do Goddesses know about the fun of enjoying a good drink." He smiled with a twinkle in His eyes.

"But the ultimate test was when one night I found a beautiful woman sleeping next to me. You see, I had vowed to be celibate for the remaining of my life. Now you can imagine my plight when I woke up one night to find this very, very beautiful woman lying next to me. She was not only really very attractive, but to add further to my woes, this woman was completely naked. She was asleep. As though nothing had bloody happened. So then I just touched her wrist to make certain that she was real and not just an illusion. She was very real. So then I got up and noticed that the doors and windows were shut tight. If this woman did not come through the door or the window then obviously she was no ordinary woman. So I sat on the bed and loudly told her 'Devi please let me sleep. Stop trying to play such games with me that too so late at night'. Immediately the woman disappeared and then Devi appeared in all Her glory. She looked at me and said 'Patri now you are ready. You have passed all tests I had in mind for you'. Saying this She disappeared leaving me wide awake, in the middle of the night."

"Baba, these Gods and Devi are very shrewd. They will test you and as you evolve, the tests will become more difficult and complicated. I mean testing a sleeping man with a beautiful woman lying all naked is not a very fair thing to do. But They will go on and on testing you. That is how God works. The more advanced you become the harder the tests. The bigger and scarier the problems. But if you have faith in Them and work to the best of your capability to stand up to your beliefs, then you have nothing to fear. Once They know that your intentions are good and you are strong enough to stand by them, then They will always be on your side. They will not let you go away from them as They have invested lots of time and energy in you. Remember, without us what will God do. Similarly, without God we cannot exist. We need each other."

We then visited another temple. In the temple's compound there is a building constructed for pilgrims who wish to stay for a few days. We sat in one of the rooms and ate a hearty meal. The meal was a very simple affair but really delicious stuff. After the meal we sat and talked about the various God men who are mushrooming from all parts of the country. Some even claiming that they are God or God incarnates.

"Shirdi Sai Baba has sent you to Me. He has asked you to write this book. At the moment His presence is very strong in this room. You know, Sai Baba never claimed that He was God. He always said Allah Malik. That means God is the Master. In the same way even I am nobody. Just a person who Devi blessed to be Her medium, so that She could work and help mankind. She is the Mother of the Universe. I am just Her agent and Her medium. All these people who claim that they are so powerful etc. are false. I am not enlightened. I don't know anything. My philosophy is 'be simple and serve mankind'. That is what Devi wants to do through me. I can't give predictions. Devi speaks through me. I have no powers. All the miracles that have happened through me are due to Devi's grace. Devi wants it to happen so they take place. Shirdi Sai Baba is with us right now. But remember, He is everywhere and not in Shirdi alone. That is because God is everywhere. Devi is everywhere. I am very close to Sai Baba of Shirdi. The only thing I disagreed with Baba was that sometimes He would cook non-vegetarian food for those devotees who ate meat. I disagreed with Him. Similarly, I have disagreed with a number of such Powers. That is why, in my horoscope I am a *Bhrasht Brahmin/Sanyasi*. As I did not agree with certain things and did things my own way, that is why in my recent incarnation I have had to undergo lots of obstacles. Take your case itself. In your last birth, Sai Baba of Shirdi asked you, to perform a particular religious exercise. He wanted you to do a particular *tapasiya*...a penance. You had nearly finished completing it, when at the last moment you walked away angrily, thinking that it was waste of time. Just for that act you have come back." For a while there was silence in the room.

"Were you always inclined to be a Swamiji?"

"Arey no! I was very happy with my life as a family man. I never knew much about Devi. The only Devis I knew were those acting in movies. I was virtually forced into becoming a Swami. At the age of forty, I was married with five children, working as an Electrical Engineer in Philips India, Bangalore. One fine day I began to get these dreams and She entered my life...but not directly. I used to get messages. Mainly that I had lived as a family man long enough and now it was my turn to return to the fold. 'Return where?' I used to wonder. Then I began to get messages of 'what not to wear, what not to eat and what not to do'. Of course I never bothered."

"What do you mean by messages and what clothes did She not want you to wear?"

"Messages would come in the state of dreams or be scribbled on the wall...yes scribbled on the walls. I have photographs that I shall show you once you are in Bangalore. Where clothes are concerned She did not want me to wear shirts and pants but the robe of a swamiji. Of course I never obeyed, so She began to burn my clothes..."

"That's cool, but how would Devi burn your clothes?"

"As I told you never mess with Devi. The moment I would remove certain clothes to wear, the shirt or pant would catch fire...first smoke would start emanating and then the clothes would be burnt as though somebody had left a hot iron on the clothes for too long. Baba, these Devis are very shrewd. Or I would wear the clothes and when I would remove them and put them on the hanger, they would begin to burn. All this was rather scary and you must remember, that all my life I have never got scared of anything. I have fought with armed men single handedly and nothing scares me, but all this was too much to take and the worst thing was that She did not bother to reveal to me who was behind all this. Then, as though burning my clothes was not enough, She then began to make all good things in life disappear. Beer and whisky bottles would disappear. I would buy the drink, hoping to enjoy it, get it home, place it on the table, go to the kitchen to get a glass and a mug of water and return to find not a trace of the silly bottle. All this was driving me up the wall and making me really angry. So I went to astrologers and tantrics and so called swamijis, as I wanted to know who was burning my bloody clothes and stealing my whisky. But all of them only told me that I was possessed and black magic had been done to me. This went on for a year and a half. In the end, I got so fed up that one day I locked myself in my room and said aloud ' whoever you are show yourself to me and tell me what on earth do you want from me?' Then our Devi very calmly showed Herself to me. I told you She is very shrewd but yes She is full of love."

The other car had by now got repaired and we continued our journey in different cars. Murli and I travelled in one, while Swamiji and Amma drove in the other. If I was not around, Murli would have certainly sat in the front seat along with Swamiji, but all through the journey, till I reached home, he made certain that I was never made to feel out of place or alone. The road to Dandeli is rather adventurous. The car goes through the State of Goa and enters the State of Karnataka. You normally pass through thick jungles and forestation. All through the road you pass huge trees and massive, tall ant-hills. You really need a tough car and a back made of steel. The roads (if you can call deep moon like craters roads), have been designed by folks with a sadistic sense of humour. Whoever is behind the construction of these roads, for sure has shares and bonds in automobile companies and has a stake with orthopedics all over the vicinity. Murli and I sat in a state of back breaking daze, contemplating various wicked, ingenious ways of deep frying the man behind such nefarious roads.

"I know this is not the time for conversation but why don't you continue your narration about Swamiji ...ouch...if not for anything than just to distract our attention from this Karnataka Road Department Torture."

MIRACLE WATER

"Okay, I get the point. As I have told you, I had bought a farm sometime earlier. Now, initially the farm had two bore-wells that yielded enough water to service the plantations. But after a while, during the months of March to May, the water from these bore-wells began to get saline. This meant the water was unfit for drinking. One day, Swamiji visited my farm and very casually inquired with my staff about anything strange happening below a particular tree. For a while, everybody remained silent and then my farm's caretaker, Abdul, informed us that sometimes he saw a flame below the mentioned tree in the night. Swamiji nodded and then selected a spot twenty five feet away from that tree. He told me to bore down to the depth of about 225 feet. He left for Bangalore. All my people scoffed and ridiculed the idea. Abdul kept telling me not to waste time and effort, but Swamiji's word is law for me. If He says something, it means Devi has said it. The boring began and at 225 feet no water was available. I rang up Swamiji and He said to bore further for another twenty-five feet. Sure enough, sweet water was found at 250 feet, exactly at the spot directed by Swamiji, without any fancy equipment used by geologists. The water from the predicted bore-well is now the only source of sweet water for the entire area during the summer. Swamiji also instructed me to construct a Devi mandir under that particular tree and whenever He visits my farm, we sit below the tree and discuss various subjects for hours. In fact, it is really great to sit and meditate below the tree."

"Do your workers believe in Devi and Swamiji's powers now?"

"Without any doubt. In fact, my farm is between two villages; Kalhe and Barapada. In Barapada, most of the inhabitants are Muslims. The headman of this village, a Muslim, is the manager of my farm. Just the other day, he came over and wanted to take Swamiji to his village, so that Swamiji could point out most sacred section of land, where they could construct their place of worship."

"Does Swamiji meditate?"

"Ha! Never. He cannot sit in one spot for a long time. He has to be on the move. No meditation and silent contemplation for our Swamiji. His meditation is mainly helping thousand and one people who either come personally to meet Him or phone Him everyday. You know another very interesting thing happened once. A number of friends have farms adjoining each other. Abdul began noticing that at a particular time, a cobra would come from another person's farm and enter our farm. This would happen at around noon. The cobra would do nothing but still you never know...what if someone working for me kills it...I mean, killing a cobra is asking for big time trouble. So I telephoned Swamiji and He, very casually, told me to place one of the Limes blessed by Devi and Him, in the very path that the cobra normally took while travelling from our neighbour's farm to my farm. By now, everybody knows that Swamiji is no ordinary soul. Even Abdul, though a staunch Muslim, is well aware of the power of Devi and Swamiji and the blessed Lime there. So Abdul, very coolly, went and placed the Lime. Next day, Abdul telephoned to say that the cobra was taken care of. He informed me that as instructed by Swamiji, he placed the Lime on the daily route taken by the cobra. As usual, the cobra came towards my farm and when it was just near the Lime, an eagle or a hawk swooped down through the air and nearly attacked the cobra. The cobra took an about turn and returned to my neighbour's farm and from that day onwards we have never seen the cobra. The Limes are like dynamite...ouuccch!"

We defied gravity, hit our heads on the top of the vehicles and landed back on our seats.

"If the Lime was ever needed to be placed on a road then I think its this one, what say Murli?"

He nodded an affirmative. Then in silence, we stared at the huge ant-hills on the right side of the road, tall trees on the left side of the road and massive craters straight ahead in the road. We groaned in unison.

After half an hour, we saw a small café and told the driver to halt for a cuppa coffee. It was nearing sunset and it was pleasant outside. We stretched our backs and in return heard our bodies give out various strange noises of protest. Murli entered the café to make certain that the joint was habitable and I entered a phone booth to call up home and tell them that unfortunately for the world at large I was still very much around and kicking. Various heroines in various stages of undress stared at me while I tried to convince the booth operator that all I wanted was Mumbai's STD code and not a room or a hot massage. Swamiji's car arrived and I walked towards it. He got out and stretched His back.

"Baba, horrrrible road!" After He made certain that the chauffeurs were also taken care of, Swamiji ordered ice- cold soda. He gulped down half the contents and then passed the bottle to me. I could make out that the journey had tired Amma too. What most devotees forget while with Swamiji and Amma is the essential fact that they both are no longer young. Swamiji is above seventy years though He still lived a life that would tax people half His age.

An hour or so before we arrived at Dandeli, Swamiji halted the cars to show us a meditation spot that overlooked the valley and the water below. It was a very picturesque sight. The sun just about to set, the valley below, the sky that kept stretching for what seemed like miles and the birds flying to and fro making a nuisance of themselves, basically telling one and all about the sun setting and the much need sleep to follow.

"This spot is very good for meditation. Centuries earlier sages and monks would meditate for months on this spot." The spot was virtually next to the road and overlooked the valley. "Of course, now if a person tries to meditate here, either he will be robbed in half an hour, get run over by a truck or for sure get very ill by the exhaust fumes." With a chuckle He got into the car and the journey to Dandeli continued.

It was already dark when the cars zoomed through Dandeli's market place. Murli informed that the entire township depended mainly on West Coast Paper Mills and that was the main reason why Swamiji paid so much attention to the well being of the company. Minutes later we entered West Coast premises;

a sprawling township, a town within a town with all the basic amenities and necessities to lead a life within its artificial womb.

Swamiji was greeted like royalty by the management and as usual, He accepted the greeting with grace while blessing one and all.

"Meet Murli, he is like a son to me and this is Ruzbeh, he is writing a book on Devi." All through out, Swamiji introduced me in such a manner. He not once tried to impress anybody about the fact that apart from Devi, He was the central figure.

We sat down in the spacious drawing room with numerous top officials of the company, all visibly delighted to have Swamiji with them once again.

"Swamiji we were really worried about the pooja what with the warnings of cyclone..."

"Has Devi ever allowed the poojas to get disturbed? Remember two years ago, it kept raining continuously but on the day of the pooja the sky was clear..."

"Yes and the moment the pooja got over and people had their meals, it began to rain once again..."

"In fact, the rains cleared all the path. Devi never allows Her work to be disturbed."

"You are writing a book on Devi..."

"Sai Baba of Shirdi has asked him to write a book on Devi and also to write down all the miracles experienced by our devotees." Swamiji looked at me and smiled.

For me it was really a memorable moment. Though all this while I had been sitting for auto writing sessions and innumerable people had benefited through the guidance of Sai Baba, for some reason, I still doubted the entire process. I was not sure whether it was really He, Sai Baba of Shirdi or just my subconscious mind at play. Thus, when Swamiji Himself informed all those seated, that I was writing this book, as per the instructions of Sainath, it was a confirmation that Baba really used me as an instrument and medium. Murli looked at me and gave me a broad smile, as he was aware of doubts assailing me regarding this entire paranormal process. In fact through out, Murli has been really supportive and never misses an opportunity to speak about how Sai Baba channels through me to help people.

RESCUED FROM A SPIRIT

Suddenly, a man and a young girl were brought from outside and made to stand in front of Swamiji. The man told Swamiji that since a few days his daughter had stopped talking to everybody and moved about as though in a daze. Swamiji stared at the girl for a few seconds and then placed His hand on the girl's head.

"Somebody died in your family or around your home recently. ..."

"Yes, our neighbour's girl... she died a few days ago very young..."

"This child of yours is being possessed by that girl. Don't worry, all will be well." All this while, Swamiji kept His hand on the girl's head. He asked for two limes and a knife. He then made three marks on the lime and after a few seconds of prayers, He gave the lime to the girl to hold.

"Leave this child alone or tomorrow I will have to take real action. Just leave the child alone. Don't stay here, just go." Though Swamiji looked at the girl, it was obvious that He was talking to somebody else; the spirit that had taken hold of the small girl. "Go away or else there will be trouble. Do you understand?" A minute or two later the girl began to cry. "Are you feeling better now?" For a while the girl spoke nothing. Then she nodded her head.

"Yes...I am better now..." She spoke in Hindi.

"Get her again tomorrow and make sure that this lime is next to her."

"She spoke after days Swamiji." The father was visibly moved and it was obvious he did not want to cry in front of so many people.

"Don't worry, that woman will not come near her now, but get her tomorrow during the time of the havan. Go."

For a while, there was silence in the hall. It must be remembered that those who sat within, to the exclusion of Murli and I, were all corporate people; in fact most of them managing either the technical or the financial aspect of the paper mill. For them, this was rather different.

"That woman who died suddenly wants to live her life through this girl. But Devi is great. No trouble now."

"Hello Swamiji!"

"Ohhh Chandakji. How are you?"

"With your grace..."

"And Devi's grace..."

"Of course and with Devi's grace completely alright. How was your journey? I see that you have taken care of the cyclone." The room resounded with laughter. "Like always, rains and cyclones play truant the moment Swamiji enters Dandeli."

For the next hour, along with coffee and snacks, preparation for the next day's havan was discussed. Mr. Chandak, Executive Director, of West Coast Paper Mills, was a handsome man who did not look as though he had grown up and married children. He looked not more than forty-five.

"So you are writing the book. It is really a very good service you are doing to lots of people, for we have seen first hand the miracles of Devi through Swamiji. We have seen how innumerable people have benefited and how innumerable people can be helped through the book, once the word spreads around. Don't get fooled by Swamiji's benign looks and sense of humour. He is a powerhouse. Really tender but with amazing spiritual power..."

"Chandakji, I am nothing. It is all the work of Devi..."

"But it is through You that we see everything happening. Of course, who can deny the love of Devi. She has time and again saved us from disasters..."

"How did you meet Swamiji?"

"See, Swamiji had first visited Dandeli for the first time in February 1988. That was really one of the most crucial periods for the company. I mean it was struggling for survival. Apart from the factory running in a loss and the financial situation looking very bleak, there were innumerable labour problems too. And to add further fuel to the raging fire, every now and then fatal accidents kept taking place in the factory. Swamiji visited our factory and immediately informed us that lots and lots of snakes had been killed during the construction of the factory. He insisted that a temple be constructed inside the factory with the idols of Lord Ganesh and Nag Devta installed within the temple. Initially the management was not very keen to construct a temple as there was already a huge Shri Ram temple located outside the factory but in the middle of our colony. But Swamiji insisted that a temple had to be constructed inside the factory under a Banyan tree, as the tree was a very powerful site as it belonged to snakes and with the worship of Ganesh and Nag Devta, most of the problems facing the company would vanish. In fact, I still remember Swamiji telling us in 1988, that a time shall come when the company shall not have enough space to expand, so well would the company fare. Frankly, I don't think anybody really believed Swamiji then, as the scenario was really bad and bleak. But within a short period of time after the temple was constructed and blessed by Ganesh, Devi and Swamiji, the entire situation changed. The financial situation began to improve, fatal accidents virtually stopped and the best part of it all was that the relationship between the management and the labour union really got better."

"In fact, initially the labour union and the workers boycotted the annual pooja and havan. They would not even partake of the prasadam as for some reason they thought that we were trying to do some black magic. But now, the entire company and the workers and their families wait for the annual pooja and have food and really it is an amazing transformation. I still remember that in 1989, one day Swamiji telephoned the Bangalore office and enquired as to the affairs of the mills and the factory. He expressed a desire that immediately the annual pooja should be performed. Of course, we all were keen to perform the pooja, but as in all commercial organisations, it takes time to get such things organised. Exactly a week later the factory had the biggest accident which could have really spelt doom and disaster for everybody. In fact, we all really believe that it was Devi's and Swamiji's blessings that averted a catastrophe of immense magnitude."

"The accident took place in the Pulp Mill. The top doom cover, made of iron, of the Digester Blow Tank No. 2, which weighs around seven to eight metric tons blew up. Now this massive and heavy doom like structure, flew in the sky and like a saucer in the air travelled about 100 odd meters and fell down near the railway tracks. It passed through by the side of the Soda Recovery plant building and fell far away from harms length. I shudder to think what would have happened if this heavy structure would have fallen bang down or any other place but from where it landed. In fact, the accident occurred at around seven in the morning, when the employees were in the process of changing shifts. I mean, God forbid if the structure would have landed on our premises, it would have been a catastrophe. Only Devi could have protected all of us and made sure that not one single person was injured and that we hardly had to incur any financial loss."

"In fact, when Swamiji had first visited our plant He had very casually remarked that this was the most accident prone site He had ever visited. The only difference being, first for small reasons fatal accidents used to take place and after the advent of Devi and Swamiji even major disasters did not lead to a single death. It took a few years for even those disasters to stop and now everything is perfectly alright. I remember around that time another miraculous incident took place. A 52 meter high iron plate chimney, which was under erection meant for the diesel generator set, suddenly crashed and fell in such a way that, neither was anybody injured nor did the company have to incur any financial loss. Had this 150 feet long iron plate landed a few feet either way, it would have dashed into live electric wires of our HT line passing through and my God that would have resulted in great disaster. You see, when you hear about all this or read these things, you might wonder as to what was so miraculous, but remember we live and work here. For that dome to fly nearly 300 feet away and fall at the only safe place or this

150 feet iron plate to land at the only safe spot once again, is not just coincidence. We know it has the stamp of Devi's and Swmaiji's protection written all over."

MAYHEM CORRECTED

"Once, after a few years, Swamiji was taking a round of the area and He passed through the area of the Contractor — Sub Contractors labour chawl. Immediately, Swamiji halted and said that this area was a trouble spot and that there were unusual things happening in this area. So Swamiji called the security guard and inquired if the man heard or saw or felt anything beyond the normal happening in this area. The guard immediately confessed, that during the night, he heard unusual noises and movements that compelled him to confine himself to the plant's building only. He confessed that whatever was happening was unusual and scary. Then Swamiji interviewed a few residents of the colony and different problems came to light. All agreed that at night this area was virtually spooky. Swamiji then visited the First Diesel Generator set, which was almost ready and a final trial was to take place. He once again expressed his displeasure and inquired if all was going as planned with the generator. Everybody agreed that some or the other problem kept cropping up every day and the schedules had gone haywire. Swamiji casually informed that there was something really weird taking place. The Site Engineer agreed. You see we are all technical people. We are more technology prone and thus feel odd and out of place when talking about anything that is out of our orbit. So, the Engineer very softly said, that one thing really weird taking place and that was out of his comprehension, was the fact that the Generator/Motor ran in a reverse direction; something that is considered highly impossible. He had noticed it about thrice. Each time this took place, he had made certain that every nut and bolt and all the accessories were in the right order and state of functioning. But the very next day, the generator would start moving in the reverse direction. Swamiji then insisted that the very next day an Agori Havan and certain poojas had to be performed. The moment all this was done, a successful commissioning of the DG Set took place without any problems. A temple was also constructed and the idols installed. Swamiji predicted that the area would now develop very rapidly. True to His words, two more DG Sets were installed in the same area without any trouble. I mean, what to say about Devi and our Swamiji. What more can I say..."

"Say that dinner is ready, Chandakji." Swamiji spoke with that usual twinkle in his eyes. Then He laughed. "You see We can tell a thousand and one things. But faith plays an all important role. The faith that you people in West Coast have in Devi and in Me is amazing. A number of times destinies are changed just because of the immense faith the disciple has in his or her Guru." We entered the dining room.

I entered last. Just a week prior, while in a state of trance, Sainath had said a very similar thing. He had said; "Your faith in your Guru should be so much that it shakes Him up. The Guru should be shaken up by your faith. That is real faith."

Woke up in the morning, with the ulcers really giving me a deuce of a bother. Looked outside and the dawn was caressing the skyline. The sun waited patiently someplace in the horizon to make its grand entry and birds flew about in all probability wanting to catch that worm who was silly enough to venture out so early in the morn. English is a strange language. All those who do not live by the dictates of the clock, are reminded of that early bird...'it is the early bird that catches the worm' so be early and about. Give a thought to that damn worm. It was caught and consumed without much culinary effort because it too was early and about, venturing God alone knows where and why.

I went for a short walk and stopped in front of the Ram Mandir. A soothing bhajan was being softly played over the mike that waltzed all over the township. The air had a bite in it and I looked at the sky to realise that not only had the cyclone thrown in the towel, but no monsoon clouds threatened to interrupt the pooja and the meal scheduled hours from now. I observed the priests performing the pooja. After a while one of the priests, got down the stairs and approached me.

"Everything is ready. You can get married as per schedule."

"Eh?"

"Just make sure that the garlands are proper...oh sorry you are not the person who is going to marry...okay okay sorry." Saying this the young priest walked away. I stood there staring at him and then turned towards the guest-house. I wondered at the reaction from the family, if instead of cashew nuts from Goa, I presented a woman from Dandeli. I returned to the guest-house and saw Swamiji seated on one of the chairs outside. I took His blessings.

"Good you got up. It is really a nice place."

"You don't sound well Swamiji? Are you all right?"

"Okay. No longer as young as before and that trip was horrrible."

"Murli is also not too well. He was feeling cold in the night. The place is really nice."

"You visited the Ram Mandir?"

"Yeah! Really well made. But I heard from Murli that temples constructed under your supervision are really out of the world? The one in Bangalore certainly is..."

"Ruzbeh, you see this is my last incarnation. My ninth and last incarnation. As I have told you, I have come back because I did not follow all that which was told to me. I have spent my early incarnations along with Saints. I have always been associated with Saints; brother saints. I was told in my early incarnations to build certain temples. Temples that are very famous now, ones in all the religious places in India... Madhurai, Kanyakumari etc were started by me. I was told to construct them. It was my karma but then due to some reason or the other I left the construction work of these temples incomplete. The temples were in the end, completed by other people, but as I kept leaving my work incomplete, I had to keep coming back to learn to complete whatever I undertook; especially as it was religious and spiritual by nature. Just like you had to come back because you did not complete your penance that Sai Baba wanted you to complete. Never take on any work and then leave it incomplete. Never. If you cannot see through a project then you can be rest assured, that you are going to keep returning till you learn the experience. Most of the famous temples were begun by me but never completed by me. That is why in this lifetime I have once again been given the opportunity to build temples and this time.

"I am making certain that I see through their completion. The temples built by me are through the directions and specifications of Devi. I do not know anything about the rituals and requirements of making temples. Over here many temples have been constructed, but where to construct them and which idol of God or Goddess is to be consecrated is something I do not know. Devi directs and I follow. Good morning Mr. Murli. "Teased Swamiji." "I was telling Ruzbeh that the temples built under Devi's specifications will obviously be powerful...."

"They are all very powerful. Of course, no temple constructed by Swamiji is as powerful as the temple of Ma Mookambika in Bangalore. It is the Mecca for Devi worshippers."

Our coffee arrived. "You know, the funny part is that most of the times the priests think that all the troubles are vanishing because of their prayers. For instance, take Dandeli. There were earlier lots of problems and now everything is all right. If you ask the priests, who come along with Swamiji as to why the troubles are being solved, they will say it is because of their prayers. They will not give Him the credit. What they do not realise is that it is because Devi directs Swamiji, in which location the temple has to be constructed and which Deity has to be consecrated and which prayers and havans have to be performed so that difficult and impossible situations get altered for the good..."

"It is the presence of Devi that does all the trick. Of course, most priests think it is because of them that the problems are getting solved. The important thing is to pinpoint the root cause of the problem and the solution to it, which only Devi can do."

I was reminded of that story about a very famous but an extremely expensive engineer. There was this man who charged the earth for solving problems that stared into the eyes of the automobile industry. But, as he was so dashed expensive, nobody would touch him unless it was unavoidable. One day he was called to solve a problem. A very expensive machine refused to work. Everybody had tried their hands and their capabilities, but the machine cared two defrosted nails. Now this specialist was called in to solve the problem. He spent a few minutes observing the machine and then lit a cigarette, then called for a hammer, banged the hammer on a nail once and then switched on the machine and that blasted thing began to work as though nothing was wrong with it. He collected a bag stuffed with cash, smiled and began to leave the premises. The boss stopped him.

"Don't you think you are charging just too much for just knocking one horrible nail." Our man lit another cigarette and scratched his unshaven cheek.

"I charged you just ten dollars for banging that nail..."

"Oh no you didn't. I have just handed you a bag full of cash..."

"Ten dollars for banging the nail in. The remaining cash is for knowing which horrible nail to bang."

We drank another cup of coffee and were about to get up when a middle-aged man, came and stood in front of Swamiji with folded hands.

DEVI'S HEALING PROWESS
"How are you Munshiji?"

"With your grace how can I not be fine."

"Whenever I come here, Munshiji comes and gives me a much need massage. Come, we shall go inside the room."

Munshiji was the local barber. He got about doing his work without much ado. He started with Swamiji's head and kept talking about various developments taking place in and around Dandeli. He, too, agreed with the fascinating change that Devi and Swamiji had brought about to the paper mill and township.

"You know something very strange has been happening with me. I am a barber but after massaging Swamiji for a few years, all of a sudden I have realised that people are getting rid of lots of aches and pains when I massage them. For a while, I thought that maybe it is all in their head, but nowadays people with aches and pains in their body specially come to me for getting rid of pain. I have come to the conclusion that it is because of massaging Swamiji and sages like Him, that God has, all of a sudden, bestowed the power of healing to these hands.

"Swamiji, just a few days back, a woman with a major neck problem came to the shop. She was really in bad shape and she said that even medicines were not helping out. I had helped a family member when he was in some pain, so he had sent her to me. I said a short prayer and gave just stroked the neck. The pain vanished. She could not believe and worse, even I could not believe it. I mean this is really strange. I do not have any knowledge about all this healing-bealing but just take God's name, remember Devi and Swamiji and healing takes place."

He continued massaging Swamiji for about twenty minutes with oil. Swamiji's cough had gotten worse and thus, Munshi applied Vicks to His chest and lovingly tucked Swamiji to bed. Murli and I entered our room. There was a long day ahead.

As the day passed, it was obvious that Swamiji was not well. But it is difficult to pin Him to his bed. There were a number of poojas to be performed and since morning, prayers had already commenced. The respect and love accorded to Swamiji was palpable. From the top brass to the workers, they all came and took His blessings. Sometime nearing noon, Swamiji realised that a number of articles needed for a major ceremony, had been left behind in Bangalore, due to an oversight. The nearest place these things could be purchased was around 100 kilometers away.

"Let's go and get them."

"But, Swamiji, you are not well. Why don't you tell the company officials to get the stuff?"

"I have to select the things. Come, lets go. We shall go in two cars."

THE MARVELOUS WAYS OF DEVI

So, once again we all seated ourselves in the Ambassadors. Murli, a company official and I, in one car, while Swamiji, Amma and others came in another car. First, we halted at the Worker's Colony, where a mandir was being constructed. They showed Swamiji around and He asked for certain changes to be done. Then we left for the city. It was a pleasant drive and we moved through the forest, the ubiquitous ant-hills, the small farms in the distance and beyond, the hills.

"Murli, continue with your experiences."

"I have finished telling you everything..."

"Bosh!"

"Bosh to you!" For a while we sat in perfect silence.

"Murli, continue with your experiences."

"You don't give up do you?"

"I have two children at home. They have perfected the art of driving people up the wall..."

"Learnt and mastered from their father..."

"Very hilarious..."

"What do you want to know..."

"More stuff on Swamiji."

"Okay, you remember my best friend…"

"Yeah, that chap who lives near the Church and who is now happily divorced…"

"Yes, same person. Well, some time back he was in Mumbai for a holiday and for some unknown reason, he climbed onto the stool, and promptly fell down and injured his head badly. He was rushed to the Hinduja hospital, where all his doctor friends work. He was really in bad pain. I mean he was literally screaming and they had to inject him with really high dose of pain-killers to just keep him calm. The opinion amongst the doctors was that he had not only suffered a hair-line fracture, but more importantly, he had injured a particular spot on his forehead which is considered very important for memory and co-ordination.

"Now, my friend is a specialist doctor in Canada. His job entails treatment and operation of premature babies, which requires super efficient co-ordination. His own friends realised that such a high-pressured job would be out of question for him now. I used to visit this friend every day and one day on my visit, I found him in terrible pain. He was in extreme agony. He sat with his head between his thigh and both hands covering his head. He was virtually screaming at the doctors asking for morphine since even high doses of pain killers had proven ineffective. He looked at me and loudly inquired as to what on earth was Swamiji doing and predicting? So, the same day, I called up Swamiji and asked Him that if He could visit my friend at the earliest. Swamiji came to the hospital in a few days and after seeing my friend, gave him a Lime. He told him to put the blessed Lime under his pillow and that all would be fine and he would not only get alright, but would be able to resume his normal activities within a month. To get fine and resume work in a month was something unimaginable, as not only was the pain severe, but he had a fracture and a nasty injury on the most delicate part of the head. All Swamiji warned my friend was, to avoid driving for a year. Within a week my friend was discharged and as predicted by Swamiji, he resumed his high powered job without any problems. In fact, he feels so grateful and obliged that he has promised Swamiji that he will come over to India and work in the hospital that Swamiji intends to construct in Subramaniya in three years time…"

"That is, if he can stay long enough from falling of stools and landing on his head."

"Should I assume this is the end of our conversation?"

"Sorry. Go on."

REMOTE HEALING

"Yes, another thing is that I have seen Him save lives of people, even sitting miles away in Bangalore. Someone might phone him up asking whether his or her family member's operation will be successful or not. Swamiji will only ask for the person's name and then not only answer whether the person's operation will be a success or not, but even whether the person should get operated and also whether the diagnosis of the doctor is correct or not. So many times he has corrected the doctor's diagnosis. At first, the doctors get angry, but later on become Swamiji's devotees. So many times he has asked the patient to just walk out of the hospital as no operation was necessary. The best part is that devotees will not think twice. Of course, many times he has predicted the time and date when a person will pass away. Many people say the time and date of death and birth cannot be predicted, but I have seen with my own eyes, Swamiji predicting the exact time and date of both death and birth."

"Is that why He never keeps the phone off the hook, even when He is ill?"

"Yes. I have seen people call him up from abroad and within India at the oddest hours. They just want to consult Him before taking any major step, especially if it is regarding their health or the health of their family and friends. I remember once Swamiji had come to Mumbai and as usual we had spent the entire day outside. We reached home late at night and both of us were exhausted. Swamiji took a bath and went to sleep. Late at night, the telephone rang and it was a lady who desperately wanted to talk to Swamiji regarding some major problem. She was really nervous as her husband had suffered a heart attack and the doctors wanted to perform a major heart surgery. The problem lay in the fact that her husband was adamant that unless and until he received the blessings and the sanction of Devi and Swamiji, he would not allow anybody to even touch his body, forget perform an operation. I, very hesitatingly, woke Swamiji and He immediately began to speak to the woman. He predicted that her husband had three blockages and should go ahead with the operation and that everything would be fine and that He would pray to Devi that all would go well. He then blessed them both, put the phone down, informed me that both, husband and wife were doctors in USA and promptly went back to sleep. In the morning the next day, the lady called and confirmed that her husband had three blockages and that he was recuperating well."

"Another aspect where Swamiji is very helpful is in cases where there is doubt regarding malignancy of tumour. So often, devotees come to Swamiji asking Him about the life span of their near and dear ones who are undergoing chemotherapy...radiation etc to fight a malignant tumour. Many times Swamiji has predicted that the tumour is not malignant and that no chemotherapy is required and has advised them to stop this painful treatment of cancer. He, at such times, advises the family to take a second opinion and I have myself seen families return with tears in their eyes, with the news that the medical fraternity had goofed up earlier and that the tumour was not malignant. Also according to me Swamiji is a Messiah for childless couples. In appropriate cases, he even advises the couple not to spend any money, as they would become parents, but only after a certain time period. Or, He advises the couple to fulfill certain promises made by their ancestors to a particular Deity, church or dargha or to go to Subramaniya to remove the curse of the serpents..."

"Nag Dosh.."

"Yes."

Our driver was in no particular hurry. He seemed content to let the car travel at its own pace with the least pressure on the accelerator. The scenary outside was very pleasant. I certainly did not miss the Mumbai traffic and the incessant attempts by cab and bus drivers to reduce the population of the city.

"Another thing about Swamiji is that He never asks for money from anybody. He has solved the problems of so many important industrialists. Saved them crores of rupees but He will never ask for a donation or any thing of that sort. Even now He wants to make a hospital for the people living in Subramaniya, but He will never ask those industrialists to help out. Never. And the worst part of it is that once people have their work done, they conveniently forget the existence of Swamiji..."

"Till the next problem arises..."

"Yes..."

"The human race is a sad species."

"You can say that again."

"Okay! The human race is a..."

"Very funny, Ruzbeh. Where was I? Yes, another thing. Swamiji does not require any sort of information. A person might telephone Him for the first time and Swamiji will describe in great detail everything about the person. He will even describe the person's ancestral property or native village and if there is a place of worship or burial and how far it is and which side it is and even draws the shape of the property...and all this without even knowing the person. Before devotees purchase any property they will confer with Him. He will once again describe the property and also ascertain whether there is a litigation or title problem. Also, if the property earlier had a place of worship but no longer was visible or even known of, and He will advise the purchaser to construct a temple in honour of that particular Deity or Sage. If there are any negative or shady powers around the property, he will describe the situation and then get it confirmed by the watchman or the constructor, etc and then direct the devotees to perform certain poojas and havans to restore peace and harmony in that area. In fact, very often He will narrate incidents that have transpired years and years ago, which even the owners are not aware of, but later on, the incidents are verified by people who have been in the area for decades. You know incidents like murder or suicide etc. But I think the reason why He gives so much importance to the matter of property is that most often industrialists approach Him and hundreds of people work on their property...this means thousands of people are dependent on the well-being of the factory or business. If something should go wrong or if the business does not make the necessary profits, then the survival and livelihood of so many families is at stake and that is why Swamiji is very involved with the matter of property. As I told you, He does not charge a rupee from anybody. All this He does for the workers and their families."

We halted for a snack and it was obvious that Swamiji was not too well, but that did not stop Him from joking and enjoying the food and the cold soda. We reached our destination and when we decided to return to Dandeli, it was my good fortune that our car once again broke down so we could travel with Swamiji and Amma. In the car as usual, I began to probe about and the talk turned towards death.

"Nobody wants to die. Everybody will say they want to die; that they are fed up with life, but in reality not many are willing to give up their life. That is the pull of this earth..."

"Is that why there are so many earthbound souls?"

"Naturally. They don't want to die, but when they have left their body, at least they want to make certain that they are still hovering around all that which gave them pleasure and comfort. Very often, people phone me up saying that their relative is dying and to see if I can do something or I can intervene with Ma Mookambika and help out. Often Ma Mookambika has postponed death. Very often, Ma Mookambika has extended the life of Her devotees, but after two years if and when that person is once again on the verge of death, he or she will still say 'just give me two more years Swamiji'; this hunger for living never dies. There is this story of a man who prayed to God with great devotion and in the end God asked this man what he wanted. The man said 'I don't want anything. But there is just one thing I am very keen on seeing and if you grant me this wish I would be very obliged.' So God tells the man 'I am God. If you want to see anything just tell me and it will be granted.' So this smart man smiles and tells God 'Oh Deva, all I want to see in this lifetime of mine is the grand-son of my grand-son sleeping peacefully on a couch made of pure gold and studded with precious stones. That is all. I don't want anything else oh God of mine.'

The car resounds with laughter. The way Swamiji mimics and says a joke has a charm that no writer can portray. "Saala (rascal) does not want anything, but virtual immortality and lots of precious stones."

73

SWAMIJI BEFORE ENLIGHTENMENT

"Swamiji, how did you get involved with all this spiritual stuff in such an advanced manner."

"Ruzbeh, I was not all spiritual and I have never meditated in my life. All this God and Ma Mookambika...I was not aware or even interested in. In fact, the only God I was interested in was Gawd, which in my language means 'sweet meat'. So for me God means Sweet."

"What made you involved with all this in such a serious way..."

"See, I was about forty or forty-one years old. My clothes started burning. I wanted to know whether there was some salla ghost-bhost around. You know some shaitan-baitan around. I wanted to know who was burning my clothes and flicking my liquor. God-bid I was least interested in and I was not at all bothered about. As I told you, I kept experimenting with astrologers, etc and finally I met Goddess. I mean I had gotten fed up of everything getting destroyed or disappearing. Bloody hell, my beer would disappear. Those days a bottle of beer used to cost around one rupee and seventy-paisa and the bottle would disappear. I used to get really mad and swear at the thing responsible for my loss of money and beer. I mean I had spent money for it. I used to shout aloud that I have not got the money from your father that you go about flicking my stuff. I used to tell the spirit that if you are a dead ghost then I am a living ghost, so don't mess with me, but all this never bothered whoever it was. I still never knew it was Ma Mookambika. I mean, She can really get up to mischief. Now you are recording my voice. If She wants, nothing will be recorded. Nothing will come..."

"Don't say that." This made Him laugh uproariously, and with twinkling eyes He looked at me.

"I was not a worshipper of Ma Mookambika..."

"But how much time did it take you to realise that it was Ma Mookambika..."

"One and a half years. Of course, those days I knew the names of girls and heroines and devis, but not this Devi. I was really a jolly fellow. God and Ma Mookambika were best in the mandir, I was only interested in having a good time. 'Let each day pass well and with lots of fun', that was my motto. But even in those days, if there was one good thing I have done, at least according to me, the only good thing done by me was that I have never lied. Even today, I never resort to lies just to please somebody or to hid my past and even in those days I never resorted to lies."

"Many devotees tell me that I must not divulge my past. They keep telling me that I must keep my colourful past a secret. I disagree. My logic is simple; Ma Mookambika graced me with Her presence and She continues to help people through me. You met me, so has Murli, so have many people. Now suppose you don't know about my past and meet a person in Bangalore. He tells you that he is in great distress and trouble. So you want to help him and you tell him, 'listen, at Mahalaxmi Layout there is a Swamiji, who, earlier used to work at Philips; go to Him and your problems will be solved.' Now you are recommending Me to him in good faith so that his problems get solved. Now, just in case that person is my 'bottle friend'. If we were drinking whisky and beer together in my days of glory, and knows me from those days. Then what will he tell you? 'Who do you want me to meet? Nayak? Philips guy. Tall and hefty. Arey baba, are you mad or what? We used to drink liquor together and now people call Him Swamiji.' Now your faith in me can be shaken up if you are under some illusion or if you have some image of me. An image that Swamiji must have done great penance and austerities to have reached this stage but when you come to know that your Swamiji used to have whiskies and beer as though there was no tomorrow, then your faith and impression will get a severe setback."

"But, suppose you know of all the facts from the beginning and if this friend of yours tells you about My past and you coolly tell him that you are aware and I have myself told you about My past glories, then the entire picture is different. You are aware of my past and even of my present. It makes a great difference. Remember, all saints have their past and all sinners have a future. That is most important. You get a diamond only from coal. Also remember, I can bring a bad name to myself but, I should not bring a bad name to God and Ma Mookambika. 'I' used to drink. 'I' used to eat non-vegetarian food but, not God. So, because of my karmas and actions, God and Ma Mookambika should not get a bad name. People come to MA for help. They come to Me, but actually they are coming to Ma Mookambika for help. Because of me, people's faith in MA and God should not get affected. Whatever I have done is all right, but the spill over of my actions should not come to God. That is what all those trying to serve mankind should keep in mind. Let your past be an open book. After reading it, whoever wants to believe in you, good for them, or else they can go where ever they want to."

"Another thing that I used to always do and still do, is help people out, who are in any sort of trouble. Thousands of people have been helped through their rough times. If somebody would come and tell me in those days that he was in trouble...either financial or medical or any sort of trouble, I would go out of my way to help the person. Whether I had money or not, I would make certain that, person got help to sort out his problem. I would get money from somebody else to help that person. I am not saying all this to boast, but just trying to tell you that before I got powers from Ma Mookambika, though I was never religious, I treated mankind with utmost respect. I used to take people who were lying on the road suffering due to illness or an accident to the hospital and make certain that they were treated."

"The third thing that I was very particular about was, about helping families to conduct death rituals. If I found out that somebody had died, I was the first to arrive there. In fact, very often I have taken care to conduct the final rites of those poor people dead on the street, with nobody to call as friends or family. Then, whether the person is a Christian, Muslim, Hindu or belonging to any religion did not and does not matter. In fact in Hubli itself, there was a Christian gentleman by the name of Mr. Kundi, the General Manager of a very big company. He was my friend and he had died sometime back. Then, his wife died and there was nobody to take care of her. So, I put her in the ambulance, packed lots of ice to make certain that the body did not decompose, and we went by road to Bangalore and then conducted the entire funeral rite. In fact, I buried her. What to do there was nobody to do this for her. After the burial, Christians gather in the house and they call it 'service' I think. They perform prayers. Then, this gentleman by the name of Major Wessley, asked everybody who I was. So I told him I was Nayak, a Brahmin Hindu. He was really shocked. He first refused to believe that I was not a Christian, then he said, something that I will never forget. He said 'Yes we all call ourselves Christians but this man is a real Christian'."

"You see, when a man is happy and has no problems, then we are not needed. He does not need our presence so much. But when he is in some trouble, then our presence is required. That is the time man requires your help. During good times, when a person does not remember God and the person does not remember God, it is okay. Even God understands. But, when a person is in trouble our presence is a must. I am called to lots of places. People keep inviting me to visit their new factory or house or farm or to be present during weddings etc I most often just bless them and pray that they are happy and healthy. I rarely visit places. But, if God forbid, the person is in real trouble then I have to be with my devotees. The presence of God...Ma Mookambika is a must whenever the devotees are in bad shape. Of course, God is very *chaloo*...He is very very shrewd. He will test you to the maximum capacity. And if you pass that test, then God never leaves you. He will always be there for you. Remember, God is in 'humanity'. God is not there in the mandir or in performing poojas and havans. The reason why we go to the temple or perform prayers, is because we want to tell Him, 'Hey Bhagvan, solve my problems. Bhagvan give me a Rolls Royce car, give me this and that and yes, don't forget that too and yes, God here take this offering, a five rupee coconut and flowers and please don't let my investment of seven rupees go to waste'. But, how many pray or visit the temple and tell God 'Listen God, whether you give or don't give is up to you. Let's forget about all this give and take and accept my thanks for everything.' Most of us pray to God only with expectations. But, if a person prays to God without expectations and tells God that 'God please bless everybody and please make sure that nobody comes to any problems' now that is true prayers, as you are praying not only for yourself, but for entire creation. If God listens to this person, then one thing is certain, that person is also taken care of as he has asked for all creation and he or she is part of 'creation'. This is the real way of praying."

"Also remember, that God is not at all partial. He is very just. Very, very fair. He is not selfish and remember one thing, God will never wish harm to anybody. How can He? We are all His / Her children. Which parent will wish harm to the child? But we, as a human race, are not very appreciative or grateful. If something goes right, we take all the credit. 'I made this and that and everything', but if something goes wrong, the attitude is 'what to do *yaar*, this God is giving me a hell of a time. Real pain'. Good things are because of the individual, but bad things are because of God. That is our logic most often. That is why, according to me, the worst creation is mankind. Even if you read our mythology or religious books, you will find that most of the times a person will do penance and get God to grant the person a boon and the moment poor God grants that person a boon, that chap immediately attacks God. Ravan took blessings from God, got lots of power and then became the enemy of God and even kidnapped Ma Sita. Then, in the end enters Ma Mookambika to take care of the situation. But you think God was not aware that this 'saala' was a chor...lafanga (this rascal was a thief and scoundrel). You really think God is not aware that the moment this chap gets a little money or power he is going to revolve anti-clockwise? But you see, God is very innocent. In fact, sometimes I think God is not only innocent, but He is a fool. You know what He does, He tries to make everybody happy and then hears their insults also. He is very innocent."

"Now, all the factory owners who call me and ask me to beseech Ma Mookambika to bless them and their factory, they want me as they are making lots of profits. You think, if they were going in a loss anybody would want Swamiji and Ma

Mookambika around? Fat chance! But we do the poojas because We know that it will benefit lots of workers and their families. I am not performing poojas and havans for the owners. No! I am doing it for the workers and their families. I mean I don't charge anybody for the time and trouble I go through. No, I don't charge a single rupee. The expense of getting me to the factory is borne by the owner, but apart from that I don't charge anybody any money. I do this for the workers. No amount of money will force me to do a pooja just so that the owner makes a profit. I will not do it for anybody but the workers. The factory is a temple; virtually like God. Never spit in the plate in which you eat your food. Never wash your hands in the plate in which you eat your food. Wash your hands outside. Simply put, if you want to understand and serve God then adopt the simple, honest path. As I told you, God is very innocent. There are plenty of things in life that you have to learn, but remember that the simple path is the best road. Don't go too deep into God and spiritualism. Serve mankind, do good for mankind, when you pray ask for God's blessings on all creation and when you eat something learn to share it with your less fortunate brothers and sisters. God is good and kind and just and selfless."

"Today a lot of people come to Me. Very rich people come to me for help. I roam about in imported cars and live in air-conditioned rooms. Now, millionaires come to me, but this same man was on the footpath thirty years ago. Yes, I was virtually on the footpath. My family and I...and that time none of these big time industrialists or millionaires came to help us. That time only God came to help me. Today, God...Ma Mookambika has given me everything and if today somebody respects me, it is not because of who I am or what I am and not because of something I have done, but because Ma Mookambika has blessed Me with Her presence. They respect the Ma Mookambika who is with me. They respect Her shakti (energy) within me. We are just instruments. That's it. Go into the basics; be simple; go in a small way and try to understand Him in a simple manner. Don't try to go too deep into spiritualism. Forget mantras and tantras. We don't have to get involved in all this;

and who has the time to get into all this deep stuff. Say simple prayers like 'Hey Bhagvan protect me. If by mistake I have done something wrong or committed a sin please forgive me. Please don't let me go on the wrong path and if I should go on the wrong path, You please get us back on the right track.' Say simple prayers. That is enough." Through out the talk, it was obvious that Swamiji was not keeping too well. His talk was punctuated with coughs and it was rather apparent that yesterday and today's long journey had taken their toll on Him.

"In fact, there is nothing much to all this. It is all very simple. The problem is that we are very self centered. We are very selfish people. It is because of this quality of selfishness that mankind has virtually ruined everything. One day, a man asked Ma Mookambika regarding a particular machine. Ma Mookambika told him that 'just as mankind has created a recording machine that records conversation or music, the same way I have created this machine which records all the deeds that you have committed not only in this life but in all the lives you have ever lived'. It is this cassette that I listen to and then give predictions. Yesterday, I compared life with a car on the highway. Today, I am comparing this cassette with life. We call it *Kaal Chakra*. There are two spools in this casette. One is full and one is empty. Whatever karmas we create is recorded in this cassette. As our life and karmas of past lives get lesser, in the other spool our karmas get more and more. The time when one side of karma gets empty life ends."

Then for a while we observed our surroundings. The driver was like Mad Max 2 and he drove like a man possessed. The journey, that normally would have taken us two and half hours, seemed to be virtually on the fag end.

GEMS AND STONES

"What about stones and vastu, Swamiji. How do stones alter one's life?"

"Stones cannot change your destiny. That is false. The Maharaja of Mysore has so many stones, but in the end he has begun to sell his furniture...."

"Then why do all astrologers insist on stones. You mean they don't even affect the person..."

"Not even by one per cent. Nonsense. All these superstitions of number, colour, etc are useless. The best precious stone is the one here." He caressed his forehead. "Brains and destiny. If your destiny is fine, then you don't need any stone. But if your destiny is not proper, then God help you. See, if you ask me, I am not an advocator of stones. Yes, what I do believe is that when sunlight or water touch the stone and the stone touches the body then some chemical reaction takes place. This might induce the wearer to behave in a more confident or positive manner and thereby make him take steps that would bring about his own welfare and thus prosperity follows. See, we have holy water in the temple. Now, what is the difference between the holy water and normal water. It is like this. You see, the holy water is first poured into a copper vessel. A certain chemical reaction takes place and that is why since ages we have always spoken highly of copper. After sometime, the water is put into the conch...dash it we forgot to buy a shell...so the water is put into the conch with tulsi (holy basil).

"What is a conch? It is nothing but calcium. So, the water first placed in a copper vessel and then placed in the conch with tulsi, once again experiences a conversion. Just like the acqua guard process. Then the water is put on the saligram stone. We say that we are bathing the Shivling. Now this saligram stone has certain qualities. It even has certain chemicals and the water poured on it once again goes through a certain conversion. Like that, all these precious stones also help certain conversions to take place when water and sunlight pass on or through it and touch the body. Even the paste, that is prepared for the pooja, is made of certain herbs, etc, which give birth to certain chemical energies. So, even in the temples what you consume as holy water or paste is actually very scientific. Chemical energy converted into spirituality. The water consumed by children is really great. Tulsi, copper, calcium, the stone with all its properties is a perfect remedy and preventive medicine for lots of ailments. It is called Jal Amrit. In fact, the paste that was earlier prepared with so many herbs was so effective that it kept all the serious maladies at bay. That is why we never heard of our forefathers suffering from cancer etc. Those days, the mixture contained real camphor, real scandal wood and many such things. Now, who can afford real scandal wood. Where do you get real scandal wood. It goes directly to Veerapan (a famous scandal wood smuggler). Anyway, whatever it contains, still is very good. But to make certain that people consume all this medicinal stuff, they are given a scare...consume it as it is holy or else there is trouble for you as you might upset God. So everybody, very quietly, consumes whatever is given to them. They don't want to upset God. Everybody is too scared...."

"Swamiji, why do you often say that there is a broken idol in your house, remove it? What happens if you keep such broken idols of God?"

"See, if you are keeping an idol that you worship as God, then you should make sure that it is not broken. I mean you should not have God with a broken hand or limb. It is not good. The scriptures say that in such idols positive energy does not enter. You should not keep all this at home as these are powers and if not taken care of, instead of positive energy, the idol might start emitting negative energy. You know, bad power radiation might take place and that is why we ask people not to keep broken idols at home. You see, there are reasons for everything but as I have told you, don't go too deep into all this as there is no end and in fact it can be very confusing."

The next morning when Murli and I had to leave for Mumbai, Swamiji was not at all well. He was running a high fever and had a nasty cough, bordering more towards asthma. The last few days had been hectic and the travelling had not made life easier, but Swamiji insisted that we carry on with our journey.

"All this goes on. Devi is with me, so worry not. I am no longer a young man and this habit of drinking cold soda is very annoying." He coughed aloud and for long, but His eyes twinkled. "I shall see you in Bangalore, Ruzbeh. Go on. Ma Mookambika be with you both."

As per the plan, I left for Bangalore two weeks later. The night had already set in when I landed in Bangalore. As my luck would have it, the chap behind the wheels was a Formula One racer, in a convincing disguise of a cab driver. By the time I reached Swamiji's Temple complex, the charlie had tried at least fourteen times to dash his vehicle with numerous trucks and buses. His sole aim in life was to reach the required destination by defying both, the laws of speed and gravity and with scant regard for human life or the spaced out passenger seated behind him. I added further grief when half way through I asked him whether he could speed up, as I had a bladder that demanded immediate attention. I might as well have told him I had a death wish. Whether it was a communication problem or a corrupted sense of humour, but for some reason the state of my bladder seemed to infuriate the chap. He spit on his palms, spoke something (that did not sound very pleasant), stood on the accelerator, dashed his balmy head on the horn, and barged through the streets as though death was behind in hot pursuit. The vehicle miraculously braked opposite the massive temple gates. A forty-five minute drive had been achieved within less than half the time. I stumbled out and quickly dispatched a prayer to Providence for the next passenger's welfare. The gate of the temple was still open and I saw Swamiji surrounded by devotees. He noticed me and smiled.

"Come Ruzbeh, did you have to arrive all by yourself?"

"Yes Swamiji, but no problem..."

"Somebody should have come to the airport for you. I would have come to receive you. Anyway, you wash up and in a few minutes we shall have dinner. "But first, He introduced me to His family."

Amma took me to Ma Mookambika's mandir where I paid my obeisance to Ma. The feeling you get within this small abode of Ma Mookambika is something I cannot describe in words. Ma's presence is palpable and omnipresent. The fragrance of flowers, the aroma of the prasad (blessed herbal water that also includes camphor), the glow of the many oil lamps burning and the vibrations that emit from Ma Mookambika's statue is a spiritually intoxicating combination and experience. This small temple, is a spiritual powerhouse that immediately comforts, protects and heals all those who come with faith and surrender.

Twenty minutes later we all sat down to have our dinner. Food is taken very seriously where Swamiji is concerned. He has, time and again, maintained First Petohba...Then Vithoba. Which, when translated, reads as Satisfy first the tummy...then all that which is Godly. Only when a person's belly is at peace can he or she really concentrate on God. Of course, as mentioned before, the real reason why Swamiji is so insistent on feeding everybody, is that He has gone through the pangs of hunger himself. He knows how it feels, not to have food, to feed the family.

The meal, like all meals partaken along with Swamiji, was tummy bursting, but that is the way Swamiji likes everybody to eat food. He keeps wondering, as how the car would move about without fuel. He insists that one must not be a glutton, but at least one should never starve oneself in search of God. Eat little, but make sure you are never hungry, is His common refrain.

After food we went to His drawing room. He personally decided who should be telephoned the next day for the interviews.

"I know many of my Mumbai devotees are not making your life easy where this book is concerned. You must not take it to heart. In the end they all are human beings. When they need help, they will call me up at two in the morning and fly down here three times in a week. When they need help it is 'Swamiji please' but the moment their work is done, it is 'Swamiji ease'. But then, that is human nature and they all are my children. But in Bangalore, you will realise that people are different. Here, all I have to do is give them a call and they will put everything on hold and come running to Me. And remember, I am talking about top doctors, industrialists, businessmen and also my numerous devotees who may not be financially very rich but their love and faith in Ma Mookambika and Me is as firm as the mountain. By tomorrow you shall be able to meet a number of them. Now you go to sleep."

My room was on the top floor. In fact, it was on the terrace and I had a lovely view of Bangalore. Trees, bungalows and the never ending sky. The room was spacious and clean and had the amenities most Mumbai folks cannot do without; the TV and the AC. I lay on the bed and glanced at the many books that I had carried along with me; books by Dexter, Wodehouse, Chase; a biography on Shirdi SaiBaba and the Holy Avesta. I switched on the TV and moaned seeing the Indian cricket team getting a trashing of their lives. If Sachin is not around, why does the team bother going all over the globe to get a hiding. Especially with Ganguly going through a bad phase. I mean how many times can Rahul bail the team out.

I woke up before six the next morning. It was still partially dark and really cold. I am not an early riser, but the persistent chirping of a sparrow, either for a blasted worm or a dashed mate, was the cause of my sleep fleeing. I stood at the window and glared at the tiny winged gramaphone. It observed me for a while in silence and then, not at all happy at the way Providence had assembled me, flew really fast, mingling with the rays of the rising sun. The ISKCON temple, dedicated to Lord Krishna and Radha, stood with head held high, fulgent in all its golden glory. Also, very close to Ma's mandir, was Lord Hanuman's temple that was visible from the window. Below, I heard Swamiji's voice. I noticed He was awake and giving instructions to the boys on how to clean the gate. He gets very disturbed if He sees anything not clean. I washed up and wearing a loose Pathani kurta-pyjama, walked down the three floors to be with Swamiji. There is a strange feeling of safety when you are within the temple and with Swamiji. It is hard to describe the comfort level, but it exists and devotees have mentioned the same, to me, during their interview. I paid my obeisance to Ma Mookambika.

Amma was cleaing the mandir and decorating Ma with lovely garlands of different colours. The blue flowers were so mesmerizing that one's eyes, on and off, kept reverting to them. I touched Swamiji's feet for blessings.

"Good, you have woken up. Come, lets go for a walk." He was, as usual in his long Kurta and lungi; hair pulled behind, and the power that emitted from Him was something that was palpable to one and all. I have seen even strangers give Him a second look. He has an aura that cannot be hidden. "Let's have coffee first." Innocently I entered the *Maha Lakshmi Restaurant;* a small clean self service joint. "I come here every morning." He spoke something in Kannada to the waiter and then He looked at me and smiled. The waiter got two plates of idli, sambhar and chatni. It was still six thirty in the morning.

"Swamiji, I am not hungry..."

"You must eat and anyway this food is very light. Come eat."

"Okay Swamiji." Ten minutes later, once again two plates, this time, hot puri with curd and onion arrived. I was about to refuse when He looked at me and smiled.

"Eat this. It is very tasty."

"Okay Swamiji." Ten minutes later, once again two plates, this time, *medhu vada,* all large, steaming and really threatening arrived. "Swamiji it is still six forty-five in the morning. In Mumbai, the first morsel is consumed at 11.30..."

"No wonder you look ill. Eat."

At seven, we both came out of the restaurant. Fortunately for me, after the third dish, only coffee arrived. Swamiji had ordered lots of food to be packed. I carried the parcel and we both slowly walked towards the temple. Though the sun had cleansed away the remains of the night, it was still cold and pleasant. It was going to be a hectic day, what with so much work to be completed in such a short period of time.

Swamiji usually spends the morning on the ground floor, next to Ma's mandir, attending to the numerous calls that pour through, from all over the country. Devotees who are either in trouble, or just calling up to inquire as to His health or schedule etc. The calls do not stop. The phone keeps the householders on their toes. The calls do not cease. They come from all over the country and also from Bangalore. Of course, there are certain devotees who call up every day at least once. Murli, Lalit, GD speak to Swamiji everyday.

"You better have a bath as I have lined up a few of the devotees who will narrate how Ma Mookambika has helped them during their times of trouble. We shall have break fast after your bath."

"What did we eat an hour back then?"

"Just some snacks." He smiled and I certainly think I heard Him chuckle.

An hour later, Swamiji introduced me to a benign looking gentle-man. A cup of coffee was served to all and we sat near Ma's Mandir, on a pleasant Friday morning and the God seemed to be in His heaven and all seemed fine with the world.

"My name is K. Devdhar. I am coming here for the last 27 years. Swamiji has been my advisor and good friend and everything rolled into one. Ma Mookambika and Swamiji have really taken care of me and my family."

"Any particular incident that you wish to share with fellow devotees and readers?"

"See, Swamiji is aware that nearly everyday I am in sort kind of trouble. Call it destiny or whatever, but troubles seem to follow me like my shadow, but somehow I am always saved and that is through the grace of Ma Mookambika and Swamiji. In fact, the whole of yesterday I was trying to get in touch with Him, but for some reason or the other we could not communicate, so first thing in the morning today, I have left all my work and am here. The moment He tells me that there is nothing to worry about, I am confident that They shall help me overcome my problems."

"What work do you do?"

"I am an ordinary businessman. We are in plantations. I mean compared to your businessmen in Mumbai, I am a very small time person but for some reason, nothing seems to be going right and one after the other problems keep gathering around me and with Their grace I am saved always. I frankly don't know what I would have done without Ma and Swamiji."

"You have been coming to the temple since twenty seven odd years. How was it in the beginning. I have been told that this entire area was virtually a forest..."

"Yes, nobody wanted to come over here. There was no temple at all. And there was no concrete building, but instead there was a tin shed and over there, was a small kitchen. Swamiji used to sleep near Ma Mookambika and in the rains, he used to get wet as the tin shed had more holes than tin. In those days not many people used to come here, but slowly with Ma Mookambika's power and grace, more and more people began to get benefited. Swamiji has undergone lots of hardship and He must have told you His story..."

"That's my biggest problem. He has not told me anything about His past. I am supposed to write a biography on Him, but He insists on changing the subject whenever I ask Him to say something about Himself." Swamiji found something humorous in my statement as He crackled with laughter. "That is why I am asking one and all to speak more, but you all seem to have so many experiences that not one comes to mind. Great!"

"I will tell you only one thing. He did not want to be a Swamiji. He was virtually forced to become a Swamiji. He tried to do many things, but Ma Mookambika always brought Him back to this path. Yes, He has undergone lots and lots of hardship. I know for a fact, that very often there was nothing to cook in the morning but with the grace of Ma, by afternoon something or the other would get arranged. Goddess really tested Him but also took care of Him and His family. I can only tell you one thing for certain...Goddess never lets you down. Yes problems come, but then they go away also. She is always there and Swamiji is there for us. What more can I ask for."

"This man," began Swamiji, "wanted to shut down His business. Everybody kept telling him to shut down this business and begin something else but Ma Mookambika kept encouraging him and predicting that he will have a secure future only with this business and as usual She was right. He is doing very well for himself.

"Yes, there was a time I wanted to sell everything I had, but Swamiji told me very clearly that even if I wanted to sell everything, Ma Mookambika would make certain nobody would buy it. And that is exactly what happened and in the end I was forced to continue and I really thank Goddess and Swamiji that I was not able to sell anything. They have really taken care of my family. Faith is the most important thing needed."

"Swamiji, describe to me how this place looked earlier. I mean now you have a beautiful building which has Ma's lovely mandir on the ground floor, but earlier what was there?"

"Nothing. There was no building. This was just a plot of land and the surroundings it was virtually a jungle. People used to get scared of visiting this place after sun set. All these buildings you see have come up recently. Earlier, I was virtually living alone with Ma over here. I used to stay in this four by six place. There was no fancy mandir, just Ma and other Gods and Goddess. During the rains, we used to put up alabaster sheets that were supported by four wooden pillars. Once, during a Chandi Havan, there were around five hundred people gathered and one of the pillars gave way and the sheet that is really heavy and dangerous was about to fall. With the grace of Ma, nothing happened or else a minimum of ten people would have died and a hundred would have got badly damaged. Imagin, one pillar is gone and still the heavy sheet balanced on three legs...the wind was blowing hard and I rushed to put things right but in the meantime Ma Mookambika took care..."

MA COMES TO THE RESCUE OF HER DEVOTEES

"Let me give you an example of how, when you call out to Ma Mookambika, She comes to your rescue. Many years back, we were coming back from Coimbatore. Now those days...maybe even now...Tamilians were very famous for pushing a cycle or even a person in front of the vehicle. The moment you stop, they grab you out of the car and rob you and there have been cases where people have been murdered. In those days it was very common. We were on such a road and I saw an old man crossing the road and I slowed the car and in no time somebody had pushed a cycle in front of the car and we were forced to stop. In no time, lots of people with weapons made us get out of the car. I was travelling with my family...wife and two daughters so you can imagine it was really very dangerous. I still remember it was 1.30 in the afternoon. These robbers made certain that no other vehicle stopped to help us. They were quite a few tough looking men and all armed and dangerous. They asked for money and I was only carrying around five hundred. They asked for jewels and I told my wife to remove the gold bangles and give it to them. Then I don't know what happened but they insisted they wanted cash and cash worth the bangles. Now, no vehicle wanted to stop for us and even in those that did, nobody wanted to help us. I realised that something bad was going to happen. It was at this time I prayed to Goddess to help me and my family. All this while I was too busy trying to negotiate with the thieves, so I had forgotten Ma Mookambika I prayed to Her and within minutes a bus stopped. The driver was a Muslim man. He said that I did not have to worry. He would leave only after we were safe and sound. One of his passengers was carrying money in the gunny bag. He negotiated with the thieves and gave them around Rs. 3000. The robbers even gave me a receipt that they have taken money for some business transaction...they had virtually legalized this whole affair. What I want to tell you is that a Muslim driver...and we earlier did not like Muslims came to our rescue and an unknown man gave me the money. This is how Ma helps Her children."

"Apply...apply, immediate reply. This is how Ma Mookambika works." The room resounded with laughter. "If you have faith then your problem has to be sorted out. 100%. It has to happen. Without faith there is no God. Immense faith and without expectations. You can ask him, the number of cases where Ma Mookambika has helped people out through situations which seemed impossible cases. We don't expect anything in return. Nor have We demanded anything from anybody. I have known him for nearly thirty years, but you can ask him whether I have taken even five rupees from him. Never. Yes, for prediction you pay whatever is charged, but that is so reasonable and that is for maintaining of the temple..."

"Also for feeding whoever comes to Swamiji. Whether one person or ten people Swamiji feeds them all. Without Him I don't know what we would have done."

"Without Ma Mookambika. I am nobody. Yes, voluntarily if devotees want to give money for the upkeep of the temple and for feeding people, it is their wish, but I have never asked people and I don't think any body who is graced by Divine Powers should ask for money. That is cheapening the Power that has graced you. Powers take care of you. Nothing is ever wanting if you leave everything to God..."

"Yes, that is true. I have seen how Ma Mookambika takes care of Swamiji. Every year before the 'Chandi Homa', Swamiji will be wondering from where so many thousands of rupees would come from but every time Ma Mookambika makes certain that the money is there to do the pooja and feed the hundreds of people who come here. And not once in a year, but four times in a year the Homa takes place and She takes care of all the expenses. Have you told Him how you established the guest house at Subramaniya."

"He has told me nothing. In fact, I think I will write another book on how I got out information from Swamiji about Himself and His life. It comes so slowly that I wish I was an accountant rather than a writer."

"Have you told him about how you brought that man back to life..."

"I was about to tell him. One day there was some work going on. We were constructing the building and this plumber fell from forty feet high and landed straight on his head. It was a single drop. Nothing weakened his fall. I was seated with lots of doctors on the ground floor and we all rushed out and saw this man lying on the ground. The doctors touched his pulse etc and told Me there was nothing I could do about it. Blood was oozing from his nose and eyes. Then Ma Mookambika made me rush into the temple, get holy water *(Jal Amrit)* and made me hold the man's wrist for five minutes. The chap got up and in an hour he was normal."

Much later, I was seated in the temple, when I was told to meet Swamiji on the second floor. I bowed down to Ma Mookambika and then once again climbed the staircase. I realised that Swamiji must be climbing up and down the three flights of stairs at least twenty to thirty times in a day; for a seventy-two year old man who was to undergo a delicate operation for a serious heart condition, He really was rather blasé about it all. I entered the drawing hall and saw Swamiji seated with a couple and they were laughing and chatting, like most people who come for Swamiji's blessings. Swamiji is a really different sage. He likes to laugh loudly, usually avoids talking philosophical and religious stuff, has no problem eating in outside restaurants and has no secretary tagging along with Him. First of all, I doubt if anybody will be able to keep pace with Him or be able to digest the odd timings and the erratic schedules Ma Mookambika keeps for Him.

"This is Ruzbeh. He is writing a book on Ma Mookambika." I did a Namaste to both.

"Hello, I am Ravi Shankar and have been coming here since six years. Incidentally it was my father who met Swamiji first in Kuke Subramaniya. In those days we were in real trouble. One of our construction approvals was stuck for the past ten years. After meeting Swamiji, the approval came through very quickly. We are now the leading Construction Company in Bangalore... Techno Art Construction Prviate Ltd. So whenever I am not out of town I come every day to the temple and take Ma Mookambika's and Swamiji's blessings without fail. Coming here we get a positive outlook, direction and hope. I can tell you one thing. Goddess is here."

The couple left and Swamiji spoke about how a number of people would not open up to a writer, as there were a lot of issues that were not meant to be disclosed to the public. He then informed me that Murli had called and inquired about my health. I sighed. If Swamiji took it into His head that I needed more food I was in dire trouble. Then Nirmala, Swamiji's eldest daughter who is settled with her doctor husband in Dubai informed us that Gundapa Vishwanath, the famous cricketer was waiting with his family.

"Come, we shall meet Vishwanath. First class cricket player. His child is through Ma's blessings. Nice man but a little shy."

"Story of my life." I sighed and then we both chuckled and walked down, to meet one of the world's best left handed players ever to have played test cricket and also the brother in law of the best cricket player in the world, Mr. Sunil Gavaskar.

I was introduced to Vishwanath, his wife, and their friends. There was a virtual '*mela*' surrounding us, as even those who had come to pray to Ma and get Her blessings, decided to stop and witness what the fuss was all about. I informed Vishwanath what my purpose was and my heart sank. It was obvious that he was an introvert, very shy and the milling crowd was not doing us any good.

"It has been about ten years since we know Swamiji. Ironically, family friends from Mumbai dropped over and told us that they wanted to meet Swamiji. They were surprised that we had never met Swamiji. I am of the opinion that you need Ma Mookambika's blessings to meet Swamiji and so we all came and meet Him. I met Him and it was a tremendous boost to our family." He then sat as though that was the end of the conversation. Vishwanath was known to have sent the ball all over the pavilion with his master stroke play, but where words were concerned he was on the back foot.

"Uh...eh...could you narrate your story in slightly more detail." I got this strange feeling that I should have stuck to editing magazines and news-papers.

"Well, after coming here once, my wife and I felt a strange pull to this place. We had gone to many places but over here I felt Ma Mookambika's presence and then there is Swamiji so...uh...so many things that I cannot tell anything more..."

"That is the problem with most people. They have taken the grace of Ma Mookambika and Swamiji so much for granted that now miracles do not need to be mentioned or thought about twice."

"Well Swamiji told us to perform certain poojas at Kuke...and then this little fellow came into our lives...after fifteen years of marriage...and the entire scenario has changed for us. I mean for fifteen years we were all alone...we were really hoping to become parents...and then we met Swamiji and then after meeting Him and with the blessings of Ma Mookambika we god our child. I am really enjoying my second innings much more than my first innings. I was always known to start my second innings in test cricket better than the first, so hopefully in life too, this second innings will be better than the first innings. Hope with the blessings of Ma Mookambika and Swamiji this innings goes on really smoothly. I believe that Ma Mookambika is Swamiji."

"Tell me one thing. You have travelled all over the world so how does this aspect of spirituality fit into your mind frame. Did you come here to Ma and Swamiji as a last recourse as medical science too was not helping you and your wife to become parents?"

"See, I have always been religious. My grand-parents, parents have all been very religious people, so God and miracles are not something I look at skeptically. And ever since Ma Mookambika...Ma has come into our lives, it is so beautiful that I cannot explain to you. I always carry Ma's photograph along with me. Where ever I am, She is with me. And whenever I have to go for an important meeting I come here to take Her blessings, take Swamiji's blessings, take a blessed Lime and then go for whatever I have to do. I always have Their photogprahs and the lime..."

"Miracle lime..."

"I don't know if one can say it is a miracle lime, but yes one thing is for sure, my work gets done. No doubt about that."

The gentle-man seated next to Vishwanath was a tall, thin, bearded person, wearing a sleeveless jacket over a blue shirt.

DEVI DEFIES MEDICAL SCIENCE

"I am Nagraj and if I begin talking about my experience with Ma Mookambika and Swamiji, then I don't think this cassette will be sufficient..."

"At last! Worry not I have a dozen cassettes waiting to be used."

"Vish got me here. When we came here the doctors had already declared that I was a walking corpse and I would die any moment. It was as though they had already declared me dead. If you see, I am wearing all these rings, then earrings etc...these have been brought for me by Swamiji through His contacts with film star Juhi Chawla from abroad. When I came here I did not believe in any swamiji-wamiji. I was dying. I just wanted to hang on. I was suffering from stomach cancer. When I came here I could not walk...I could not eat. Vish and his wife and everybody around bowed to Him but I did not. I saw Swamiji and outside I saw his car NE 118 and told Vishy that this was a fancy Swamiji and Vish told me that 'I have brought you here so that He can repair you'."

"Fortunately for us, that day with the grace of Ma Mookambika, we got into the mandir for predictions. Swamiji lit a camphor and then began to tell me all about my past things only I could have known. Then He told me all about my present residence and how many Ganesha idols there are at my house...basically, He was trying to reach me. Then he told me something that I had forgotten, what with my own suffering due to cancer. He told me that one of my brother's had died thirty years back and he had died an unnatural death. I could not remember but Vishy knew about this...then Vishy reminded me that he was talking about Arun...my brother. Then He told me that my ancestors had killed many snakes. You see, at this moment I am very humble but in those days I was rather brash and I told Swamiji that I was not responsible for my ancestors. They could take care of their own mistakes. But Swamiji insisted that I would have to do something to make peace with the snakes and also for the welfare of the entire family. So Vishy told me to offer to do pooja...you see I was still in a daze. Here I was in front of a man who could read my past and present in a flash and accurately. I had never met anybody like Him. After that He told me that till I did not do the pooja He would not go ahead with future predictions. He had told me all about my past and present but the future, He said, He would predict, only after the pooja. So I told him frankly that though I did not believe in pooja I would do so to please Him but I had a serious problem that needed an urgent remedy. I told him that I had not eaten a proper meal for a year. I told him that doctors were all sure that I was going to die. But I wanted to eat food. I was hungry but could not eat. Is there anyway I could eat...for that meant a miracle itself. So Swamiji gave me a lime and told me to go upstairs and eat. All this really happened. Vishy, our wives they all were present. That day I looked at Vishy and scoffed with a look that said 'what was wrong with Swamiji'. I mean just by giving me a lime and telling me to eat I was not going to be able to just eat. I was suffering from the last stages of stomach cancer and not indigestion. But these people did not talk anything. We went up and my wife and Kavita sat on the other side and Vishy and I sat opposite them. Then we were served lovely chutney and food...I still remember that beautiful day...and I began to eat...not just eat, I began to bloody hog the food. Then after a while, I noticed that I was sweating profusely and Vishy was slowly passing his hand on my back so as to make certain that I relaxed and everything would go all right. I, then raised my head and saw my wife and Kavita looking at me and both of them were crying. It was unbelievable. From that moment on, I began to believe in Him. In fact, I believed in Him so much that I did not want to go. I wanted to stay with Him. But Swamiji insisted that I must do the pooja at Kuke Subramaniya. The very next day, Vishy and his family and I with my own family left for Kuke. In fact Swamiji is so loving, that He agreed to come along with us just to make certain that everything was done right. After that pooja I have never looked back. Trust me sir, in those days not only was I told I was going to die, physically, but also financially, I was in a bad shape. Just thinking about those days makes me shudder. But Swamiji has helped me all through out. He has stood by me and seen that I have come out of the mess I was in. I had a loan of 15 lakh rupees. Today, I have paid up all the loans and am doing so well that my family will never have to worry about comforts and even luxury."

"How's your health?"

"First class. Around four years back I went with a friend of mine to Apollo Hospital in Madras. I did not go for a check up. My friend is a very big doctor from US. He had come and insisted that I come along with him. My friend wanted me to go through the Cat scan. It is a very expensive test and takes a long time and I refused. But my friend was adamant. After the scanning, the doctor told us that my malignancy is just a few millimeters away from my liver. Once it hits my liver I will be out. But the doctor kept saying that he could not believe that I had been in this state since so many years. He kept saying 'I can't believe it that you are still alive. You should have died many years ago'. All this took place four years ago and let me tell you I am still going great guns. I can eat food and live a normal life. Not bad for a man who was told nearly a decade earlier, that he was a corpse and certainly dead. There is nothing that I have asked and not got. I can tell you that Ma is over here. Believe what I am telling you and that is if you want to find Ma Mookambika, go to that small mandir and you will find Her. We feel Her talking to us and it is for real, that if you keep faith She will talk to you."

SWAMIJI: A BOON TO THE CHILDLESS

"Let me tell you a strange incident. I am ever grateful to Vishy and Kavita for having got us here. One day we were praying in the mandir and whilst returning home, I asked her what she had spoken to Ma Mookambika and she told me that she wanted a baby. Naturally, I asked what Swamiji had predicted regarding the child. So Kavita said that 'when ever I ask Swamiji about the child He does not give me a firm answer'. So I told her, that we would go there in the evening and we would not leave till we had a firm answer. So in the evening, my wife, Kavita and I went to the mandir and spoke to Swamiji. While speaking to Him, Kavita broke down. She really wanted a child and after fifteen years of marriage, the longing for a child had only grown more intense. So she was crying her heart out. Swamiji got up, put His hand on her head and told her that before the year got over she would have a child. It really happened. In fact, how ever trivial the problem may seem, He does not take it lightly. Like once we lost our Alsatian dog. My wife came crying to Him and He promptly gave her a lime and told her that within three months you will get your dog and not to worry, the dog was not dead. Within three months we found our dog. Or for instance, take the case of a friend who lost his car. We called up Swamiji and He calmly told us that next day at 3 p.m. the car would arrive home. Next day, at 3.15 p.m., Kavita called up Swamiji to inform Him that the car had not yet arrived. Swamiji jokingly told her that maybe the driver had stopped to have a cup of coffee. The moment she put the phone down, the car arrived. Miracles are happening. It is sheer magic. If miracles don't happen, then Swamiji is not in the mood. Ma Mookambika is here. Just go and ask for something reasonable and tell me if it does not happen. Not possible. Swamiji is our father, our God father. Whatever He says is the law in our house. Sometimes my stomach hurts. Whenever it does, I come here and Swamiji gives me a blessed Lime and tells me to make lime juice out of it and in moments the pain is gone. Yes, it is gone. I don't go to any doctor. No medicines. Nothing. Only Ma Mookambika and Swamiji. Sometime back, my wife was suffering from severe leg pain. No pain killers were working, so we came to Swamiji. Swamiji lit a camphor, did something, then Ma Mookambika made Swamiji kick her leg and believe me she began to walk as though nothing had happened to her. My wife and I are like the North Pole and South Pole. We only agree where Swamiji and Ma Mookambika are concerned. Whenever she comes to pray, she will bow down to Ma and immediately, a flower will drop somewhere near her.

"I will tell you a very humorous story. A friend of mine came from Australia and he was going through a very bad patch in his marriage. So I took him to Swamiji who gave him a lime and told him to put it in the house where his wife was presently living with her father. This silly man did not do as told. Instead he threw the lime from his own house and it fell on a man who was working for him. This happened ten years ago. This man on whom the lime fell is still with my friend but my friend's wife divorced him soon afterwards." The room felt as though it would burst with laughter. "The lime fell on this man's head. So even now, my friend will tell this person to get out of his life and never to show his face again to my friend but moments later all is well. Now my friend has bought a cell phone for this man. He even stays with him. He has given this man a car. The man travels by plane. Everything is fine with both of them. But I still say that if you had thrown it where your wife lives, you both would still be together. Another thing I will tell you honestly and that is not only Swamiji but His entire family is so hospitable. They always take care of you. They never send you away without making certain that you have been fed. They keep serving coffee. I mean they are really caring. Another thing I have noticed is that many times very simple people are given predictions very quickly but there are very very rich people...big shots...big industrialists who have been waiting for a long period of time but with no luck. So you have to be very lucky to be able to get inside and get Ma Mookambika's darshan. Another thing is that Swamiji does not need any details. He gives predictions on the phone and they are cent per cent accurate."

When Swamiji and I were alone, eating jack fruits that were making the rounds of people waiting for Swamiji to begin His predictions, I felt extremely fortunate and protected. A number of people had expressed surprise that Swamiji had allowed somebody to pen His story. I inquired as to the reason.

"Maybe the time is right for people to know the power that is over here in Ma Mookambika's temple. Or may be my time is getting over and Ma Mookambika wants to help as many people in the shortest period of time."

"Don't say such things Swamiji. People need you a lot."

"I know but we shall leave that to Ma." Saying this, He entered the small powerful mandir and sat down for predictions.

"Hello, my name is Bhupendra Seth and I am coming here for the last four years. You see, I did not believe in any Swamiji. I came here because a friend of mine kept insisting that a lot of people suffering from various diseases are cured after having Ma Mookambika's and Swamiji's darshan. I was suffering from severe back and neck problems and the pain was really killing me. Also, three reputed doctors insisted that I had to undergo a major operation, but the chances of success were not very encouraging. Either way, I was in a fix. If I did not get operated, I would have to live with this pain that was killing me and if I did get operated, there were chances that I might get bedridden.

PAIN FLEES

So one day, I came here and had darshan of Ma Mookambika and took Swamiji's blessings and once again left for home. Half way through the journey, I realised that I had forgotten my neck belt at the temple. So I returned and once again was fortunate to meet Swamiji, who asked me to come back for three days continuously. He also very casually told me not to bother about anything. I would get cured and that no operation was needed. You see, if somebody were to tell me casually that I was going to get cured without an operation and that too within three days I would have not believed that person, but the fact was, that for the first time without a belt, I was already feeling better. I had not put on the belt for an hour or more and the pain was bearable, something that I had not experienced since a long time."

"Who recommended the operation?"

"Dr. Dholhakiya from Mumbai, who is a known surgeon, then one of the best doctors from Madras...uh...I cannot recollect his name and Dr. Srinavasan from Bangalore. They were all of the opinion that the operation was a must, but the chances of my becoming paralytic due to the operation being unsuccessful was very high. But, it took just three days for Swamiji to cure me. Just three days of coming here and He touching my neck and back and the blessed Lime to cure me. The doctors were all shocked. Then, I got my entire family and Swamiji took one hour for the prediction. He drew my house in my native village that is more than a 1000 kilometers away and described in great detail my village and house and everything.

"Once my daughter was in a very serious condition. She was pregnant and she fell very ill. They were at their native place and they were to travel back to Madras. Swamiji told me not to wait for them, as they would not make it to Madras and that instead, I should go where they were and that all would be well. Just as Swamiji had predicted, they could not make it to Madras and I met them over there and the delivery went without a problem. But the doctors informed us that my daughter's kidney was badly affected. I, immediately telephone Swamiji and He told me that the doctor's were wrong. There was nothing wrong with the kidney. The problem lay between the kidney and the liver. Some fluid had collected and the moment the fluid was removed, the problem would be solved. When we informed the doctors, they got very angry and said that they did not believe in all these predictions or Swamiji and that we should keep out of their medical business. One hour later, they came to us and very sheepishly informed us that the reports confirmed that there was fluid between the liver and the kidney and that nothing was wrong with her kidney. Then, even the head doctor was shocked as to how could our Swamiji, could predict so accurately, on the phone, so many hundreds of kilometers away, without any medical knowledge?

"There is something divine in this temple. Ma Mookambika's presence and Swamiji's grace can be felt by those who have faith. Just observe people who enter the temple and when they come out either after prayers or predictions. There is so much of a difference. They will enter with worry and come out with a certain assurance that they are being looked after. One funny thing happened. Swamiji has led a very colourful past. One day, I brought a friend of mine to meet Swamiji. Ironically this friend knew Swamiji very well but not as a God man but as Nayak. So, when my friend saw Swamiji, he immediately told me 'you have brought me to this 420...this man, with whom I have shared so many strong pegs of liquor'. But after Swamiji spent sometime in the mandir, predicting and guiding his old friend, this person was all shocked and in a daze. He could not believe that his friend had become so powerful. I tell one and all, 'everybody says there are seven wonders in the world. I can assure you the Swamiji is the eighth wonder'."

Swamiji came out of Ma's temple looking visibly tired. He had sat there for more than two hours and it was obvious that He was in discomfort. He limped towards us, red in the face, tired, but as usual smiling. He spoke to a few people who had come from Mumbai, a large Maharashtrian family and insisted that they all eat lunch and go. Sometimes people have asked aloud why Swamiji charges Rs. 150 for a prediction. What these people do not realise is that the money is spent on feeding them and their family and friends as well as a number of needy and poor people, who are certain of getting food if they enter Ma Mookambika's home. For instance, though the prediction was only for one person, at least six members of the family had accompanied the person. Swamiji's policy is very clear. Eat your meal and go. So, the entire family was fed and there was no limit as to how much you could eat.

"Something the matter with your leg, Swamiji?"

"Sunil had a major problem last night..."

"Yes, Sunil...yes the person who is of great help to you...brown hair..."

"Yes. He, on and off, gets a major problem in the leg. It affects him badly and there are times he cannot even get out of the house. Last year he had come over and Ma Mookambika cured him. Now, after more than a year, again the problem had resurfaced. He had come in the morning. He came limping and dragging his foot and went back smiling, walking straight..."

"And you took the pain..."

"What to do, baba. For one's children one has to go through a little pain and discomfort."

The lunch was, as usual, a simple but delicious affair. We all sat on mats laid down on the floor. The dinning room is a huge corridor like area, of a thousand square feet or more. To the extreme left, is a huge kitchen, where food and coffee are continuously being prepared, from early morn till late at night. When meals are served, banana leaves and steel glasses are put before you. Then, one by one the boys start serving the food. The meal begins with pickles...Swamiji is a connoisseur of pickles...and then different varieties of vegetables and pulses, rice, curd, on and off roti, keep being offered and you eat till you can eat no more. Very often, hot milk is offered to end the meal and if you are sitting next to Swamiji, nobody offers you anything, they just keep piling up your plate. I learnt it the hard way and as and when I could, I always allowed somebody who could eat steel and glass sit in between Swamiji and me. You had some chance of refusing food.

After the meal, we sat for a while in the drawing room and along with Amma, Nirmala, Mangala and Ravi and chit-chatted about life in general. A plate brimmed with guava and jack fruit was passed around and I glimpsed through a few old photographs of the family. It was apparent from the old black and white photographs that Amma had gone through a struggle to maintain body and soul. A photograph showed a visibly tired Amma, with dark circles around her eyes, standing in front of a stove. In the background the walls are dark with soot and I felt immense sadness at the realisation that both Swamiji and Amma had lived a hard, testing life. I looked at both of them. They looked, now, like contented grand-parents, all smiles and happy, but certainly, life had not treated them always so lovingly and with such tender grace. Behind all the comforts that now were visible to one and all, lay years of thorns and soot and a kitchen that barely contained with a kilo of rice to feed five young, hungry children. Swamiji entered His room for a little rest, that is if the phones did not keep Him awake anyway. Nirmala must have observed me staring for a shade too long at the old photograph. She smiled and offered me some more fruits.

"That is our old home. Ma Mookambika really tested us for nine and more years. We really have lived a hard life, especially my mother and father. Though they have tried to make certain that we did not lack anything, but for nine years Ma Mookambika put us through hell. I know She was doing all this for our own good but at that time, when you're young and have no food at home and no proper clothes to wear to school or college, it can really be very frustrating. Though now, Ma Mookambika has given us more than we could have ever dreamt of, but both Mangala and I always say that we had to pay a very heavy price for the present comfort. My father and mother used to often wonder where the next meal would come from. Ma Mookambika made certain that my father could not work outside. He had to serve Her and the needy people. So where would food and basic necessities come from? Yes, She never allowed us to sleep on an empty stomach but it was a constant struggle. We have been virtually brought up on second hand, hand me down clothes. Rarely have we worn new clothes when we were small. So, now, when people say we are so lucky to have Swamiji as our father and have Ma Mookambika as a Guardian Mother, they don't realise what we have gone through to arrive at the present state of comfort. "Saying this, she stood up and with a smile left the hall. I looked once again at the photograph and then sighed. Nothing comes easy. Certainly not 'nirvana'.

OVERCOMING FINANCIAL HURDLES

I spent sometime at work and was then called down to the mandir as somebody had come to meet me. Sometime later, I was introduced to Umesh Shenoy, who divulged that he had been introduced to Swamiji five years ago.

"Swamiji, at our first meeting, told me everything about my past and also where I lived and how many Ganesh idols I had at home in our small mandir. Even I did not know that we had five Ganesh murtis in the temple. He told me my ancestral history. Everything was perfect. He then told me to go to Subramanyia and perform certain poojas. He said that after the poojas the problems I was facing with my factory would be solved. You see my factory..."

"What do you deal in?"

"Manufacturing recycling plastic. This factory was closed for three months and I had to pay more than five lakh rupees. I was really in a bad shape. Swamiji assured me that after the pooja, not only would my factory begin to operate again, but I would pay off my debts and be on a more secure footing. That time it was unbelievable that I would ever be able to restart my factory. He further informed me that somebody who I knew, would come forward and help me restart the factory. Exactly as He had predicted, after the pooja within a very short period, friends of mine stood guarantee for me with a bank and I had enough capital to restart the factory and I paid off my debts and now am on a firm footing. At present also there is a certain problem and He has assured me that within a week the problem will be solved. If He says it will be solved then with the grace of Ma Mookambika the problem will be solved. Whatever Swamiji says is 100 percent perfect. That much I can tell you from my experience."

ALL YOU NEED IS FAITH

Swamiji joined us and we took His blessings. We were served coffee and then Umesh took our leave and in walked Mr. Gupta, one of Swamiji's regular disciples. We were introduced to each other and I knew that I had somebody who would not be niggardly with words. I was not wrong.

"I know Swamiji since ten years. The best part of our meeting was that nobody arranged it. I think Ma wanted me to be blessed and She organised a meeting with Swamiji. You see I wanted to take a flight to Jaipur. But for some reason or the other, for three days, I could not get a seat on any flight to Jaipur. At last, I got one seat and entered the airport. In the lobby I saw this man with long hair and beard, wearing a kurta and lungi. I did not know He was one of the most powerful men on earth. Swamiji just looked at me and laughed. In those days I used to get irritated very quickly. So, I went to Him and asked Him what was so funny? So Swamiji looked into my eyes and laughed again. He then told me that I was really worried about a certain problem and that I should not be worried as that problem was not as serious as it seemed. He also told me that in my house, there was a broken Ganesh idol and I should immerse it immediately; preferably the next day, as it was the first Monday of the month of Shravan. I was rather taken aback. Then He told me that the job for which I was flying down, should not worry me, as what I feared was not true. I realised that this man is no normal person. Saying this, He went away."

So, what transpired was that Mr. Gupta immediately telephoned his wife and inquired, as to whether the Ganesh idol that they worshipped at home was broken? She, very lovingly told him that he must really be sleep-walking through the prayers, if he had not realised after years that the Ganesha idol they worshipped had a broken trunk. His daughter had brought the idol and a chip had come out of it and she had decorated that part with *haldi*. So, Mr. Gupta informed his wife as to what to do with the idol and then rushed back into the lobby to hear his name being announced. It was the last call for him. The voice announcing his name did not sound very happy about his truant ways and indirectly implied that if he didn't get his butt into the airplane fast enough, he could jolly well walk his way to Jaipur.

"Now I was in further tension. I did not know whether Swamiji was going to Jaipur or some other part of the country. I really wanted to speak further with Him. I rushed into the airplane and you won't believe that my seat was next to Swamiji. Amma sat near the window, then next to her was Swamiji's seat and next to Him was my vacant seat. On the flight, Swamiji once again told me not to worry. I asked Him as to why did He keep mentioning that I should not worry. So He then told me that I was going to Jaipur for my brother's operation that was to take place within a few days. But He insisted that my brother would be fine but on the condition that he would not be operated. He kept insisting that my brother should 'not' be operated. 'If he gets operated it could be fatal for him' He said. He then gave me a lime and told me to place it below my brother's pillow and that all would be well. Then, I think, Ma Mookambika wanted to give me another surprise. So, my connecting flight to Jaipur, due to some reason was postponed. I followed Swamiji and saw around 150 people, all waiting for Him. Some garlanded Him, some touched His feet and I wondered what all this was about.

"So, I took a man aside, it was G. D. Shah, and asked him who this man was? So GD inquired as to how I had met Swamiji and I narrated my incident. He then asked me whether Swamiji had given me any *prasad* (usually blessed coconut and sweet meats). I said that He had'nt but instead had given me of all things, a *limbu* (lime) in my hand. So GD insisted that I do exactly what Swamiji had ordered, as the very fact that I had travelled with Him itself was a very big occurrence. By now, I had understood that Swamiji was a different sort of sage. Not the usual type to be surrounded by yes men and that even his way of speech and behaviour were like normal people...only, underneath the guise of normalcy, lurked a super power."

"Anyway, I left for Jaipur the very next day and reached the hospital in a few hours before the operation. I, immediately placed the blessed lime under my brother's pillow and then, with my sister-in-law, went to five Shiva temples to pour milk and perform abhishek. Swamiji had insisted on this being done. Now Swamiji had insisted that my brother should not undergo the operation and I told them about my meeting with Him. But, the family kept insisting, that after months they had managed to get a date for the operation as Dr. Dharkar, one of the leading surgeons, was a very busy man. Anyway, the doctor arrived sharply at ten and instead of operating on my brother, he insisted that a few more tests were necessary. We all found this very strange as such a prominent doctor had not thought of these tests before hand. He informed us that, for some reason, he now felt such tests important, as these tests were not mandatory. Thus, for three days, the operation could not be performed. I realised that Ma and Swamiji were at work, but how to convince the family."

"Anyway, on the third day, we had to take my brother to another place for a test. So, we put him on a wheel chair and arrived at the place. The door was shut, so I opened the door and instead of a doctor, I saw a sadhu sitting, in, with a mala in his hand. Later on, we found out that the sage was around 110 years old and was a powerful soul. Anyway, the Sadhu looked at me and asked 'who has let you in and what are you doing here'. The door was open and our entire family and friends had, coincidentally had gathered. In front of all of them, this sadhu said the same thing that Swamiji had told me on the plane...'don't go for the operation or else the results will be very bad. Paralysis, blindness or even death'. He said this and then shut his eyes and began to pray. I, once again told my family, but they inquired if I had lost my mind to listen to 'Swamijis' and 'Sadhus'. My brother was all for me, but no body wanted to listen to us. But the worst thing to happen was that, due to some negligence, the blessed lime that Swamiji had given us got misplaced. I searched high and low, but the lime was not there to be found. On the fourth day, my brother was operated on. Six months later, he passed away. He was a six footer, hefty, handsome man. Looked like a film star. I really tried to save him, but I was all alone. He was the only person on my side. Ma Mookambika and Swamiji tried Their best to prevent the operation. First, the meeting with Swamiji, then the doctor delaying the operation, then the Sadhu telling the entire family not to get my brother operated on...but when the lime disappeared, I guess the battle was lost."

DEVI GUIDES YOU ALONG

"Do you live in Bangalore?"

"Yes. I deal in Honda Generators. Doing very well with the grace of Ma, God, Swamiji...every Sunday, me and my family pay a visit to the temple. If Swamiji is there, then we speak to Him or just bow to our darshan of Ma. You see, one thing is very amazing - Swamiji's casual and jovial way of giving predictions. So many times I have gone to Him with major problems and He very jovially says, 'Go, your work will be done in such and such a time'. So, I ask Him, 'what Swamiji this is really serious and how it can be done so soon?' and He just smiles and says, 'I told you, now go the problem will be solved' and believe me, the problem is taken care of. Not only my troubles, but so many devotees will vouch for the fact that their problems have been taken care of by just Swamiji saying so. Remember, over here people come with all sorts of problems and Ma Mookambika, through Swamiji really takes care of their problems."

"Once my son wanted admission in Saint Joseph College. I approached Swamiji and He gave me a Lime and told me to go to St. Joseph College and throw the lime in the compound. I told Him, 'what Swamiji, if I get caught, You will have to come and see me in the nearby jail', so He laughed and told me to do what He had ordered. I did as follows, but I was certain that my son would not get admission in the college, because for the admission, the important thing needed was the admission application form which the college had stopped issuing and thus, the chance of him getting admission were zero. Also, date for admissions, had closed and it was a lost case, but as Swamiji had asked us to go and meet the principal, we went ahead.

There was a large crowd to see the principal, but somehow we found ourselves third in line from the principal's office. Then, the person before us went inside. The door was slightly ajar, so we could see what was happening inside. This chap removed money from his pocket and put it on the Principal's table and said 'take this money and make certain we get the admission'. The principal lost his fuse and told him to immediately pick up the one lakh rupees and go away. So the man began threatening the principal. I don't know what happened to me...I am sure Ma Mookambika and Swamiji must have given me some sense...so I entered and told that man to leave immediately. So he looked at me and threatened me. He told me, 'you don't know who I am and my connections are very powerful and I will make you disappear'. He kept threatening me but I held onto the blessed lime tightly and told him to go to hell and took the Father principal's hand and we left the office. Now, the best part is that the principal came along with me without a word. We sat in the car and after a while, the principal told me to drop him at a particular nursing home. When we reached the nursing home, he asked me for my card and inquired as to what I was doing in the line. So I told him that I had come for my son's admission. He asked me to hand him the admission form number. I sheepishly told him that we did not have any form. There and then, in my own car, he began to scold me as though I was some kid. After scolding me really well, he took my card and told me thanks once again. I, of course realised that my son would have to try for admission in another college, as I thought to myself, what could even the principal do if we did not even have the admission form. Three days later, the principal himself called me up and said 'Mr. Gupta, come immediately to my office with all the required documents and photographs'. In the office, he handed me the form and told me to get it filled immediately in my car and within ten minutes hand it over to him. Half an hour, later my son had got his admission. This is the way Ma and Swamiji work. This lime that he gives, is like an atom bomb. The explosion takes place very quietly but the impact is really tremendous. Faith is the main thing."

"Take my daughter's case. She was in Bangkok and she had an accident. She fell down and hurt herself very badly. Really badly. She was admitted to a hospital and her condition got worse. I approached Swamiji and He told me that there was nothing to worry. The only problem was that the place where she was admitted, was not good enough and that there was a nursing home on the other street and my daughter should be admitted in that nursing home. So I immediately called my daughter in Bangkok and asked her if there was a nursing home near by. She was shocked that Swamiji could know even such details and said that at the time of the accident, she wanted to be admitted in the nursing home, but it was filled to capacity. Swamiji asked her to try for admission once again and she got it the same day. I left for Bangkok and as advised by Swamiji, I made my daughter drink the juice, mixed with water and within a few days she was discharged, completely normal and out of danger."

"Why talk about things so distant. Let me tell you what happened this morning..."

"About the sweet meat..."

"Yes, you were there in the morning." He turned around to narrate the incident. What had transpired in the morning was uncanny and if it is a coincidence, then it sure was a long shot. Swamiji telephoned Mr. Gupta in the morning, asking him to come over and meet me. Then for the first time in His life, Swamiji wondered aloud that Mr. Gupta should get something sweet to eat. This was the first time in His life that Swamiji asked Mr. Gupta to bring something. So, the latter was ecstatic and asked what he should bring along. Swamiji laughed and said 'bring me some petha from Agra'. Mr. Gupta virtually shot out of his skin, as that very moment, in one of his hands, he held the telephone and in the other hand he held a box of petha that had arrived from Agra.

Coffee arrived and I was rather tired. I could not possibly light a cigarette in front of Swamiji and that, too, in the temple. Finding myself all alone for a while, I entered Ma's temple and sat alone in the sanctuary; sitting in the small mandir, with the fragrance of flowers and the many lamps burning perpetually, with incense sticks inviting powers to reside...it is a heady combination. Very often I have entered this spiritual womb and have been enveloped with love and security. It really feels as though nothing in the whole wide creation can ever harm you or hurt your loved ones. It feels that God is in heaven, Ma Mookambika is here and all is well with the world.

Often, I have sat with Amma, while she chanted prayers or decorated Ma's idol. It is during such times, I have felt, that really, God is one. The moment you strip aside the cloak of religion and be left with only the inner garment of spirituality, all differences disappear and what is left is one large family and the feeling of universal peace and love. How does one explain to fanatics belonging to all religions, that there is no greater sin than spilling blood in the name of God.

"My name is Dr. Ganesh Naik. You know, I was toying with the idea of writing a book on Ma Mookambika and Swamiji. Whenever I am here, I meet so many people and each one has had such fantastic experiences that it is really amazing. I met Swamiji about seven to eight years ago. A patient of mine, Mr. Sharma, who used to work in Dandeli..."

"At West Coast?"

"Yes. Have you gone there...oh you have...good. So, Sharma would go on and on praising Swamiji and once he told me how because of Ma Mookambika's and Swamiji's grace, lots of lives had been saved. You know about that furnace blast that fell on the railways tracks away from people...so in the end I decided to meet Swamiji. I met Him and it turned out that Swamiji, as a child, used to visit my home in Mangalore. He knew by name, all my six uncles and everybody in my family. It was really amazing. I used to meet Swamiji sporadically. Then, around two years ago, I got this strange urge to go and meet Swamiji. Now for some reason, I had not met Swamiji for more than a year and this strange urge to go and meet Him was not understandable. So next morning, I went to meet Him."

"Now, the funny thing is that since the previous day, when I had this strange urge to go and meet Him, Swamiji had been trying to contact me to fix an appointment for Himself. He had been asked by Ma Mookambika to have a check up and He was trying to contact me and had even left a message at my office, about which I was never informed. The power of Ma Mookambika is so much, that when I did not get the message, She virtually dragged me over to meet Swamiji. But the point I am trying to make is the humility and the simplicity in Swamiji. He did not have to come to the clinic. I could easily have come home and done the check up, but yet He does not want to bother anybody. When He speaks with people, love, humour and care are so clearly visible...no wonder so many just come to be near Him. They have nothing to ask or seek...they just want to be with Ma and Him. Now I come as often as my work permits and spend an hour or two with Him. It really relaxes me and gives me great confidence to handle the responsibility of being a doctor. I am a heart specialist."

Dr. Ganesh Naik, is really a nice, warm gentleman. He is one of the leading Heart specialists in Bangalore, but is too modest to say it. I have seen him interacting with other doctors and professionals and he is soft spoken, very humble and a good listener. In fact, Swamiji holds him in very high esteem and more importantly, He likes the bespectacled doctor a lot.

"You know a year or so back, my cousin brother and I wanted to start a small business of our own. Actually, I wanted him to handle it and I was basically there to make certain that the banks would fund the project. We were supposed to supply minerals to a company in Mumbai. All the paper work had been completed. The next day, the company officials were coming over to Bangalore to sign the M.O.U. The bank had passed the loan and I was supposed to sign the papers and collect a large sum of money. I don't know what got into me, but I insisted that we go and seek Ma Mookambika's and Swamiji's blessings for this project. Of course, I was doing it at the last moment, but I wanted to seek Their blessings. It was a big project and the money involved was not small. The moment Swamiji heard about the proposal He shook His head and said that the project was not going to take off and that I would incur a great loss if I got involved in the project. Swamiji's word is law for me. Rightly so, we got a call a few days later that the project was being shelved. If I had not listened to Swamiji, I would have really got in a mess as the money involved was huge. I can go on giving you many such examples."

HEALTH AND WELLNESS

"Take, for example this incident. One day, I got a call from a close Bengali friend of mine. He was the Chairman of a society of which I am the Director. He told me that he had a problem while swallowing. Immediately, we got an endoscopy done and we found that he was suffering from cancer of the food-pipe. In fact, I myself operated on him and when I opened him up, we found he had an inoperable advanced cancer. So, we could not do much about it. I got him to Swamiji after two weeks. Now, I had not told anything to Swamiji. We sat in front of Ma and Swamiji began His predictions. The first thing He told my friend was that he had difficulty in swallowing anything and that he had a tumour. Swamiji told him that He saw the tumour was in a very advanced stage. Both, my friend and I, were really taken aback. I mean here we had gone through considerable expense and my friend had undergone lots of pain to find out

113

what he was suffering from and Swamiji, in fifteen seconds, gave us the same diagnosis. Swamiji told my friend that this was the last stage and that his chances of survival were virtually nil. But, Swamiji informed my friend that if he survived three months...to be precise ninety days...starting from that very day...then he would survive but Swamiji told me in private, that it was a lost cause. On the 89th day, my friend's wife called me up and said that just one more day was left and after that, all would be well. My friend did not survive the night. He died on the 89th night."

"What difference has Swamiji made to your life?"

"Well, as you know, I am in the medical profession. It is really a very responsible job. Apart from the responsibility of having the lives of so many patients constantly on your shoulder, now we doctors have to always look behind our shoulder for legal notices being slapped onto us. The consumer forum has gotten so strong, that for the minutest grievances we doctors are being hauled to court. It is not the fear of the court or the reprisal or the compensation that bothers us, but the constant tension of being accused of negligence even though most of us put our heart and soul in our profession. So, whenever I find myself in trouble or feel that a problem might lead to a legal tangle or even when the cases are very complicated, I remember Devi and Swamiji and everything gets alright. I always carry the limes with me. They are there in the car, in my coats, wherever I am they are there with me. Also, my practice has improved considerably after meeting Swamiji and being blessed by Devi and Him. Take my daughter's case. You know, since birth she had been suffering from a skin problem that refused to be cured by medicines. She was leaving for America and it was then that Swamiji told us to do a pooja over here. After the pooja, the skin disease has vanished. You see I am a doctor. I am doing very well and supposedly I have a very good reputation as a doctor, but there are, often, cases where medicine has no answer. At that time, Their blessings are the only salvation."

Dr. Naik and I sipped hot coffee and chatted about various things. He mentioned the need for doctors to spend a part of their time on serving those who cannot afford their treatment.

That led to the discussion regarding the hospital Swamiji was keen on setting up. He then received another phone call and softly informed me that he had to pay a visit to one of his patients. Though he tried to make a quick exit, he was caught and made to consume a plateful of assorted snacks. He made an attempt at convincing one and all that he had eaten a heavy lunch, but I knew he was fighting a losing battle. He then, like the wise man he is, threw in the towel, quietly but quickly ate the delicacies, took Swamiji's blessings and then dashed away. It is hard to escape the culinary roadblocks laid down by Swamiji and His family.

I have noticed a great difference in the attitude of the devotees in Mumbai and Bangalore. Mumbai devotees are usually more interested in their balance sheet or making their 44th crore rupee or buying their 13th factory or 6th farmhouse. In Bangalore, the scene is different. Firstly, most of those who come to meet Swamiji are professionals and middle income bracketed folk, but that is not where the difference lies. It is in their attitude towards Swamiji. They do not treat Swamiji, like a golden goose that needs to be pampered and humoured for the golden eggs, that are astrally and paranormally laid, so frequently! The devotees in Bangalore treat Swamiji like their father and family member; friend and counsel; guide and philosopher and also somebody who is great fun to be around. When they talk about him, tears gather, and very often roll down in streams of gratitude. They are unabashed in their knowledge that though Swamiji may not be their biological father, He certainly is their Spiritual father, anchor and friend all rolled into one. Out of every five people spoken to, at least three of them, certainly cried or were misty eyed, when tallking about Him.

It does not mean, that in Mumbai, you do not find such devotion. Of course you do. Sunit and Meena, Murli, Lalit, Sameer, Yatin and their entire families, to name just a few, are as staunch devotees as they come, but the ration favours Bangalore. Why do I mention all this? For the simple reason, that I learnt through my interaction with various people, that even devotion comes in various packages and sizes. That it is one thing to claim to be a devotee and another thing to totally annihilate one's ego and surrender to one's God/Goddess/Guru.

DEVI: THE ULTIMATE GUIDE

"Hello, I am Sonal Chaya. My husband and I have been coming to Swamiji for the past six years. I was introduced to Swamiji by a close friend called Sheela Rao, she shall be meeting you hopefully tomorrow. Her story is filled with fantastic miracles. Anyway, she kept telling us to meet Swamiji and I kept putting it off. I am a practicing Eye Surgeon and did not believe in Swamijis and God men. You keep hearing about how they psychologically brain wash you and I did not want to get into any further problems as I was going through a really hard and trying period. I am a believer of God...especially Devi...but as I was going through such a bad phase in life, I realised that I needed help or else I would do something fatal to my life. In fact, every time I sat down for prayers I would ask Devi to end my life. Now I know modern society usually scoffs at snakes and how dangerous it is to kill them, but I have experienced first hand the curse of killing a cobra. You see, a cobra came into the compound of my in-laws' house. My husband hit the fatal blow on it's head. The next day, to our horror, another cobra entered our house. You see we had been living in that house for three years and never had we seen even a small snake, leave aside a cobra. But this cobra began to virtually haunt us. It kept showing itself to us and would slide away. And then, the problems began for us. Just thinking of those days gives me the shivers. In the end, we went to meet Swamiji. On seeing my husband, Swamiji immediately told him that 'you are a naagard' (Gujarati Brahmin known to be Cobra-Naag protectors). He told my husband ' you are supposed to protect *naags* not kill them'. I immediately began to cry. He told me that we would have to go to Subramaniya to perform the required pooja, but immediately to send a money order of just Rs.11 to the temple."

To send money to a religious place is a symbolic act. It basically implies that as one cannot physically be present and make offerings to God, the money is a small token of offering, till such time the person can make time to be physically present. In this case, as Sonal and her husband could not possibly leave everything and dash to perform the Naag pooja, this was their white flag...their humble offering to Lord Subramanyia, in the hope of a truce and eventually forgiveness.

"We told Swamiji that there was this other cobra who for the past twenty days, was avoiding all attempts to be captured. Swamiji told us that the cobra would be captured and that it was a female of the specie and wants to leave its eggs in our compound...a sure sign of further disasters. Will you believe it, the moment we reached home, the snake catcher who had been unsuccessful for so long, had eventually caught the cobra. He informed us that it was a female and yes, it was pregnant. Since then we have been coming here."

"How's everything in your life now?"

"I can't believe that I am the same person who had visited Devi and Swamiji, six years back. I mean...those days were like nightmares...I would not wish them on an enemy. "I shut the recorder. Tears flowed freely from her eyes and I looked outside the window and saw Lord Hanuman's temple dome. It felt so strange. This was the beginning of the twenty-first century. Mobile phones, internet, and cloning was the order of the day and here I sat in this peaceful temple, and heard real life incidents, that involved curses inflicted by cobras, and limes that cured stomach cancer and poojas that eradicated skin diseases as well as different sorts of maladies. The best part of it all was that there was not an iota of doubt. Neither the devotees doubted these phenomenal miracles that took place with mundane periodicity, nor did I. Life moved on, but here it seemed as though it had been caught in a pleasant time wrap. Hearing people who opened their hearts to let me get a glimpse of their lives; especially a glimpse of days fraught with tears and heart ache; made me realise that for each, his or her cross seems to be the heaviest. Helping and sharing with each other is the best and the only way to make this long and uncharted journey of life bearable and God-help-us-all...even enjoyable at certain times."

"In all honesty, both my husband and I are certain that we are alive because of the help and support from Swamiji. There is no ambiguity in our minds. The best part of it all was that everything happened at its given time so beautifully. Very often, we behave like spoilt children. We want instant gratification of all our desires. But when I look back, I really thank Devi and Swamiji that they allowed things to unwrap at their given time. You see, many times devotees get disappointed as they want instant nirvana and all their wishes to be granted instantly. I think Devi really separates, beautifully, the grain and the chaff. Also, another thing that I have found so remarkable about Swamiji is that you can call Him at the oddest hours. I have personally called Him up at two in the morning; four in the morning... during His afternoon nap time...and I know how irritating sometimes these odd hour calls can be, as I am a doctor myself and receive such calls. But Swamiji never ever gets upset. He never distinguishes between the rich and the poor; the famous and people like us...nobodies. I may feel I am nobody, but Swamiji has never ever made us feel that way. His love is boundless. That is why, every devotee living here has to meet Swamiji at least once a month or we begin to feel all disoriented."

DEVI'S BLESSINGS:
THE PERFECT ANTIDOTE FOR CANCER

"Once, my mother telephoned from Mumbai telling me, that she was in acute discomfort regarding some problem on her tongue. She wanted me to be with her, so I went to Swamiji just to ask if all was well with my mother. Swamiji told me that He was not getting good signals about my mother's tongue problem and He even mentioned that I should be prepared for a harsh diagnosis. He showed me exactly where the problem on the tongue lay; he pointed out a spot on the left side of His own tongue. But He assured me that whatever the diagnosis there was nothing to worry, Devi and He would make certain that my mother did not have to suffer or her life style be altered adversely."

"I reached Mumbai and will you believe it the abrasion was at the exact spot that Swamiji had pointed out. Also, it was detected as cancer. Now usually the prognosis where tongue cancer is concerned is very poor. Also the quality of life suffers drastically. But will you believe it till date my mother can still sing, her speech has not been affected; her lifestyle has not changed dramatically and though thrice the abrasion had to be removed it is still on the superficial level. Swamiji has kept telling me that the medical profession...my own world...can say what they want but where Devi and He are concerned my mother is not suffering from tongue cancer. It is true for if she was the pain and discomfort to her would have been hell and unimaginable. Also whenever I think of Him, He will call up. Like today I am leaving for Hyderabad for a conference and in the morning I thought to myself that I must meet Swamiji before leaving. Minutes later I get a call and He tells me ' come over, Ruzbeh is here' and when I told Him that I was thinking of Him, He as usual just chuckled. We don't take any major decision in life without His approval."

"Another thing that you must know, I wanted my parents to settle down in Bangalore. With His approval granted, I began to search for the right house for them. I must have searched for two and a half years. Each and every house He refused. People thought I had gone mad. But do you know something. Every time I talked to Him about a prospective house that I had liked He would describe in great detail the same house. I don't know how He does it. I mean I must have seen around two hundred houses and I would get him either the name of the owner or in which area the house was and He would sitting in the mandir describe the house to the minutest detail. He would say 'there is this type of basement in the house' and I would say ' yes yes there is' and then he would tell me that a snake had been killed there so many odd years ago. Thus for two and a half years our hunt went on. By that time all real estate agents in Bangalore refused to speak to me. My relatives thought I had gone completely off my head. Every time He rejected a house, He would only ask me one thing, 'you want something quick or something good. If you trust me then have faith in my judgement or else go ahead'. In the end He gave His approval. My mother had just to come to Bangalore and immediately settle in. The house is tailor made for her. In fact so tailor made that the old refrigerator of ours matches the tiles. We did not have to change a thing. There is a pooja room...everything is perfect. We all live together. In fact we always say it is Devi's house. One thing that affects me greatly is His total disregard to His comfort and health. You are Shiridi Sai Baba's worshipper. So am I. Since childhood we have great faith in Shirdi Sai Baba. Just as Baba would never bother about His comfort, similarly Swamiji is not bothered about what happens to Him. Both of Them are present in spirit form the moment you call on Them. I see a lot of similarity in both of Them."

Mr. Gupta walked in and told me that he was leaving. He spoke to Sonal for a while and then we resumed our talk.

"Take Mr. Gupta's grand child. She is a mentally challanged child. Four years back she could barely talk but now if you see her, she sings, works on the computer and even goes to a regular school. We have a friend from Mumbai. He is an industrialist. His son was born with a series of seizures...you know epilepsy...and he too was mentally challanged. Swamiji asked the family to perform certain poojas and now the same child goes to a regular school and though the child is slightly slow, he is like all normal children. When they came here the child could not speak at all...and they had consulted speech therapists etc and now if you see the child you will say it is a miracle. But nothing happens in a day. You have to really have faith..."

"Like Baba says, *Shrada and Saburi*..."

"Yes, faith and patience. Through experience I have learnt that faith and patience are the only things that matter."

Sonal left to check on Swamiji's health. She regularly monitored Swamiji to make certain that He was not neglecting His well-being due to the constant flow of devotees and perpetual tinkling of the ubiquitous telephones. I was seated in the drawing room. Swamiji was unable to take His afternoon siesta as He had to arrange for a generator to be sent to His guesthouse in Subramanyia.

Swamiji was very often directed by Devi to inform devotees and those who flocked for predictions that they needed to perform certain prayers and poojas at Subramanyia. The temple is a Government owned religious site and Swamiji has no say in the running of the temple. As very often a few days are required for the completion of the pooja, the devotees had no option but to stay in the extremely inhabitable sheds that disguised themselves as guesthouses. Those days, spending a few days at Subramaniya was a true parameter of faith as the conditions made people made of steel cry for basic comforts and sanitation. One day, Swamiji took a loan from the bank and decided to make a small guesthouse that would provide devotees with the comforts that they had taken so much for granted. He was immediately cheated and though the work on the guesthouse had begun, its completion looked as probable as finding an amused mule that comprehended Einstein. By then Swamiji, had as usual gone overboard, and devotees like Lalit, Murli, Sameer, stepped in and made certain that the work on the guesthouse eventually got completed. Now the guesthouse provides city dwellers with the comforts they are used to and staying in Subramaniya does not make strong men swirl with vertigo. Coffee arrived and Swamiji introduced me to a gentleman who tried to pronounce my name seven times and then decided that he would rather enjoy the steaming coffee. A few minutes later, another gentleman introduced himself to me.

SPIRITS BANISHED

"Namaste! My name is Sudhir Goyal. I know Swamiji since 1973. In those days I had a major problem with my hotel. Basically, something to do with the evil eye. There was no cure for the problems that kept harassing me and in the end, a person working for me told me about Swamiji. So one day in the morning, I arrived here. At that time, this place was deserted. In fact, in the nights, people used to get scared to come over here. There was no building. Just Ma's mandir and a small kitchen very close by. That day Swamiji was in a trance. I did not know anything about trance and all this, but I sat down and the first thing Ma told me was that I should come in the evening and Swamiji would accompany me to my hotel. I took Her blessings and in the evening...actually around 8.30 p.m., I arrived with a box of sweetmeats. I did my namaste to Swamiji and waited for Him to guide me. One hour passed and I asked Him if I should come some other day. He nodded in the negative and told me to wait. So wait I did. Another hour went by. It was now 10.30 at night. As I told you, this place was deserted. It was dark and nobody was near by for a long distance. But Swamiji told me to wait. Now, this was the first time I was interacting with somebody like Swamiji. I mean frankly, I did not know how to tell Him that it was too late and I could certainly come another time. At 11.30 p.m. in the end, Swamiji told me that it would be better if I came again some other time. I was not disappointed. I bowed down to Ma and told Her that as asked, I had come and took Her blessings.

"The moment I opened my car door, I heard a loud noise outside. I looked around and saw Ma's trishul, a coconut and a lime fallen in front of my car. All this was, minutes earlier, near Ma. Before I could really understand what was happening I heard Swamiji come running. He told me that Ma wanted Him to visit my place that very moment. He then told me to go and see what had happened to the sweetmeats and other offerings I had brought for Ma. I went inside and saw all that I had brought for Ma was burnt to ashes. Then we started our journey. A little while later, the brakes of my car failed. There was a car behind my car and a scooter in front of us. The inevitable occurred. There was a crash, but somehow nobody was injured. Fortunately for me, the scooter driver was a person who regularly came to my hotel and the driver behind was a friend of Swamiji's. We all parted amicably, but minutes later my steering wheel began to rotate on its own volition. I mean I did not know what the hell was going on. Swamiji told me not to worry, this was expected as the force that He was being sent to remove, was trying its damn all to make certain

Swamiji did not reach my hotel. Eventually, Swamiji performed whatever He had to do and after a small pooja we reached His mandir at 1.30 a.m."

VANISHING PAIN

"After that day the problems ceased and since then no decision is made without Ma's and Swamiji's approval. So many times when I have been praying here, the Lime will fall down, the flowers will fall and roll towards you. I have two hotels and I know that my success is all Her doing. She is my mother. She will never let Her son down. Once for six months, I kept falling ill...mainly pain in the chest and maybe around a hundred x-rays were removed and an equal number of tests, but the doctors could not find out what was really the matter with me. In the end my doctor advised that I should get an operation done, as he felt the problem was caused due to two lobes which had got affected. I was admitted in the hospital and the next day my operation was due. I began to feel very uneasy and thus I got myself discharged, reached home and told my brother to take me to Ma and Swamiji. Due to some reason or the other, I could not make contact with Swamiji...I am talking of a number of years ago. I reached the temple and Swamiji went into a trance... those days even for predictions Swamiji would go into a trance and Ma would only communicate through Him in Kannada language. So Ma informed me that nothing was wrong with me. That the cough had dried up very badly and thus, had affected my health...as it had affected my breathing and had caused my chest to pain. She advised me to take a very simple ayurvedic medicine found in all shops and told me to chew a particular part of the pineapple...the centre part of the pineapple, that is hard and is usually thrown away. She told me to chew that part and spit it away. She told me to do this for three days. On the second day itself, late in the night, I coughed badly and then vomited. The dried cough came out and I was completely all right. For six months, I had unnecessarily suffered. I must have taken every cough medicine in the bloody market. This had happened in the 1980s."

"You have been coming here since the early 70s. Did Devi test Swamiji really hard?"

"Oh very hard. You know when I began coming here there was nothing. All this fancy building and car and big time people were not around. Swamiji used to stay alone in the building near by. Devi really tested Him. Swamiji was a fun loving man. He liked His drink and His enjoyments. He did not want to become a Swamiji, but when Ma wants something done, nothing and nobody can stand in Her way. She used to burn His clothes. His liquor would disappear. She made Him give up driving the motor bike. No smoking. No non-vegetarian food. Of course, Swamiji really tried to resist Her but then Ma wanted Him to lead life Her way. There have been times when He has not had food to eat or feed His family. In the morning He would wonder from where the food would come and by afternoon, Ma would make certain that He and His family had food to survive on. If you were there your eyes would fill with tears. But Ma changed His life. Not actually by force. What She did was, changed the direction of His energy. A Mother knows best for Her child. First He used to spend His energy in other things. Ma redirected His energy in such heavenly activity. He had really led a rough and tough life. But all through, whenever somebody would die, He would be there first to make certain that the person gets a decent send off. I mean most of us do not take the time off for our own family and friends but He would be present whenever He knew or heard that somebody had passed away. He really has suffered a lot. I remember, His children would all come to meet Him. They would travel a long distance in a crowded bus and then walk all the way here. After He was better settled, He confessed to me, that many times He had come to meet me at my hotel to ask for help, but His pride and His faith in Ma always prevented Him. He often did not have money even for oil to burn the lamps.

"Another thing is that He does not hide His past from anybody. He openly says that He has led a very colourful life. He has done it all and seen it all. Before Ma entered His life, Swamiji used to earn a lot but then squander it all away on enjoyments of

124

life. In a confrontation, He would first bash the person and then bother to ask questions and reasons for the fight. Even now He cannot tolerate fools. Amma, was telling me, that His no nonsense nature has still not left Him. He will not think of the consequences. Amma was telling me that if ever I wanted to remove anybody from my hotel, who was giving me trouble, I should give the task to Swamiji. You see, He is very straight and that is why He cannot tolerate any sort of deceit. And He is like a child. One day I showed Him this nine stoned precious ring. It is called *Nav Ratna...* made of nine precious stones. I asked Him whether this *Nav Ratna* was good. You know what He told me? He said that the best *Nav Ratna* is to feed the poor and hungry people. He is the most practical Swamiji you will ever meet. According to Him, the third eye is nothing but one's own brain and mind. And yes, you don't have to show Him anything or come personally to meet Him. One phone call and He tells you everything. That is why He is so down to earth. That is why He is so approachable. He understands the pain of all those who come to Him because Ma has made Him experience everything. He has gone through every possible hardship and that is why He understands the pain and suffering of all those who come to Him. Of course you have to go through your karma, but in coming here even the intensity of your karma is reduced."

TO AMPUTATE OR NOT TO AMPUTATE

"I will give you an example. One day a friend from my village came here and he was in great pain. His leg was completely gone and it was obvious that gangrene had spread through the leg. The doctors advised that the leg should be cut. Now this person had just married two months prior. He told the doctor that instead of cutting his leg, he might as well cut his neck off, as for a newly married man, his manliness and pride are so important. I asked this man whether he believed in God. He said he did. I gave him Swamiji's card and told him to meet Swamiji and if Ma wanted to save this man's leg then well and good. He came here and Swamiji gave him three limes and told him everyday to squeeze the lime in water and drink it. He then told him that on the fourth day, he could go back to the same doctor and show him the leg and get the doctor's opinion. On the fourth day, the doctor was shocked out of his wits. The leg was virtually all right. Just one finger had to be cut and not the whole leg. So you see, in the person's karma, amputation was written but instead of a complete leg, with the grace of Ma and Swamiji, just one finger got amputated. Ma is phenomenal. We are nothing. What does a man do? Just depletes ration...nothing else. And mankind is just running to and fro. Often Swamiji says that mankind now does not bother about butter...we want to run after oil. We leave God and run after money. Sad but true.

"And yes, the kind of trance that Swamiji goes through is amazing. Once my mother told me that I should not keep bothering Swamiji about everything and thus she told me not to go to Swamiji for a prediction. I still came here and Swamiji went in a trance. The first thing Ma tells me: 'when your mother told you not to come her, why did you disobey her...next time if your mother tells you not to come I don't want you to disobey her...she is also your mother'. I had not told anybody what had happened at my home. But she is the Universal Mother. She knows all that is happening every where. These are facts, not just my imagination." Then Mangala, Swamiji's daughter, sat down and for a while we spoke about the Chandi Havan that was to take place in a few weeks.

"You know I still remember, uncle had a major problem with his palms. He could not eat or hold anything. The doctors were totally foxed..."

"Yes. How could I forget this incident. You see I could not even hold rice in my fingers...so bad was my condition..."

"He would sit in the mandir and spread out his hands and tell Ma to cure him." Informed Mangala.

"Devi really cured me. I was suffering with this problem for seven years and Ma cured me. No medicines worked but the grace of Ma did the trick. I feel that if you have any problems sit in front of Ma."

"But let me tell you that She is a very strict Mother," informed Mangala. "Just because we are graced by Her, does not mean we can take any sort of liberties. Sometimes we get angry at certain things or subconsciously wish something that is not right or good. Immediately She points that out to us, either through my father... Swamiji, or through a dream or even when we bow to Her in the temple. She is extremely loving but very strict. She tolerates no nonsense from anybody. She is very disciplined and very difficult to understand. Most people want instant gratification of their wish. If they don't get it, they begin to doubt Her power and Swamiji's power. That really upsets me. Also, most people the moment their wish is granted, disappear only to be seen again when they are in trouble or want another wish to be fulfilled. Most people come here come for material benefits...I don't blame them...but very few come here for spiritual benefits. They benefit tremendously. But you cannot take advantage of Her. You cannot play with Her emotions. But, if you surrender to Her...She guides you very well..."

"You know, She has directed Swamiji, as to how Her image should look like in the idol. She has directed Swamiji in the entire planning of Her idol, as well as the planning of the entire mandir...."

"You mean Devi has actually directed Swamiji in making Her own image?" I inquired.

"Yes. Often, She would point out that a particular thing was not looking good or the nose was not shaped properly or this was not right or that was too long, etc. She directs Swamiji for everything and He does not do anything that does not have Her approval.

"She will continue testing you. You have to submit yourself to Her. You have to say, 'Ma I leave everything to you'. She is really phenomenal. I have done clinical psychology but I still cannot understand Her or my father. She only wants love. Ma has always insisted that 'even if you don't do my pooja it is okay, but make sure all those who come to Me are fed.' Feeding the hungry, is according to both, Ma and Swamiji the most important thing. And yes, one thing you can be sure of and that is She is there protecting us all...everybody who comes here." Informed Mangala.

"You know sometime back, Ma through Swamiji, forbid me to eat in my own hotel. Somebody has done something there. She told me not to even drink water. She said that somebody has done something in such a manner that only I would get affected. So for six months I did not touch my own food or water and then on Her own, one day She told me that I could now go ahead and do as I pleased." Informed Sudhir.

"Ma is really out of this world..."

"See, there is no doubt about the power of Ma, but Mangala, one thing is certain and that is I have never ever seen a Medium as powerful as your father...I think Swamiji is really one of the most clear and powerful Mediums." I could make this statement as I had met a number of mediums and though all of them were damn good; Swamiji was galaxies above them.

"Though, He is my own father and often we have our differences, I can tell you that He is the most large hearted person I have ever seen. Yes as a Medium and Swamiji, He is really very extraordinary but even as a father and friend and confidant, you will not find many like Him. I am really very lucky to have Him as my father. Even before He became a Swamiji, He would spend all that He earned in making sure we were well fed and happy. Yes, when He could not afford it, He would make us eat food and stay hungry Himself. He treats everybody like His family. In fact, I fight with Him often on this regard. I tell Him very often that, 'You treat your devotees like your family and have more time for them than us, your real family'. And He always tells me that 'now everybody is my family as I am a Swamiji'. He is engrossed in solving the problems of His devotees and engrossed with Ma Mookambika. Though you will never see Him consciously pray or do pooja, His very life is a prayer. In fact sometime later I shall write a book on my experiences with Ma and Swamiji. You know something...in my childhood, teachers kept complaining that I was very slow in my work. In fact, many thought that I was a slow learner. One day Ma Mookambika came through and told Swamiji that nothing was wrong with me and that I would really pursue education with a zeal. So for a child who was called slow and thought to have a

128

defect, now I have done my Doctorate in Clinical Psychology. I really used to get horrible marks earlier. I still have those mark sheets."

"Was your life very difficult?"

"Yes earlier we went through a hard life. All of a sudden, our entire lifestyle changed. People began to talk strange things about our father...accusing Him of abandoning us and neglecting us. Initially we did not understand what was happening, but after a while, we knew that something phenomenal was going on; out of the ordinary. Yes, life was hard, but Ma kept Her word of taking care of us. We may have, in those days, not lived in luxury or even comfort, but our basic necessities were always taken care of. She had once told my father, that a time will come when you will feed hundreds of people and your family will be so settled that people will envy you. Of course those days we barely had enough food to eat, but She kept Her word like She always does."

"That is why Swamiji eats anywhere, as long as the place serves only vegetarian food and it is clean. Then it can be a small restaurant or a palace, it does not matter. He is without any fuss. That day Swamiji was washing the car and somebody had come here for the first time. So he asked my father where he could find Swamiji? My father kept washing the car and told the person that Swamiji must be inside, whiling away His time doing something or the other. He loves to make people laugh. He will never laugh at somebody's expense, but He is so jolly that there is never a dull moment with Him. He does not teach some serious philosophy, but in a simple, jovial manner He will get His and Ma Mookambika's point of view across. And yes His memory is so phenomenal that it is amazing. People can come here after years and He still remembers them and why they had come earlier. For instance, you know how fast He drives the car. He is like a race driver. He will wave to so many people and I have to turn around to see, who He has waved out to and how He saw those people. He has the reflexes of a young man and the memory of an elephant. Also, every morning He goes for a walk and then, on and off, He visits this restaurant..."

"Don't mention that restaurant. I was with Him today and He stuffed me with so much food that I shall never look at a South Indian restaurant ever again."

"Oh! you were with Him. Then there is no way you can get out of the restaurant without your belly bursting. There is no excuse that can be used to avoid eating the food put in front of you. He will eat and make sure He will feed all those with Him."

"Yes, Murli was telling me the other day that if a journey normally takes four hours, with Swamiji it takes six and more as He would like to experiment snacks and coffee at various joints..."

"One day, Swamiji and I went to Delhi together. He told me that there was this particular mountain that He wanted to visit. So I agreed. We went by car and on the way, Swamiji felt hungry. So we stopped at a small dhaba (a small road side stall) got food prepared, He forced us to eat along with Him and only then did we continue the journey. As a hotelier, having more people like Swamiji is a dream come true for us."

"Talking about journeys, one day we were travelling out of town and passing through a forest. It was raining very heavily and we all were sleeping. Suddenly, His door slowly opened and He immediately closed it and then woke me up saying 'Mangala be careful, your door is going to open now' and you won't believe it, the door opened that very moment. Luckily my mother held me tight and we got the door shut. Ma Mookambika had opened daddy's door and then given Him the message that my door was going to open. If daddy had not warned me, I would have certainly fallen off the car which was travelling really fast. It was really great. All thanks to Ma that I got saved...."

"Even the suggestions given by Ma are so practical. As you know, I own hotels and She goes on telling me 'that if you feed the people good food, they will keep coming to you, but if you feed them poison, will they ever come to you again? You don't worry. I am there taking care of you and your interests'. She is really handling everything. Whenever I come and inquire if I should expand my business interests, She will say 'yes go ahead, I am there' and you won't believe it, She really takes care. How I started and now the position I am in, are two different planets virtually, but with Her grace and support I know all this major expansion work gets completed successfully."

"You know, He is a Swamiji to the world, but for me He is my father first and that is why, very often I get upset at the way He allows His health to suffer. You know I sit down and just take appointments and in a limited manner, deal with those coming for predictions. I get exhausted. Imagine He has to sit in the mandir, and for hours give predictions and answer each and every question...and He never hurries up anybody..."

"To do that, at His age and absorb all the negativity that He deals with, is not funny..."

"So many times He takes the pain and suffering of His devotees. You remember I told you that I had this bad cough..."

"For six months and Ma told you..."

"Yes exactly. Well I got cured within three days, but for the next fifteen days Swamiji kept coughing badly. His health suffered and His cough seemed not to go. You will not believe it, but He was coughing blood. What do you think happened? He took it upon Himself. Then fortunately, Ma made certain that He got back to normal. How many people will do such a thing?"

"But Ruzbeh, why does this happen? I mean why does it affect my father?"

"See, I have been often told when Sainath comes through, that energy has to be absorbed. If Swamiji is removing an illness...illness is negative energy...then where does that negative energy go? Energy says 'okay you are removing me from here, now where am I to go?' The Master absorbs the energy. Energy cannot be destroyed. Also healing is dangerous, as you are dabbling with energy and transference of energy. If you touch a live wire, no matter how noble your intentions may be, you will get a dickens of a shock. That is the law of energy. And if you see, the more emotionally attached Swamiji is to a person, during healing He will be affected more, as He has touched a live wire without the required protection. Protection means, you have to be detached during the process of healing. With you and Sunil

He is greatly attached and immediately He took on your problems..."

"Yes, we had asked the Goddess regarding this...that when He is healing people, how can we protect Him? And Ma said that the only thing that can protect Him, from contracting the person's disease, is to make sure that Swamiji does meditation..."

"I can't see Swamiji tying Himself in knots doing meditation." I am as certain of this, as I am that the sun is a blazing ball of fire. "The reason why Ma asked Him to do meditation was that meditation brings about a sense of detachment. Illness is transferred when you are attached to the person you are healing. For instance, you or like today, this morning, He took on Sunil's pain. He is attached to both of you. Swamiji, so often tells the Goddess that 'I am not interested in karma, cure this person'. The Goddess says fine ' but who will take upon the problem'. Somebody has to and our Swamiji, on and off, keeps falling ill...little wonder."

"But why does it happen that every time during healing, though the person gets cured, nothing happens to Him?"

"You see I have been told that while healing somebody, you have to tell your Guru 'if You so desire please cure this person or give the person strength and wisdom to accept whatever God has in store for him/her'. At such times, if healing takes place, God/Goddess or the Guru in the spirit plane, absorbs the illness and being in the spirit plane they do not have to undergo the same gruesome agony. But suppose Swamiji tells Ma 'I don't care about karma-dharma, you have to cure this person' then Ma says fine 'you take on the problem then' and it is at such times Swamiji gets badly affected. Or if Swamiji knows that due to whatever laws, His devotee cannot be cured, He voluntarily takes on the disease."

By the time the talk concluded, it was late in the evening. Swamiji had still not arrived. He had been out for a few hours just organising that the work on the generator got completed, so that He could send the generator to Subramaniya the next day itself. Apart from helping the vast number of devotees, who thronged the temple and kept the telephones blaring at the oddest hours, Swamiji spent a lot of His time and energy handling work that could easily be done by, either an efficient assistant or the family itself. But for some reason, help was always wanting and He who helped one and all in their daily life, unfortunately very often, had to soil His hands with mundane work. Very often I have seen Him absolutely exhausted, what with predictions, healing, counselling and then making certain that cleanliness is maintained and the guest house functions like clock work and what not.

If there is a Sage, who is perfectly content and involved with the spiritual and the physical aspects of survival, Swamiji is the chosen one. I took a short walk and attempted to call up the family. The lines were busy and by the time I returned, it was already dark. Swamiji still had not returned. Managla met me and informed that Swamiji had called and inquired if I had been fed and taken care of. She also informed me that He wanted me to go and meet Dr. Sudhir Vinekar and his wife, a doctor too. They lived twenty minutes away. I took down the address and paid my obeisance to Ma. Amma was once again saying her prayers. Seeing her devotion, made me realise the shallowness in most people's lives. Most of us are so caught up in our small crab like world, where according to each individual, the sun and the planets revolved only around 'I, me and myself'.

I hailed a rickshaw and spent the better half of ten minutes trying to convince the driver that I had no intention of going, either to the railway station, the airport or the blasted museum. We both spoke different languages and in the end, an exasperated hawker, after watching both of us make asses of ourselves, intervened. I watched, fascinated as he, in top speed, with lots of vocal modulation and physical hand movements, that did hint towards the use of violence, explained the dash blighter the destination I wanted to travel to.

So off we travelled, with the driver muttering under his breath, certain things I am for sure I was better off not knowing. He stood on his brake and announced something. I looked around and found the place I was looking for. The receptionist announced my arrival and within a few moments, Dr. Sudhir Vinekar stood in front of me, shaking my hands with sincere warmth and regard.

I entered his cabin and felt overjoyed to see an enlarged photograph of my Guru, Sai Baba of Shirdi. We both spoke about Sai Baba and it was obvious that he and his family were great devotees of Master Sai. His wife entered and we were introduced.

TO YOUR 'RIGHT' DESTINATION

"I think we met Swamiji in 1976. We had studied and become doctors in Mumbai, but as my parents were in Bangalore, we decided to settle down here and start a nursing home. We arrived here in 1975 and a year later, met Swamiji through a common friend called Krishnan. The first time I met Him, I must confess that I was scared. I mean, He was in a trance and His voice had changed and buddy, I was shit scared. Those days, Omen 1 and Omen 2 had just been released and frankly, I did not know what to make out of it. I met Swamiji as we wanted to start a nursing home that was ideal for mother and child-care. My wife's mother died in child-birth. My wife was just thirteen then and that inspired her to become a doctor; especially become a gynecologist. That is why our nursing home is called The Ideal

Nursing Home. But we were not very rich and did not have any financial backing. Though both my parents were doctors...they would earn hundred rupees and give away ninety-five. Now we wanted a real top class hospital or nursing home.

"Ma Mookambika, in the trance, spoke through Swamiji. He then asked for a sheet of paper and then drew in detail, what the property that we would eventually buy, look like. He even went to the extent of describing what the front of the house would look like and said that it would have a peculiar design done on wood and showed us how that design would look like. He said the entire property would be in the shape of the word L. He also said that the property would face the road and it would be on such and such angle and He went on and on. I was very young and I thought, 'how on earth can somebody conceptualize not only what I might buy in the future, but also draw the design that would be in the front of the house?'. Plus the weird shape of the house itself stumped me. For, me it was something mind blowing. So I kept quiet and assumed that He was pulling my leg. But He said that 'you are Devi's child and that Devi has her blessings on us and that She would make sure that at the right time we would get the property'. The same property, that was for some odd reason, shaped like a blooming L. Devi, speaking through Swamiji, is something now I do not take lightly. In fact Devi's first message to me was that 'your family Goddess is Shanta Durga', something that was cent per cent accurate and also something not many people could have known of."

"My search began and nothing seemed to happen. Two years went by, but still no progress. Swamiji kept insisting that we would find the house that Devi had predicted. The problem with us was that we refused to give any black money to buy our house. Then at last, we were told that there was a house for sale. So in the end, we came over here and an old woman, around ninety-five years old opened the door slightly and I could see through the door, two ferocious looking Doberman dogs staring at me. She asked me what I wanted and I told her that I wanted to buy her house. She looked me over and, still with the door slightly ajar, she told me that I would have to meet two required conditions. First condition was that she wanted all the money by cheque...no black money. I sighed with relief. But the second condition stumped me. She said that I should be married and also be the father of a daughter. That clearly left me speechless. I had, by then, got into the house and stared at her with my jaws wide open. I mean where on earth was the connection of buying a house and being the father to a baby girl. So she told me, that she came to India in 1911 from France. This house had a history that whenever a daughter was born in this house, the father of that child passed away. She gave me the entire list of all those men who had possessed this house and passed away a few years after they became father to a girl child. So she was scared that I, too, would pass away, if and when I would get a daughter, thus she wanted to sell the house to a man who already had a daughter and was still kicking about like a horse. I asked her, as to how many of these men had passed away in this house? She told me of the five men just one man had passed away in this house, while all others had died at other places. I concluded that it could not possibly be the land that was the cause of their premature demise, but some other reason like a genetic problem or even karmic problems. She scratched her chin and nodded and concluded that maybe...just maybe, I had a point."

"I made an agreement with her and paid her a down payment and then rushed to Swamiji. He mentioned to me that this was the very place that Ma Mookambika had spoken about and had I not checked the wooden gate and the design on it. I had first visited the place in the evening, so I immediately set out for the bungalow. Exactly as He had said two years before, I saw the same design and the same wooden latis work that He had drawn the first time I had met up with Him. We had still kept the wooden work...it is made of Burmese wood that is not available now.

"Anyway, when I went to meet Swamiji again to finalize everything, He told me, that before I could buy the place, I would have to do something. He mentioned that if I just wanted to buy the place to live in, then I could go ahead and purchase the property. But if I wanted to build a nursing home, then I would have to seek the permission of the king cobra that resided in the garden. I nearly fell off my chair. I mean, I was a doctor, not an African witch doctor, who could communicate with snakes and seek their permission. But Swamiji was insistent that I should go back to the bungalow, and in the garden, seek out a jasmine tree. Once I had found the jasmine tree, I should say a particular mantra and then throw the lime near the tree. A King Cobra would appear and then I was supposed to ask the cobra if I could build my nursing home. Swamiji informed me gently, that if the cobra nods its head thrice in the affirmation, I could go ahead and buy the place immediately. But if it hisses angrily, then I should not waste much time and get the hell out of the garden and say goodbye to the bungalow and my down payment.

"Frankly, I thought this whole thing was way out and the idea of losing my hard earned down payment did not appeal to me. But Krishnan agreed and we arrived at the bungalow and began to search for the jasmine tree. There was every dash tree in the garden, but no jasmine tree. So we went back and told Swamiji and He phoo-phooed the idea that there was no jasmine tree. He told me to go back to the bungalow and get the floor map of the entire premises. So off we went and returned with the map and He took a pencil and then made a point on the paper and said 'there is your jasmine tree'. So off we went again and this time we took a measuring tape and in the end, arrived to the exact place that corresponded with the pencil dot Swamiji had made on the floor map. On the exact spot, stood a six inch jasmine baby shrub, that still had a long way to grow into a tree, but the fact is that, on the exact spot specified by Swamiji a jasmine plant had bloomed."

The doctor's good friend Krishnan, asked the doctor to chant the mantra and throw the lime near the jasmine plant. The good doctor had totally forgotten the mantra but fortunately, his friend remembered it. He spoke aloud the mantra and threw the lime near the tree and they both waited for the cobra to arrive and begin a tete-a-tete. No cobra with a penchant for chitchatting with mankind, arrived. So feeling a little silly, they both turned to report back to the Spiritual Headquarters that 'Operation Cobra' had fallen flat on its head.

"We must have taken two steps forward when we both heard a clear hissing coming from behind. We turned and we saw this huge, brown cobra, with its hood in the air...it was right in front of us, next to the jasmine tree. The cobra looked to me like a damn army tank. I forgot everything after that. Forget asking the cobra a question, I even forgot my name. I had achieved instant samadhi. I just kept making these strange sounds and staring goggled eyed at the huge cobra. Krishnan, by then realised that I was out of circulation. He was made of sterner stuff. Krishnan told this serpent in Kannada, that his friend who had become dumb and deaf at the moment, wanted to build a nursing home and that we wanted its permission and that if the permission was not granted, we would leave this place in a flash. The cobra very beautifully nodded its head thrice. Just like Swamiji had predicted and then after nodding thrice in a flash it turned around and slithered away. The last I saw of it was, it slithering away out of the compound and disappearing between two rocks at a distance.

"Now the main problem arose. The problem of buying the property. I had paid the first down payment and within six months, I was supposed to pay the entire sum. As days turned into weeks, no bank wanted to give us the loan, as frankly, we did not have anything to give as a security to the bank. So once again, I rushed back to Ma Mookambika and Swamiji. He very casually informed me, that funding for such a venture was no problem. He gave me a lime and told me that when I was with the bank manager, I should slip the lime under the manager's chair. This once again stumped me. Swamiji coolly informed me that I should not be worried about being thrown out. He showed me a simple manner of achieving this objective. He said, 'you first drop your pen...or drop the manager's pen...then you bend to pick it up and slowly slip the lime under the person's seat and pick up the pen and voila'. He told me that the next day, the person would call me up and sanction my loan." By now, Sudhir was a firm believer of Ma Mookambika and Swamiji. Though Swamiji's operandi, first hobnobbing with a cobra and then slipping limes under Bank Manager's seating arrangements, were unconventional, Sudhir agreed to conduct Operation Lime. He had reached a stage of no return. Apart from blind belief in Swamiji, he was running out of time. He would have even skinned the manager alive, if that would have got home the bacon.

"I, somehow managed to slip the lime under the charlie's chair and the very next day I got a call from him saying that my loan had been sanctioned. I mean, if I tell this to a foreigner he will immediately make plans of locking me in an asylum, but all these are facts. So with the funding in place we got an architect and an interior designer and really planned a jazzy place...for which we would have to break down the bungalow and build two different structures...one for us to live in and one for the nursing home. It really looked impressive on paper and also fitted our budget. I showed it to Swamiji, who in two seconds flat, told me that I would never be able to complete this project. In fact, He told me that I would not even begin this project. I asked Him why and He just shrugged His shoulders and said 'wait and watch'. But this time we were very keen to have it done our way and we were about to begin work when, for some cuckoo reason, our country decided to host the Asiad Games.

"All the cement meant for everything else was redirected to Delhi and then cement was rationed and the stuff available in black, costed twice the legal rate. Also the cost of everything else increased and we realised that Swamiji was bang on right, once again. So then, we once again made alternations and decided not to break down and reconstruct, but make modifications. We made modifications and went back to show the plan to Swamiji. He okayed the plan and then informed me that the property I had bought came about once in a eon. I should try my best never to dispose it away or even do too much of alternation. Then He told me that my plan was all right, but I would have to tilt the structural planning as He did not want anything to happen to the little jasmine tree. I was aghast. That six-inch jasmine plant could be relocated, I pleaded. He said no. So for that little jasmine plant, the entire planning had to be redone and everything had to be modified, keeping in mind that nothing ever happened to that jasmine plant.

"So at last the nursing home was established and everything was going on smoothly. We had to start repaying the loan bank in a few months time and in the first few months, itself, we were earning enough to take care of our needs and the needs of the nursing home. But the problem was that, as months went by, we kept earning the same Rs.20,000. In a few months our monthly installments would begin and then this twenty grand would fall drastically short to pay the loan, maintain the nursing home and our family. So off we went back to Ma Mookambika and Swamiji. Swamiji said that Ma had asked Him to come over and do a pooja. In the pooja Ma Mookambika spoke through Swamiji and inquired as to why a particular door had been removed from the room. It was true that there had been a door and we had removed it and shut the place up. Nobody could have noticed that, but then for Ma Mookambika and Swamiji, all these are trivial points. So Swamiji told me that I would have to put a door. We had completely shut up the area and after a little haggling of where the door could and could not be placed, it was finally agreed to place the door at an approved junction. Will you believe I did not have money to buy the door that cost us Rs.18,600. Our neighbour helped us out. But from the next month onwards, instead of the usual Rs. 20,000, we began to earn more than Rs. 50,000. I mean, we did not do anything. Just paid heed to the advice of Ma and Swamiji and bang! the income more than doubled. At every stage Ma Mookambika and Sai Baba of Shirdi have been holding our hands and helping us to cross the ocean of maya and karma."

OVERCOMING ALL OBSTACLES

"Now take my son. When he passed out of the university, he got seventeen gold medals. At no time has any medical student got seventeen gold medals. He was called by the national papers as the 'golden boy' and believe me, he truly is a golden child of God." For the next hour, the good doctor spoke at length about his son, who he loves and holds in awe. I have never seen a father who is so genuinely proud and so much in awe and love with his son, like the way Sudhir Vinekar. It is an amazing love relationship. "So my son said that he wanted to build an eye hospital. Something like the India Institute of Science. An eye hospital, where even the poorest of the poor are treated and we should never say no to anybody. It should be the Mecca for eye problems and I don't mind if we don't earn a rupee from it, but we need to build the hospital.

"I, immediately remembered Swamiji. Years and years ago, He had told me that after I had made success of the nursing home, I shall get involved in social work of international standing. That I would devote my later years to social service and be content with serving people. And my son had the same views, though I had told nobody about what Swamiji had predicted more that twenty years ago. I also remembered my father who had become blind at the fag end of his life. My son had promised him that he would grow up and cure his blindness and build an eye hospital. Maybe, just to make my son serve countless blind people, my father had to make a sacrifice...something planned in the spirit world, beyond our comprehension. I have now bought acres and acres of land far away from here to start the eye hospital, to serve those afflicted with eye problems. Its main aim is to serve the poor and the needy. What Swamiji had predicted about us getting involved in social work, twenty years ago, has become a reality. He is truly amazing.

"My son had won 17 gold medals and he wanted admission in All India Medical. He appeared for the examination and we were all shocked when we learnt that he had stood 170th. We knew there was a mistake, as he always stood in the top rankers and thus, we got the papers reevaluated. There we learnt, that in an important score sheet, his pen had smudged everything and as nothing was visible, all those marks which he was certain to have earned, were lost. Those lost marks would have propelled him to the front rank, but it was an unfortunate accident and though everybody were unhappy about the state of events, even they could do little to help us. So he had to appear for the Chandigarh exam, but to the horror of everybody, the entire pattern of the question sheet had been changed. There was just one seat available and there were around 8600 people appearing.

He said that there was no way he would get it and he was really depressed that he had not got into the All India Medical. He had a fever of 103 degrees and believe me, for a boy who has earned 17 gold medals, all of a sudden nothing seemed to be going right. That is the time I went to meet Swamiji. He said that 101% my child would get admission in Chandigarh. So after a lot of encouragement my son sat for the examination. The next day was the result and he had stood 125th rank out of 8600 students. Two days later, the boy who had stood in the top five, took the seat that my son was hoping to secure. Then, the first two hundred rankers were called in and they were asked to write their preference.

"I got in touch with Swamiji and told Him what had happened. I told Him that there was no way on earth my son could now get the Chandigarh seat. The seat was taken by the kid who stood third. But Swamiji told me to have faith. He insisted that my son would get admission. For the first time, I thought that Swamiji's prediction would not fall true. Then a month later, we got a call from the Chandigarh people, telling us that my son had got admission as MS in Ophthalmology. We could not believe this. It was virtually impossible for the 125th ranker to get the seat of his choice. It seems what had occurred was that, the boy who had chosen the seat, got a marriage proposal from abroad and decided to move out of the country. He did not join and thus, his seat was not offered to those just below him. Directly it was given to the second person who was desirous of the same seat in Ophthalmology ...and that was my son. Just before my son entered the campus, he gave us a call. He said, 'Daddy, I am just about to enter the hospital campus and want yours and mummy's blessings'. I had tears in my eyes. I knew that Ma , Swamiji and Sai Baba had worked a miracle. 'What more can I say about Them?' When I went to meet Swamiji and told Him that my son had really got the admission, He just coolly looked at me as though, after Ma telling me that my son would get admission, there was any way the authorities would dare refuse him admission. He is so confident and casual about miracles, that it is not funny."

Sudhir showed me around the nursing home and it was obvious that he and his wife had put their blood and sweat into the venture, thus making it a success. All the while, Sudhir kept talking about his son, his young daughter and his adopted daughter...they seemed to be his very existence and it felt nice to meet a couple, who though so very successful, still had their roots so well entrenched in Mother Nature.

By the time I reached the mandir, the gates were locked. It took me a few minutes and different voice modulations to attract attention and ten minutes later, all washed up, I sat in front of Swamiji, who had not yet eaten dinner, as He did not want me to sup all alone. These are the little gestures that makes one feel good to be still above Mother Earth rather than few feet below, within her womb.

We ate and discussed various people who had been interviewed. It was obvious that Swamiji was exhausted. After dinner, we went to the sitting room and Swamiji gave instructions to Nirmala and Mangala about their three day trip out of Bangalore. Except Swamiji and Amma, all were leaving in the morning and they would spend a day sight seeing through the forest and Swamiji spoke to each one, making certain that they had taken everything essential for the trip.

"You have had a long day and so, you go to sleep now. You, too, look tired. Tomorrow we will go for a walk." He smiled and after blessing me, entered His room. A little while later I lay on bed with assorted books lying around me, watching television. Once again our cricket team had got their living daylights thrashed and a selector was justifying why a few of the boys had been selected and why a few had not made it to the playing eleven. Hoping that somebody wise enough would boil the selector's head once and for all, I switched off the television and diverted my mind into a novel written by a gentleman who should have been effectively strangulated at birth. I read a few paragraphs from Sai Baba's book and moments later, was in slumber land.

Once again I was roused from sleep, much before six, by that persistent sparrow. Today the little bugger sat on my balcony, looking at me rather accusingly and blaring its little chest out and creating bedlam. Through sleep brimmed eyes, I peered at that cantankerous delinquent and told it to bugger off. Wrong move. It took a deep breath that really made its chest puff up, till I thought it would burst and then it let out a barrage of what appeared to me as abuses. Then seeing me sufficiently awake, glared at me and then flew away.

Sleep was out of question. I stood up and did my *pranam* to Lord Krishna and Ma Radha and Lord Hanuman. Then looked below and saw a few of the boys already washing up the floor outside the gate. I washed myself, changed into a new set of clothes and then went down to say my Namaste to Ma Mookambika. Amma was already doing her pooja and decorating Ma. There was a soft bhajan lilting out from a small taperecorder. I might forget everything associated with this trip, but these activities in and around the pooja room in the early mornings, shall always be etched in my mind... Amma saying her prayers; the fragrance of fresh flowers of different colours; the aroma of the incence sticks that give the entire place a spiritual aura; the oil lamps burning bright; the soft bhajan in the background; Swamiji either on the phone helping a devotee through his or her problems or standing near the gate making certain that cleanliness is maintained; passerbys bowing their heads in obeisance; the boys cleaning the statues of various deities...it really makes one feel blessed to be present in such an environment.

Swamiji blessed me and after a few minutes, He said we would go for a cup of coffee. We once again entered Maha Lakshmi Restaurant and once again, I was fed three dishes and a cup of coffee and I staggered out of the restaurant, vowing once again never to ever put either an idli or a vada or a dash dosa in my mouth ever again.

For an hour or more, I sat beside Swamiji, reading the paper or just hearing Him talk to the various devotees, who telephoned

Him asking for blessings or advice or to invite Him to come and grace the opening of a factory or something or the other. Usually, Swamiji only gave His blessings. Very rarely did He travel to inaugurate some new venture, unless He felt His presence was absolutely essential. Of course, He usually ascended to the wishes of the inner cirlce, namely Lalit, Murli, GD, Samir, for they were truly close to Him and had often shown their solidarity at those rare times that their need was required.

After bath and saying my prayers in front of Ma, I was once again called by Swamiji to partake of breakfast. I looked at the boy who had been sent to give me this unbelievable culinary brimmed message. I shook my head and told the boy that obviously there was some serious communication problem, as I had just eaten a breakfast at six fifteen that could have killed a weaker man. He smiled at me and said that all the communication channels were open and working fine and that my breakfast was already laid on my plate and Swamiji was waiting anxiously for my arrival. I climbed up two floors with the obvious intent of refusing to bread once more. Half an hour, later I moaned down two floors, having stuffed myself once again on dosas, vadas, fruit and pipping hot coffee. If I lived like this for a week, I would have to be crane-lifted into the aircraft.

BUISNESS AND SUCCESS

Sometime later, I was introduced to Dilip Kumar Manea, a businessman who had a short story to narrate regarding the power of Swamiji's presence.

"I was having trouble in renting two of my godowns. They had been lying vacant since two years and though a number of people had come to rent them, for some reason or the other, the deal would never materialise. In fact, because the godowns were not being leased, I was going through my own share of problems. I requested Swamiji to come and pay a visit to the godowns. Fortuantely for me He agreed. He saw the place and for a few minutes, spent time in each godown. Seven days later, one godown was leased and then again seven days later, the second godown was also leased. Just His presence and in a fortnight both the godowns that I was not able to let out, were leased with the least effort on my behalf. This is the shakti of Ma Mookambika and Her messenger, Swamiji."

Such incidents are common occurrences where sages are involved. Their very presence is enough to take care of persistent problems assailing the devotee. Very often, even the devotee does not realise the favour the Guru has bestowed upon the former, for all the times small miracles are not visible. Very often a major catastrophe might be in store for the devotee. Due to the presence of the Guru, the disaster either gets nullified or its impact gets inconsequential. In both the cases, many times the devotee is in a state of comatose, regarding the protection the Guru has accorded him/her.

I approached Swamiji and once again we discussed about who was to come over. The discussion returned to Dr. Sudhir Vinekar. The incident where they hobnobed with the cobra was still very clear in my mind.

"You know once, Anand, Dr. Sudhir's son, got convulsions late in the night. They took him to their doctor but to no avail, the convulsions would just not stop. Both the parents are doctors and they know many doctors so they took Anand to a specialist and even he could not prevent the convulsions from coming and going. At two-thirty in the night, Sudhir realised that if the convulsions would not stop, it could be fatal for his son. So he removed the packet he always carries of Ma's limbu and kumkum. He prayed to Ma and remembered Me and then just applied the kumkum on his son's forehead. Within a short time, the convulsions stopped and never reoccured. In fact, Ma had told him the exact date and time when his father and mother were going to expire. She is just too loving and powerful. They were having certain problems with the nursing home. After the old lady died, her family began laying a claim on the property. Ma told them not to worry, all would be sorted out in their favour and this is exactly what happened. All She told them was that, once a year they should treat one poor patient free of cost. They are doing that..."

"You have told him that he would be in social work..."

"Yes and now they are planning to open this massive eye hospital and serve the poor. Of course, they have a lot of faith. Faith is very important...faith and God.

"You see Ruzbeh, there are different types of problems also. There are problems that come about from one's own destiny and then there are man made problems. Man made problems are really hard to solve..."

"What about problems that arise due to one's planetary positions?"

"Oh they can be handled and solved."

"How? Through prayers?"

"Yes, prayers and poojas can take care of planetary problems, but what can one do about man made problems? I mean, suppose a person just has ten thousand rupees in his pocket and conducts business of ten lakh rupees. If the business flops, then he and others are ruined. These are man made problems. There is a saying that 'slow and steady wins the race' and also 'never put a ladder to the sky'. Go slowly. Most people are too much in a rush to make money and become successful. Take me, for example. Many bankers and people tell me that 'Swamiji take how much ever money you want for your Hospital project'. All this is very good, but I know one thing and that is if I cannot pay them, they will be the same people who will come home and start carrying away my furniture and television." We both enjoy a chuckle.

"Another thing to be kept in mind is that, everyday is not a Sunday. There will be times you will have everything going for you and then there will be times that even if you touch gold, it shall become coal. So you need to be careful and never in haste or greed while doing anything in life. Otherwise, a lot of man made problems arise. Take the case of buying things in instalments. I know so many people who have bought these fancy cars on monthly instalments. For a few months they pay up on time as their work and business is doing well. Then slowly the business begins to suffer and they realise that after a few months, they cannot pay the monthly installment. So what happens, the bank people arrive and take possession of the car. As they have your signed post dated cheques, they file a case against you and to top it all you have lost your fifty thousand or one lakh rupees that you had paid in your previous installment schemes. How do you know that seven months from now in what state you are going to be? Apart from all the financial loss, there is a loss of face and reputation. I can understand you decide to pay off somebody in one or two months, but taking two or three-year schemes are not sensible."

"Take the case of family planning. I have heard couples say that they are going to wait for five years before having a child, as by then they would be more secure and their future would be more settled. I always wonder if those people are Gods or really advanced souls to know what might happen five years hence. Who knows what might happen five years later? Maybe their yoga or their time for having children may dry up. Maybe they might be afflicted with some physical problem that makes certain that they will not become parents. Who knows if they are together or not? I believe, that do things when the time is right and forget planning too many months or years in advance. What does the present tell you? If you can afford a car now, buy it or travel by public transport. If you can have a child now, have it and after having two issues you shut close the manufacturing unit. Man makes too many mistakes, planning years ahead or depending too much on the future. Live in the present. Damn all this family planning and planning years and years in advance.

"Yes, if you have somebody who can guide you well, like astrologers or swamijis, then it is a different matter, as they can see into your future and guide you that way. But if you don't have anybody to guide you, then let your present moment guide you. If you can afford something, indulge. If you can have a child now then go ahead. Because very often, man creates his own problem.

"See, when people come to me and Ma Mookambika tells them to perform a pooja, I advise them the cheapest possible method in conducting the pooja. Poojas can be conducted lavishly or in a very simple manner. If you don't have money but yet borrow it and call lots of people and spend lavishly and perform the pooja, then it is very foolish. I have made sure that poojas have been conducted in just fifty rupees and the same pooja has been performed in 50,000 rupees. If a person is already bankrupt and still borrows and spends lavishly, then he or she is a damn fool. Don't do that. Yes the moment you are on your feet and can afford a lavish pooja, go ahead and hold another pooja and call everybody and feed them. That should be the attitude. I shall give you an example. A devotee of mine, inspite of my warnings, invested two crore rupees in building a house. Now he does not have money to complete the house and does not have money to put petrol in his car. He is neither here nor there. This is how man makes mistakes and creates his or her own problems. He has built a palace, but has no peace of mind.

"Take, for instance, my own devotees. Sometimes when a person is going through a real trying, problem that person will come here every day. He will give me a report of what is going on...so often people come from twenty five or thirty kilometers to report the progress going on in their lives. They might tell me that they don't have money to pay their children's school fees or they don't have money to pay the electricity bill or even have food to feed the family. I will allow that person to come here for five days maximum. Then I will tell the person not to come here from the next day. I mean he does not have money to pay for his children's education or feed his family but still comes here either by car, rickshaw (three wheelers) or bus, spending so much money to give me his status report. Instead of spending so much money I advise the person to utilise the money for his family and spend just one rupee and telephone me and inform me of what is happening. I know so many people who will travel from out of town, spending hundreds or thousands of rupees and stay here for so many days, again incurring so much expense. Instead, they should stay at home and keep me informed about what is going on. They might come to me or go to any other swamiji, but I still think it is wrong and even foolish.

"It is so much cheaper, that they stay at home and take care of their family better and pray to God and just keep me informed on the phone what is transpiring. If it is necessary, I will call but

I don't advise people to come here every day. No. There were many people who used to come here every day in a car. Imagine, they don't have money for the child's schooling and they will spend hundred rupees everyday coming here. No I don't encourage such things. Yes, when I learn that certain families don't have even basic food to eat, then they are supplied ration and the money is collected from me. I know what hunger is, so I cannot allow Ma Mookambika's devotees to sleep on a hungry stomach. Every month a certain amount of ration goes to those people who cannot afford the basic necessities of life. Swamijis are meant to take care of their flock. Only then, does faith and love arise for God and for all humanity. Many of my devotees have told Me that they have not seen Ma Mookambika, but they see Ma Mookambika in me. They see the Divine Mother in Me and as a Mother, I should behave like a mother, and I should bless them like a mother, love and protect and guide them like a mother."

Coffee was served. Swamiji refused, as He had to begin giving predictions. He does this on an empty stomach and thus, usually does not eat anything for an hour or two before predictions. He entered Ma's mandir and I could see and feel the tension and eager anticipation of those who awaited their turn. Lives and destinies have been revealed and changed in the small abode of Ma Mookambika.

I completed some work and then returned to the ground floor. Swamiji was still giving predictions and I really marveled at his stamina. During autowriting sessions, I know the state of one's energy level. You feel as though somebody has sucked the very marrow from your bones and removed the prana from each cell. At Swamiji's age, to be involved from morning to night, solving and counselling, plus taking care of all the worldly affairs and then spend a few hours giving predictions is a herculean task, that really requires the strength of a legion of horses. It may seem as though I am exaggerating but you need to wear the shoe to know where and how badly it pinches. Also, the level of clairvoyance and clairaudience that Swamiji functions on, is something that I do not think can be imitated, by many, if at all by anybody.

He came out of the inner mandir, looking extremely tired but His eyes glowed with the presence of Ma Mookambika. Once outside, He again gave a few pointers to a few devotees who had been guided by Ma Mookambika. Then He introduced me to a number of devotees who had gathered to speak to me about Swamiji and Ma Mookambika.

SKEPTICS TURN INTO FIRM BELIEVERS

"I am Arun R. Tandon. My son-in-law, Pakuj Mehra, is in Tokyo. He buys old cars in Japan and exports it to other countries. With Swamiji's blessings and permission, he began an office in London. But, since he began his office in London, something or other made certain that the work did not move on smoothly. Either recession or bad luck or some other problem kept cropping up and the business was not doing too well. So, my son-in-law telephoned me and told me to ask Swamiji..."

"Ask Goddess..."

"But, Swamiji for us Goddess and you are one..."

"Goddess is everything..."

"Okay Swamiji! So, I was told to ask Ma Mookambika whether my son-in-law should shut shop in London as it was barely breaking even. I put forward the question to Ma Mookambika. For a while, there was only silence and then Goddess told me 'I shall not answer your question now...ask me this same question two months later'. Within two months, my son-in-laws business has shot up beyond his expectations. In fact, he is wondering whether this is a temporary phase or is it permanent. That is why, I have come here today..."

"Since when have you been coming here?"

"Twenty years. That is why I have come here today..."

"I was introduced to Ma and Swamiji, by a friend, who did not believe that miracles and predictions were possible. So, he brought me here but himself did not enter the premises to get Ma's blessings. I thought that it would take me fifteen minutes or so and had not informed anybody about my whereabouts. Those days this place was barren and Swamiji used to go in a trance and only then give predictions. Goddess used to speak through Him

151

on three days...Tuesday, Friday and Sunday. I remember I had first come here on Friday, generally known as Goddess' day. Instead, of fifteen minutes I was here for a few hours and reached home at 11.30 in the night. Those days there was no telephone over here or any telephone nearby so I had not informed my wife that I was in the temple. She really blew her fuse on me and had got really worried as I had left my office without any intimation. When I told my wife that I was with a Swamiji and He had lots of powers etc., she got further angry with me, saying that I was so gullible that anybody could make a fool out of me. I told her to come and see Swamiji herself and if she felt that there was nothing authentic about Devi or Swamiji, we would not visit the place ever again. She is very astute about recognising people. So, on Sunday, we both once again visited this place and in minutes my wife fainted. Swamiji was informed about the happenings and He did something and sprinkled some water and my wife came back to consciousness. Swamiji told me then that she had not fainted but that Devi had entered her.

"After taking rest and drinking some coffee we sat in front of Devi in Her inner mandir. Swamiji lit a camphor and I asked a question. I got the shock of my life when instead of answering through Swamiji, Devi answered through my wife. I kept asking questions and Devi kept replying using my wife as a medium. Then, Devi presented my wife with a saree (a garment draped by women in India) that had been draped on her image. We still have the saree and every time there is an important religious ceremony in the house we bring out that saree. So many people have commented regarding the power and peace that emanates from the saree. Since that day we have been firm *bhakts* (believers) of Ma Mookambika and Her messenger, Swamiji.

"But, I must tell you something honestly. You see even after my wife went in a trance and Devi spoke through her, I was for some reason not cent per cent convinced of the authenticity and the powers of Devi and Swamiji. For some odd reason, I kept doubting everything and wondered whether it was all mind reading going on. One day, a business associate, a Muslim gentleman from Kashmir informed me that he was going to Mysore to undergo a piles operation. He said, that there was no other go as the pain and discomfort was unbearable. So, I informed him about Swamiji and also disclosed my doubts. I told this Muslim gentleman, that there were lots of people, who had got healed in this mandir and why not kill two birds with one stone. If this place was really genuine he would benefit and if it was not then I would be convinced regarding my doubts. So this man agreed.

"We decided that as he was from Kashmir, he should only converse in Dongri, the native Kashmir language. If Goddess really appeared then She should not have any problems understanding the language. We sat in front of Ma Mookambika and Swamiji. To my great surprise instead of my friend speaking in Kashmiri, Devi began to speak to him in his own native toungue. It seems, She asked him to think about his home town and ask any question regarding it. Before my friend could ask Her any question, Devi began to describe his hometown. She said that a river flowed behind his house and that there was a burial ground very near by. She then described all his family members and told him that he was worried about the marriage of his daughter. She then, in detail, described his daughter and told him that she would get married after a few years and that a man would knock on his door to ask for her hand and when he did that my friend would not be at home. She even told him that in his dreams he has often seen a man in a white robe and flowing beard. My friend agreed and then Devi said that it was She in that form.

"She told him that now he no longer saw the person and he agreed. She told him the reason why now he no longer saw that Powerful person was because he had stopped saying his prayers since some time. He said that he did not have the time for namaz. She then scolded him gently telling him that if his wife and daughter can say the namaz four to five times a day why could he not say his prayers just once a day. She then told him that if the Powerful man was not around he would have been dead sometime back. Then my friend asked Devi regarding his piles problem...remember all this conversation took place in Kashmiri language. So Devi told him that he had been suffering from Rahu (a planetary position) and that Rahu would leave his astrological house within ten to twelve days and that the piles problem would vanish and he did not have to have himself operated. Fifteen days later this is exactly what happened. This Muslim gentle-man was astounded and really impressed by Devi and Swamiji. He met me some years ago and informed me that what had been predicted about his daughter's marriage happened just as Devi had informed him. A man did knock on his door and asked for his daughter's marriage. He was not around at that time. His father looked into the matter and then informed my friend regarding his own daughter's marriage. What can you say about all this. It is truly out of this world.

"People go on saying that birth and death cannot be predicted but where Ma and Swamiji are concerned all these things do not apply. My sister's son was admitted to a hospital and I had come to ask Ma regarding his health. The answer came that I should catch the first flight available and go and meet my nephew. In fact, She said that even if I had to charter a flight I should. In the morning, I got a call at 5.30 in the morning that my nephew was no more. Then one day, a friend's wife got very ill and her son and I came to the mandir and put forward the question to Devi regarding the woman's health. At first no answer came and then She said that if immediately poojas are performed She saw no danger. But, four days later I got a telephone call that the woman has cancer and it is in the last stage. I once again came here and asked Devi as to why had She said that all would be well. So, She said that though she was aware that the boy's mother would die on the day of holi...seven days from that day...she could not tell a son that his mother was going to be no more. She said that on so and so day the mother would be no more.

"Exactly, on that same day the mother expired. Forty-five days later the son came once again to meet Ma and Swamiji. Ma blessed the boy and then informed that within a few months there would be a marriage in his house. We all were shocked. The mother's pyre had not yet got cold and Ma was talking about a marriage in the house. The son told Ma that it was impossible that he would get married so soon after his mother's demise. In India we have a year or more mourning period and the son was certain that he would never marry in that period. Ma smiled and told him that She saw a marriage in four to five months. Three months later instead of the boy, his own father got married again. You see there was a small child in the family. The age difference between the boy and the last child was huge. The father decided that the child needed a mother and got married. Ma had also predicted that after the marriage peace would return and yes peace has returned. What more can I say about Ma and Swamiji!"

MA' S GRACE KNOWS NO BOUNDARIES

"During the Asiad, which was held in India, the Pakistani team had arrived in Bangalore. We were seated in the club, when we were introduced to a number of Pakistani ladies who had accompanied the delegation. One of them asked me my opinion about a famous God man, as she wanted to seek His help for her failing health. I mentioned a few of the amazing incidents of our Devi and Swamiji and she was very keen on having a sitting with Swamiji. So, the next day we went to pick her up. She was not alone and requested us that we allow another Pakistani friend to accompany us and meet Swamiji. This second lady's name was Faujia. Though Faujia had come mainly to accompany her friend, Ma Mookambika took her first. I had to be in the room as those days, I am talking about seventeen years back, Swamiji went in a trance and Devi only spoke through Him in Kannada language. So I accompanied her as a transalator.

"The first thing MA told this Muslim lady was that her forefathers were Goddess or Devi worshippers. I was rather shocked as she was a pure Muslim and looked every bit of a traditional Muslim woman. This lady agreed. She revealed that her forefathers were from Kutch and they were Hindus earlier but had converted to Islam decades and decades ago. Then Ma Mookambika told this woman that her grand-father had done a very noble thing by distributing free water to those in need of it. She was shocked. She said that yes, in Tanzania, her grand-father had built tankers, where water was distributed freely to all those who need it.

155

"Ma asked her if she was aware that her husband had a major affair before their marriage. She said that she was aware of this fact. Then what followed was a shocker. Ma then asked her if she was aware that her husband was still having an affair with another woman. This woman was stunned. She had no idea of this fact. So she pleaded to know who that other woman was. Ma said 'if you want the remedy then leave everything in My hands. If I tell you who the woman is, you will spoil your case and lose your husband forever'. Then Ma told her to light a *diva* (lamp) for seven days in the mandir. Ma also assured her that She would make certain that after all her problems would be over, Ma would call this woman back to this temple to pay another visit to Her. When this lady asked Ma how she would communicate with Her from Pakistan as that time Swamiji did not have a phone and for a Pakistani to visit India was very difficult, Ma had told her something very beautiful. She told her, 'you have your holy book covered in a black cloth', the woman agreed that her Holy Koran was covered in a black cloth back home in Pakistan. Then Ma told her 'every Friday, light a candle, open the Holy Koran and on which ever page it opens, read one para from the Holy Book and then shut your eyes and whatever you want to tell me, say it to the Koran and it will reach me. I will immediately hear you and guide and help you'.

"Years later, I met Faujia in the temple once again. Her husband, as told by Ma was having an affair with another woman, but through the grace of Ma Mookambika now everything was alright with them and miraculously she had been granted a visa to visit India, though how she managed this, only Ma could answer. Ma had promised the woman that She would make sure she returned to meet her personally and thus it had to happen."

"Now, about the first woman who was facing health problems. The next day she was asked to come into the inner mandir for predictions. The first thing Ma asked her was that 'why are you not following your husband's religion'. I was stunned. As far as I knew, this woman was a staunch Muslim and her husband was also a Muslim, so where was the question of her not following her husband. But the woman kept quiet. So Ma told her that 'after marriage the religion of your husband becomes your religion'. Then Ma told this woman that her husband used to visit a Dargah (the tomb where followers pay obeisance to the body of the sage/saint/wali/peer buried within). The woman agreed that her husband used to worship at a Dargah, but as she had never taken interest in his religious beliefs, she was not aware where the holy tomb lay. So Ma explained to her that the Dargah was 40 kilometers east from where she stayed presently. A river flowed just behind the Dargha and that if she made enquires she would find it without difficulty. She was asked to offer anything she thought befitting, at the Dargah. Ma told her that after she accepted her husband's religion and did the needful, at the Dargah her troubles would be behind her and she would be cured of the disease that ate into her body. Then the woman confessed that her husband was a follower of Aga Khan and she was a staunch Muslim who did not believe in anybody but Allah and His prophet, Mohammed and that she was suffering from cancer. This woman, after a year or so, wrote to me that whatever Devi had predicted was cent per cent true. There was a Dargah, forty odd kilometers east to her home and that her husband used to visit this Dargah very often and then was even a river flowing behind it and that now she was cured of cancer."

FAMILY REUNION

The last incident Mr. Tandon mentioned, showed the way divinity works and understands the fragility of the human mind and thus acts accordingly. One day, Mr. Tandon got a call from his banker, where the latter insisted that he be met at the earliest time that very day. I have, on purpose, not mentioned the banker's name for obvious reasons. For the sake of convenience, we shall call the Manager as M (not very innovative but what the hell).

This was the first time Mr. Tandon had even spoken to M and the fact that the latter wanted to meet him at the earliest, was disturbing. So, off he went and found himself in the Manager's cabin and instead of discussing balance sheets and credits and financial mumbo jumbo, M confessed that he was in real trouble and would Mr. Tandon help him out. Then M revealed that since two and a half years, his wife had left him and M had not seen his five and a half year child ever since. So, immediately Tandon took M to Swamiji. Devi, first and foremost, promised M that he would have his wife and child back, but he would have to do a few things. M agreed. So Devi informed M that in such and such place, there lived a real snake. M was to pour milk where the snake resided, for seven days continously. M being a financial man, was slightly taken aback. He thought it would look mighty funny if people saw a bank manager pouring milk down a snake hill, but desperate to be united with his family, he agreed. For seven days, M did as directed. He was rather impressed that Devi had the residential data of the reptile world. After a week, he once again sat in front of Ma Mookambika and the Goddess told him to wait, as within a short time everything would be all right.

A month passed and nothing happened and so M went back to Devi with a letter in his pocket, addressed to his wife pleading that she should come home. Ma Mookambika told him that she knew what the contents of the letter were and that try how hard, he would not be able to post that letter and even if he did post it, Ma would make certain, that the letter would never reach his wife. She then told him something that made M realise that Goddess was truly omnipresent. She told that even if his wife did return, the root of the problem that had propelled her to leave M, still existed. Till the problem was not solved there was no sense having his wife back with him. It was then that M confessed to Mr. Tandon that the reason his wife had abandoned him was because M had become impotent. M then revealed that he had tried every possible medicine in the market to help him overcome his physical disability, but to no avail. M's wife had walked out on him after realising that M's impotency would remain lifelong.

Two months later, M. called up Mr. Tandon, telling him that a miracle had taken place. Without any application or medicine, he had been cured of his impotency and he cried out that he was a normal healthy man again. He knew that this miracle was due to Ma Mookambika's grace and now His faith was rock solid. Inspite of all this, it still took another two years for M's wife and child to return to him. They are now all living happily and are Ma Mookambika's staunch devotees. When Mr. Tandon had inquired of Devi, as to why did it take two long years for M's wife to return and why had Devi kept telling M that his family would return very soon, the answer he received needs attention. 'When a person is going through a very very difficult period and I tell him something that he will not be able to handle then I am doing him more harm than good. Depending upon the person's capability to withstand reality, I reveal the truth. He has got his family back as I had promised, but if I had, then, told him it would take him two years, to get his family back, he would have broken down and not recovered from the shock of so long a wait'.

Swamiji asked us to join Him for lunch. Already, twenty odd people were just completing their meal. We waited for them to wash their hands and for the banana leaves on which they had partaken of the meal to be cleared by the number of lads working round the clock. I sat next to Swamiji and Amma. Nirmala, Mangala, and Ravi had left for the short vacation that included a safari. The meal as usual was hot, delicious and filled with variety. After the meal, we sat upstairs in the large sitting room and Swamiji inquired as to how I thought the book was progressing. I was not certain as to how I should frame the book. I wanted Devi to give me some sort of an indicator, as there are a hundred ways to write a biography but on a topic as vast and as phenomenal as Ma Mookambika and Swamiji, the options only increase ten times further.

"You write it as though you are the hero of the book..."

"You know, I am not comfortable with that and that would not be fair to the poor reader..."

"You don't worry about the reader. The book will go to whosoever Ma Mookambika wants it to go to. It will be read by only those, who Devi wants to reach out to, so worry not. It should come through your eyes and not anybody else's vision. It

is your story about Ma Mookambika and Swamiji. I might tell
you so many things, but I want you to write the book as you feel
and see things from your perspective. Come, eat these fruits."

Then the phone once again seeked His attention. I heard
Swamiji tell the person on the other end that, 'within fourteen
days everything will be all right. Devi is there with you. Yes, I will
pray for you'. He put the phone down and informed me that it
was an industrialist who had been rescued so many times from a
financial mess that it was not funny. He revealed that sometimes
during the construction of a house or a factory, unwittingly,
snakes are either killed or made homeless. Projects that take place
on such land never yield fruits and there is never peace in such
homes and businesses. Of course, there are remedies for all such
maladies and after poojas, or in some cases building of a temple,
miraculous results have always followed.

OMNISCIENT DEVI

"I am Ramesh Upadhaya and have been a devotee of this
place since the time this temple has been installed. During those
days, we used to meet each other very often. It had just started
and we used to have food together, every alternate day. All I can
say after nearly thirty years is that Devi is divine and She has
come here and made Swamiji Her medium so that people can be
served. It is what we call *Lok Kalyan* (service to mankind). When
I came to this place I was working with a company and due to
certain problems I resigned from the company thus I had lots of
free time. I used to come here very often and I used to travel on
the motor bike. I had never told Him that I had come to a
situation where even money for the petrol was becoming a
problem. I did not tell Him because in those days He himself was
going through such a bad period financially that my problems
seemed small in comparison. But whenever I was really in bad
shape He would enter the mandir and come out with something
in His hand. He then would open His hand and there would be
some money and He would say 'here this is for the petrol'. I still
don't know how He knew or where He got the money from
within the temple. That is why when my good times arrived

I never forgot Devi and Swamiji's help in those days of trouble. I believe that whatever we all are today is because of the grace of Devi, Swamiji and God. Nothing belongs to us, and why simply get proud over something as trivial as money. She is there and She will take care of us.

"My wife was suffering from diabetes and other complications. It was she who actually introduced me to Devi and Swamiji, and she had been a great devotee of Devi since years. But due to her health problems, in the end, I had to bring her here in a wheel chair. One day, Devi through Swamiji, said 'I will make you walk and you will come here walking'. In a year's time, though the doctors said that it would be near impossible for my wife to resume walking, my wife began to walk a bit and she walked from the gate to Devi's temple and bowed down. Devi really has done a lot for us. Of course, She tests everybody. The way She has tested Mr. Nayak (Swamiji) is no laughing matter. Yes, my friend was also so independent in thought, that many times He created trouble for Himself."

DEVI AND SWAMIJI

"I still remember this incident, when one morning I arrived to ask Him a very important question. But one look at him and I realised that there was no way He would be able to sit in a trance. His knees were swollen four times the normal size and He was in really great pain. Then a man came and told Mr. Nayak that his son was very, very sick and he needed the Blessed Lime. So Mr. Nayak, though He had not had his bath, still limped into the temple and stood for a while with the lime in His hand and began to pray to Devi to charge the lime with Her energy and vibrations. All of a sudden, when He began to do the pooja, then to my disbelief with his knees virtually four times the normal size He still sat down for prediction. So then I asked the Goddess, 'why are you troubling Him so much?' So Goddess told me, 'who are you to question Me? 'Then I told Her that with Him in so much pain how will He recover fast enough for Her to help those in need. Because if He was not well how could Devi help her other children?' Then Devi spoke through Him. She said, 'Doctors, from far, are coming here to seek My advice, but this man does not want to listen to me. I have told Him not to drive a two-wheeler, but He is so fond of the motor bike that He continues to drive it and as accidents are written in his destiny on two wheelers what can I do about the pain that He is going through. More so, after not listening to me He goes to a doctor for advice. Those same doctors, who come here for medical advice, My patri (messenger) goes there. And even after going there He does not listen to them. They have told Him that there is water in the knee and they will have to puncture the knee to remove the water and He will have to be hospitalised for seven days. He does not want to listen to them and He is not listening to Me so what can I do. So why should I help Him?'

"So I told Devi that She must help Him for all of us who are so dependent on Her and Her messenger for moving on in life. So in the end, She said ' Okay apply this medicine to his legs and pray that He should be cured. I will cure Him and that too without any puncturing of the knee'. So His wife and I applied the simple medicine. The next day, when I told Him what Ma had adviced, Mr. Nayak told me ' You don't listen to Ma. She will blabber anything. I have to go through the pain not Her. I am going to another doctor to get his opinion'. Saying this He began to tie a cloth around His knees. They were in bad shape. He told me that till He was not completely cured He would not sit down for predictions.

"Five minutes, later His friend arrived and next thing I see Him once again in the temple, once again sitting down and Devi had begun to speak through Him. When He got up from the prediction, the swelling had gone and He was cured. No swelling, no pain, it was as though nothing had ever happened to His knees. So, during those days, Ma and He had this constant tussle going on. But, He has sacrificed a lot to make Her happy and She has always helped Him. Always."

"Let me tell you a very nice incident and you will understand how Devi used to help Swamiji in making sure that His dreams were realised. Whenever Mr. Nayak, went to Subramaniya, He came back with the realisation that there were no good facilities for either staying there or for getting medical assistance. Since years, I have been hearing Him say that two things He will do before Devi calls for Him, is to make a hotel that will offer pilgrims a decent accommodation and make certain that a small hospital is set up so that people do not have to travel fifty kilometers or more just to get an injection.

"Mr. Nayak had a Christian friend who wanted to sell his house and land and Mr. Nayak was keen of buying the property. He quoted a figure, but his friend found that too low and so they never discussed this subject ever again. One day, this gentleman came to meet Him and Mr. Nayak told his friend that his wife was not in good health. So the Christian friend told him that his wife had been bedridden for a long time and her health was deteriorating as time went by. So Swamiji gave His friend a Blessed Lime and told the friend that he should make certain that the lime was with his wife all the time and that the moment if and when she got cured, they should go to Vallankanni, a famous and powerful pilgrimage spot for Christians. It seems this couple had made a promise that they would make the pilgrimage, but for one reason or the other, had forgotten to keep their word. Swamiji told this man that the moment his wife got all right, they should make the journey.

"The Christian took the Blessed Lime and went away. A few hours later, he came running to Swamiji and touched His feet. He said that though they had known each other for such a long time he had never known how powerful Swamiji really was, till date. It seems, within a few hours his wife who had been bed ridden for a long time, not only began to feel better but she got this strange feeling that she would be able to get out of bed and walk. She did just that and now she was so grateful to Swamiji that she insisted that the property would be sold only to Him and that to at the earlier price decided by Swamiji. But this is not all. Even the first down payment for the property was arranged by Ma Mookambika."

What transpired was typical of how Devi operates to get Her work done. Swamiji, due to His lack of business acumen, has often landed in business deals that would make MBA students want to go flying out of the window. His devotees usually enter the business transaction, when they realise that if they don't, pandemonium will reign. So due to the insistent of well wishers Swamiji agreed to get a document drafted and signed by both parties concerned. He had around five thousand rupees, which he had kept aside for the down payment. It was a small amount, but His Christian friend had no problem with the amount. Swamiji was just moving towards his friend's house, when He met a family. One of the members quickly prostrated himself to touch His feet.

It was obvious that this man was really ecstatic to meet Swamiji. The reason was that a casual off the cuff remark from Swamiji had saved the man lot of physical pain, emotional discomfort and hard cash. It so happened that this family had visited Devi's temple to pay their respects to Ma Mookambika. This man met an acquaintance and began to discuss his health problems. Swamiji was nearby and He overheard the conversation. It seems that this man was advised by his doctors to undergo an operation. It was a major operation and very expensive too. Swamiji very casually, as is His practice, as though He is discussing the weather or ordering coffee, told the chap that he did not have any major health problem and that he did not have to undergo any operation. The man was rather shocked as to how a man could so coolly tell him that he was first of all in perfect health and that his battery of expensive doctors were all mixed up. Then, Swamiji further predicted to this man, that when he went for his operation, the same doctor would insist on some tests to be performed and then claim that due to some reason, the disease no longer existed and the operation was not necessary.

The man and his family went away bewildered. But as is so common with Devi and Swamiji, this is exactly what transpired. The patient's very doctor rejected the notion of performing the operation and told the patient to levitate out of the hospital as soon as was humanly possible. Swamiji had told this family that as and when the operation was cancelled, they should come to Subramaniya and perform a small pooja. Thus, this family was also around during the same time Swamiji was finalising his purchase deal. The man placed a stack of currency in Swamiji's hand. He told Him that this was the first instalment he was supposed to pay the doctor for the operation and treatment, but as the very operation was cancelled he wanted Swamiji to accept the money and use it for whatever He thought best. It was a sum of seventeen thousand rupees, no small amount, even in this galloping inflation era. So Swamiji continued His journey to His friend's house and instead of just five grand, handed His surprised friend a sum four times more than was agreed upon.

LOST AND FOUND

"I must also tell you, that once Goddess gives Her word then the world may get upside down, but She will keep Her word. One day, a friend of ours who is a widow, came to me and cried that a diamond ring costing those days over one lakh rupees was missing and she was certain that the ring was stolen by a guest, who had stayed at her house for a few days. The problem was, that this diamond ring, was given to her by her mother-in-law and anytime, she could be asked to return the ring. She was very worried, so we got her to Devi and Mr. Nayak. Ma, through Mr. Nayak told her that she would get her ring in a fortnight or so and that she should just have faith.

"Fourteen days passed and there was no sign of the diamond ring. A month passed and still no sign of the ring. So this lady arrived one day in her car and entered the mandir. Mr. Nayak had gone to Mumbai and even Amma was nowhere to be seen. This lady was all alone in front of Ma Mookambika. She was very upset and sad and asked Ma that how could She be wrong and that She had promised her that within such and such time, the ring would be found so where was it. This friend then heard a woman telling her to go back home and open her cupboard. Our friend at first looked everywhere to see who was speaking to her but saw nobody. She shut her eyes and once again she heard a woman telling her to go home and open her cupboard. So my friend went home very disappointed and depressed. She had been opening her cupboard ten or more times a day for the past month and was certain that the ring was not

165

around for sure. She opened the cupboard and the first thing she saw was her diamond ring. It was as though it had never left its place. My friend yet cannot understand how it came into her cupboard as the cupboard was always under lock and key and she has the key with her. Just imagine Devi whispering into her ears. Amazing is not the word."

INJUSTICE CORRECTED

"My name is Poovaiah. I retired as Director of Secondary Education of the State of Karnataka. I had a problem when I was still in employment. You must have heard of the major Marks card Scandal that rocked the state of Karnataka. It involved examinations, for which I was in charge. And this was a State level examination, Pre-university board, and I was in charge of the entire examination and it was a very responsible post. This happened in the year 1982. I was working under a Director, whose integrity was under question. It was unfortunate that I was directly working under him and however much I tried to straighten the system and rid the system of mal-functioning I was unsuccessful. Instead I got caught in the fire of two opposite camps; one that worked above me and one that worked below me. In between both of them I was caught in the crossfire. In fact, I was sacked from service. You can imagine my plight.

"The irony of it all was that though the Government found me innocent, they still had to punish me. In fact, even the Court found me innocent and the judge wrote that 'it was not correct to have dismissed me' but the wheels within wheels work in strange manners and I was punished for no fault of mine. The Cabinet did not pay heed to the Court's order because according to the State Cabinet, this entire scam was a team effort and they wanted all those associated with the team to be punished. I was not a part of the team that had conspired to make money illegally but in the end I was dragged along with them. I was distraught and virtually at my wits end. Remember, for me it was not just the question of losing my job but it was the question of losing my dignity and self-respect. We are a part of society and no matter how much we say we don't care about what society thinks about us, the fact is that it really matters a lot. Eventually, I was told by a well wisher that there was this temple where Devi really dwelled and that there was Her medium who they called Swamiji who was really powerful. I was asked to go there and lay my case before Goddess Ma Mookambika and Swamiji. In fact, the first thing Goddess spoke through Swamiji was that ' I know you have come with clean hands. I know you are innocent and have been wrongly punished. I will bring you back to glory. And when all this trouble is behind you, the glory will be greater and your respect in society will increase much more than ever'. Whatever She spoke that very first day happened exactly as predicted though it did not happen overnight. Nobody can change the wheels or the time frame that destiny has laid down for each of us.

"In fact, the first miracle took place the first night after I visited Devi and Swamiji. I had become an insomniac and was really suffering due to tension added with lack of sleep. The first night after I had bowed down and pleaded Devi for justice, I began to sleep as though nothing had happened. See for an honest person who has served his employers for more than two decades, to be punished for no fault of his is something that eats into his very soul. But from the day I bowed down to Devi my health that was deteriorating very badly began to get better. Just the assurance from Devi that I will get back and in greater glory was itself a balm to my bleeding heart. She told me that it would take time and to continue my efforts for justice. For me the Governor was my last hope as the State Cabinet had also turned its back on me. The Governor was my only hope. He was on my side. In fact there was a big fight between the Governor and the State Cabinet. In fact it became a Constitutional issue. The Governor insisted that I should be given back my job.

"The Cabinet refused and it became an ego issue. The most important thing is that through it all, Devi made certain that my health did not suffer. That I slept well. That whenever I was really miserable, Her call was so powerful that I had to come over here and bow down to Her and She would fill me up with hope, strength and the will to move on without doubt or anger. I know that without Her and Swamiji, I would have in all probability succumbed to a heart attack or some other health problem. Believe me, it was a miracle that I got back my job and as She had promised me I got back my job in greater glory."

"In fact, She told my father that if I don't get you back to your job I shall not sit over here henceforth." Informed his daughter, Dr. Pravin, who had come along with her daughter, an angel of a child. "I still remember we were still kids and we were all worried about his health and when he came back that day after meeting Devi he was a changed person. There was strength and the will to hold on and fight, within his eyes. The words of Devi kept ringing in his head. He kept telling us that ' imagine Devi has promised me that if I don't get back my job She will not sit in that temple'. In fact both the men who connived and cheated and were the cause of the trouble died soon thereafter. One person died immediately after the scandal came out into the public eye. The other person also immediately fell seriously ill and after lots of suffering died. Devi and Swamiji took care that I pulled through in the best possible health and frame of mind."

"My children were all young. One of my son's had just completed engineering. The other was still in tenth standard. We wanted to marry our daughter and it was during this time that the catastrophe hit us and trust me without Devi and Swamiji I would not have survived. And to get back my job and with due respect and for the authorities to admit that they had blundered in my case is something unimaginable especially in our country."

"I got into medicine the moment he had lost his job." Informed Pravin. "I did very well and then to my bad luck I had the worst experience with the most miserable head of the department. He was such a horror that he virtually hated me. He was really not a good man and he did not like my attitude of selfrespect and my disinclination to be a ' yes-woman'. He was not a clean man and he tried his best to abuse me and insult me in front of the under graduate crowd or anywhere he could get the opportunity for that matter. One day I came to this haven of security and bowed down to Ma and I was in a mess. Believe me I had begun to harbour suicidal tendencies as the man had hurt me so badly that I had once left my unit and travelled overnight just so that in the morning I could be in front of Devi and Swamiji."

"That day Swamiji lit a camphor and Devi spoke through Him. She said ' I know your problem is with that man. He is *chanchal* (restless) and if it is 8'o clock he will argue it is not. But don't worry He cannot do anything. ' I went back reassured and in the knowledge that Devi was with me as I had not told Swamiji anything about my problems. The fact that on Her own Ma talked about this man meant She was omnipresent and aware of what was happening. Sometime passed and then in front of many undergraduate students and all my colleagues this man said ' I will see how you get your MD this time'. The fact was that he was the Chief Examiner for eight consecutive years and he was the ultimate in our department and his word was the law. In fact the word went around that I was certainly going to be casualty because of that man's hatred towards me.

"I was very hurt and to top it all even other professors assumed the worst for me. In fact they even informed me that I would get three attempts and if he failed me in all of them I should approach the court. Court will have to give you the MD. I was a good student and I deserved the MD."

"Was your father still fighting his case?"

"No. With Devi's grace and Swamiji's prayers he was reinstated with honours. His problems had got solved and my problems with this man began. Anyway when all this took place I immediately came over here. Swamiji lit a camphor and immediately Devi came through. She said 'keep this lime and call for me whenever you need me. As for that man, he will not be in front of you during your exam. She repeated that the man will not be seated in front of you before and during the exam'. I said that it was not possible as since the last eight years this man's word was the law and he was present during every such exam. So She said ' go back and study. I will take care of everything'. I went back with the knowledge that if not anything I shall at least keep my word to Devi that I would do my best and study as though nothing has and will happen. Though frankly in my heart I knew I was not going to pass with that man around. Ten days before the exam the Department's list came out and his name was very much there. Everybody told me that in the end I would have to approach the Court. Four days before the exam I was studying in the night and a junior honks from his car and calls me down. I went down and he tells me that there is a rumour that this man who was troubling me is sacked. It was not possible as this man was virtually the law out there. I still thought it was impossible for him to be sacked. This same man who had sat for eight consecutive years could not be sacked over night. Everybody said that I had used some very high influence..."

"It could not have got higher..."

"You bet. Anyway on the day of my examination, I took my file and walked into the cubicle and I did not see this man anywhere. I saw four different examiners and one lady from the department who was very fond of me. As I sat down in front of them, she looked at me and said loudly 'she is the best candinate of the year'. Late that night the results were declared. I had topped. No sign of this man. Believe me, I had my Blessed Lime with me and I knew that Devi was working over time with me before, during and even after the examination. In fact six months later this man was back at the job, back at the examination. It is history that only during my exams he was nowhere to be seen. You know what he said when I walked out of the Degree Room. He looked at me and said 'whichever God you pray to is very, very powerful'. I just looked at him and said 'don't do this to another woman as there is a Great Power taking care of all'. This same doctor came for the wedding. Imagine.

"Even where my marriage was concerned She helped out so beautifully. I kept insisting that I wanted to live in Bangalore after my marriage as I wanted to be close to my parents and family. Devi had promised me that She would make sure that I would marry and settle in Bangalore. But my husband was in the army and he kept insisting that it was impossible that the army would relieve him as they had spent a huge amount on a particular course Every time I came over here and cried my eyes out. She then told me that by September She would make sure that he would be with me in Bangalore. September 4th he was back with me in Bangalore. Once again the impossible had taken place. Even now, my husband cannot understand how the army relieved him."

"I was blessed with a son. But, unfortunately he got jaundice and his levels were so high that we all began to think of the worst. I kept calling up Swamiji for help. He kept telling me that you are the daughter of this temple and he is your child how can anything happen to your son. He then told me that in the evening when the report comes in again he will be perfectly all right. As was predicted the 4.30 pm report showed that he was completely all right. Even now my medical colleagues keep wondering how such a high level of jaundice could vanish so soon. Then after a few years, I wanted to mother a girl. So, on one of the Chandi Homas, when Swamiji went into a trance, I asked Devi for a daughter. He looked at me and through Him Devi said 'everybody who comes here wants putradan (son child) but you have asked for me. I shall come'. Soon my daughter arrived. What more can I tell you about the grace of Ma Mookambika and Swamiji?"

"You know, when I got back my job, within a matter of six months I got a raise and then another raise shortly. I also got all the pending salaries of the last four years that had been denied to me. In fact, just as He had predicted, I was reinstated with full honours and my career progressed in leaps and bounds." Informed Mr. Poovaiah.

"Apart from my father and my case, I have sent so many people who were trying to become parents for years and years without success. Though I am a doctor I have sent a number of childless couples who have tried everything medically to become parents but to no avail. Then they have fallen at Devi's feet and beseeched Her and Swamiji and they have become parents. I tell you, this place defies logic and medical science." Pravin stopped speaking and touched Swamiji's feet.

Swamiji had just finished an hour and a half of predictions and He seemed drained out of all energy, but as usual, His eyes were shining and His face had an aura of divinity that has to be seen. He smiled and inquired as to how things were moving. His leg was once again aching, but He said it was much better than yesterday.

DEVI AND SWAMIJI

"Swamiji, your beard looks real neat!"

"Oh this beard also has its own story. You know, once a favourite chain of mine had been stolen. In those days, I had no money to buy another chain and the worst part of it all, was that I knew who had stolen the chain. I put forth the case to Devi. I told Her 'I know who has taken my chain. I also know that as the chain has been stolen by a woman partiality will be there'. Devi will always support ladies as She herself is a woman. So, I told Her that 'this time I am not going to ask You for my chain back as I know you are supporting women'. Then, I told Her that the moment I have my chain back, I will go to Dharmastal and present my chain to God and till I don't get my chain back I will not shave. Though I hated a beard, I said this out of sheer anger. That was a wrong move because Devi wanted me to have a beard and my promising that till the chain was found, I would not shave was exactly what She wanted.

"Days turned into weeks and my beard kept growing and people began to get scared of my appearance and many told me I looked like an angry lion. Devi is just too shrewd. So, in the end a few of my devotees got together and bought the same type of chain and requested me to have a shave and put their chain on. So, I decided to go to Dharmastal have a shave and put on this new chain. In the mean time, the main people who managed the Dharmastal Trust came over to the temple. You know Hegde, well his brother came here and wanted to ask certain questions. He informed Me, that his mother's jewels, costing around 25 to 30 lakh rupees were stolen. This was the first time in the history of that temple that a robbery had taken place and they wanted to catch the thieves. So, they came in and Devi gave them respect by giving them dhotis and after all this got over She told them that the jewels were stolen by five people who were at the present moment at such and such place, go there and you will get your gold. They went there and later informed me that they had got back all the jewels.

"After they went away, Devi told me, 'My *Patri* (messenger) is going there for a chain of 6000 rupees, whereas they have come to Me for jewels worth 25 lakh rupees. Who is greater, He (Shiv) or Me? And he wants to get his chain, so that he can shave but I don't want Him to shave, so he will never get his chain. He may not like it but I am very happy'. Then I said, 'Ma, but give me permission at least to trim the beard,' so She said, 'that is allowed'.

"Devi's ways are not easy. They don't work by force, but by wisdom. She always says, 'don't hit your enemy by force. If he is dancing, first let him dance, then give him one slap he will fall flat as he is already tired. No sense using force whole time'. Always use your common sense. It will go a long way.

"There is a big stone, don't try to push it you will not succeed. Put a small stone under that big stone and then push the big stone in all probability it will roll down.

"I have learnt everything from Her. No books and no Guru for Me. She has been everything. In fact, now She is *Patri* (messenger) and *Patri* is Devi. I am within Her and She is within Me. Whatever I say..."

"Will happen..."

"Yes, I cannot explain it."

"How does She look, Swamiji?"

"A very beautiful woman...I see Her very often, but on 2nd August, I can see Her all the time. I can see Her on other days also but on that particular day, She is very clearly seen and sharp. One thing is sure, and I say this with all modesty, that the kind of predictions and miracles that take place here do not take place anywhere in the world. Nobody in the world can give predictions the way We are doing here. It is impossible. Also predictions on any and every subject are given. Anything and the prediction is hundred per cent accurate..."

"Yes, Swamiji, you remember that man who used to bring a chart and tell You and Devi that he was a water diviner and he wanted to know where to dig the well."

"Yes and Devi would tell him dig here and dig there and after doing it he would come back and say that at the exact spot that Devi had shown, he had struck water. One day, I made him go in a trance and made him go deep into the earth and made him tell us what he saw and what he felt. Finally he went so deep that he got scared and came up and then out of the trance. All this has been done here only We don't talk much about it. So many times, Devi just to prove that She exists and that She is present, enters either the person who is a doubting Thomas or enters a relative of the skeptic person. So many times She will not enter me but enter the person who has been doubting Her or Me. Some times people who are waiting for prediction grumble that why should they pay for predictions as Devi does not require money. They grumble that, 'Devi is giving predictions and Swamiji is charging money'. Now, I don't know what is going on outside the inner room. But, the moment they sit down, Devi will tell somebody to give that person the prediction money back. If they ask why they are being given back their money then She says 'what were you saying outside? What is the income of this temple? How can My *patri* support the expense of the flowers, oil, limes and the food that He feeds all of you?' Just imagine we feed everybody who comes here. A person can come with the entire family and they all are fed. A simple meal costs not less than twenty-five rupees. Then limes and the coconut and the flowers and the oil and the constant electricity that is required, has to be paid for. These people are not bothered about all such expenses. Anyway, come all this talk about food must have made you all hungry. Come let us go have our lunch."

DEVI APPEARS BEFORE HER DEVOTEES

There were around twenty-five people, who ate lunch along with Swamiji. The prediction session had tired Him but Swamiji was more tensed about the generator that had to be sent to Subramaniya the first thing in the morning. After lunch and a short nap He left to organise the transport while I continued with my work. At around four-thirty I was informed that Mrs. Nagrajan, (the wife of the man suffering from stomach cancer, who ought to have died years ago but still kept defying the medical fraternity) was waiting in the sitting room to speak about her experiences. A few minutes later, I was seated on the chair opposite her and had my recorder switched on.

"You see, some people might consider our experiences weird, while some might consider them divine, but I am certain that my husband is the living proof that miracles still do happen. He has baffled each and every doctor by continuing to live and tell the tale. With his kind of advanced cancer to still live for years when doctors had predicted he would not live for months itself is a miracle. Hopefully after reading your book more and more people will come to this beautiful place that houses Ma and Swamiji. Not just to get the problems solved but to bathe in the divine atmosphere that is prevalent over here. In fact the best part for me is that Ma has so often communicated with us in Her own way. So many times I have bowed down to Her and that very instant, flowers have fallen down and that too have fallen in front of us. So many times limes have fallen down and rolled towards me. I mean what more proof of Her divinity and Her presence is required. And where Swamiji is concerned He is like a father to us all. Anytime and anyplace, He is accessible and without any fuss. However tired He may be but He will speak to us and calm us down. His predictions are legendary. I don't even think I need to get into the phenomenal predictions that all have come true. It was after I began coming over here that I began to go in a state of trance. I could do little about this state. I could not come out of it and Swamiji would get me back to my normal state. But after falling into trance I began to get more and more religious and spiritual. I got more into poojas and meditations. I began to get up early in the morning to meditate.

"Also, you don't have to tell Devi or Swamiji anything, still They know what is happening. Like for instance I had lost my dog and Devi had promised that it would come back. Just as She had promised me we got our dog back but I forgot to thank Swamiji and Devi. A few days later, the Chandi Homa ceremony took place and I bowed down to Swamiji who was in a trance. Devi came through and told me 'so you got your dog back'. I felt guilty but was also astonished that though there were so many people She still remembered something so trivial. But the next thing She said stumped me. You see, as my dog had got lost I had begun neglecting my pooja and a number of spiritual activities, though of this, only I was aware. She told me 'you have forgotten to keep milk for your *Nag Appa-Amma* (Snake God)'. That did it. I began to cry. Only somebody who was omnipresent could have known such intimate details. I tell you She is divine.

"You know, once I could not attend the Chandi Homa. I was devastated. I really wanted to be there for some reason I could not make it to the ceremony. So I cried out to Her that I was sorry for not being present. Suddenly I began to feel very sleepy. I lay on bed and then there She was standing in front of me, smiling and blessing me. The next thing, I knew was that I was fast asleep. When I woke up, I was really confused about what had transpired. I mean I did not know whether I had dreamt the whole incident. So the day I could go and meet Swamiji, I did and asked Him to sit for a prediction. He did so. My first question to Ma was whether She had really blessed me or had I dreamt the whole thing? She told me, 'You called on to me. I came to you and now you don't believe it'. I was so thrilled, you can well imagine.

"Another time, a similar thing took place. Once I was praying in the home temple and I really wanted to feel Her presence. So I lit an oil lamp and prayed to Devi to show Herself to me. What happened next was that outside our house gate, a huge cobra appeared out of nowhere and my dogs, all four of them, began to bark at them. It was a really huge cobra and it did nothing but stare at the house with its hood all up. My dogs would have usually attacked a snake but this cobra they did not attack; they just kept barking at it. My man Friday came and told me what was happening and I understood intuitively that the cobra was none other than Devi Ma. So I ran towards Her and pleaded that She should go away. I ran back to the mandir and lit the camphor and prayed to Devi that She should leave or else I feared the dogs would attack Her. The cobra left immediately. I forgot about the incident and after many weeks we went back to

Swamiji for a prediction and Devi came through. Her first sentence to me was 'I don't know why but every time you call Me, I come and then you get scared and send me away'. I had forgotten about the incident so I assumed She was talking to my husband. Then my husband told me that Devi was talking to me and was referring to the Cobra incident. Swamiji was not aware of the incident mind you. Just imagine, She remembered and spoke about it weeks after it had taken place. Can you imagine how powerful Swamiji is as a medium?

"Once, during those really trying days of ours, when all the doctors insisted that my husband was going to die any moment and financially we were in a mess, we had to vacate our house. Days passed and we could not find a house that appealed to us. Just four days left and I charged into the mandir. Swamiji must have sighed with disbelief for I was always troubling Him. I only came with problems and that too as though it were the end of the world. So, He sat down for predictions and Devi came through and said 'why are you worrying. There is a *Nag* temple near your house. Go pour milk to *Nag Appa* and pray that you want a house. You will get a house you like by this evening'. I rushed back home and found the *Nag* temple She had referred to. I did as told and then went back home.

"If, within four days, we would not vacate the house, they would chuck our stuff out. It was really a hard time. So, I just casually picked up the newspaper and began to read the estate agent advertisements. I had in the weeks preceding this, contacted every real estate possible and seen countless houses but none had appealed or those that we liked were out of our budget. Suddenly I saw a small advertisement from a real estate agent that had somehow skipped my attention earlier. First, I hesitated and then decided to call on. Within four days I had got the house that appealed to us and also fitted our budget. Imagine we had tried so hard all these weeks and with just four days left within a few hours we got what we desired."

By the time, Mrs. Nagragan left for her residence, it was already dark and there was still no sign of Swamiji. I went to my room and after a wash up lay down on bed watching a ghastly serial made by a director who should have been flogged publicly for subjecting innocent tired author's with such mushy nonsense. I switched to cricket, but that was like watching a horror show. The way our boys were getting a thrashing made me groan. On some wildlife channel, I watched for ten minutes how certain animals fought each other tooth and nail only to be informed that the channel was showing its discerning viewers the sex life of these various animals. By God, there is at least something mankind does with more taste and style than those silly four legged animals.

After a knock on the door Ganesh informed that Swamiji had arrived and wanted me downstairs for a cup of coffee and some snacks. By the time I reached the hall He was seated on the chair, as usual speaking to one of His devotees. He looked exhausted but managed a smile and beckoned me to tuck into the tiffin. He had not touched anything obviously waiting for me. These little gestures, made one feel warm and wanted.

"So, how did it go?"

"Rather good, but a lot of what was told to me was regarding SaiBaba of Shirdi and her own personal growth as a medium, so there shall have to be lots of editing."

"Why do you worry about editing. Whatever Devi wants will only be printed. If She does not want you to print certain things then rest assured that will not be recorded."

(Just for the record, that is exactly what took place. Months later, when I began to transcribe and write the book, a huge chunk of Mrs. Nagarajan's conversation had not been recorded. In fact, it has happened a number of times that what Devi has not wanted to be included in the book has not been recorded. This is something that as an author I can vouch for. No exaggeration or no arm twisting. Out of the dozen and more cassettes that were recorded only portions that She has not thought necessary have been deleted. Ironically, before beginning transcribing those very sections and oblivious to the deletion, there would be a debate in my mind whether to include those sections or not. Obviously, Devi helped me out by making sure those conversations were not recorded.)

"You know Ruzbeh, very often, people have taken photographs of Me when I am in a trance and they have taken photographs of Devi too. Very often, they have not asked for Her permission and believe Me, every such time, those photographs have either got spoilt or they have not been captured on film. In fact, once a person tried to tape Her voice and She told him that he was wasting his time. True enough, though every other thing got recorded, Devi's voice did not appear on the cassette. So, you do not worry, whatever She wants only that will appear on the cassette. You see, sometimes things will be deleted as those things might be too private or She might not want it to be published for the welfare of the person (as in the case of Mrs. Nagrajan, I assume). Anyway, I have to again leave as the driver still has not reached the garage and tomorrow he has to leave for Subramaniya. Do you want to come with me or would you like to take some rest?"

"I am with you, Swamiji!"

So off we went. Swamiji drove fast but in firm confidence. He was not called the oldest teenager for nothing. The roads were packed with traffic but He detoured and kept a constant flow of talk, especially about how hard it was to get good honest staff. This was an issue that bothered Swamiji as He really treated His boys well but for some reason or the other very often due to their ignorance they bungled up and Swamiji is not very famous for tolerating fools. He does not like to be cheated or lied to and apart from that his staff really have a free hand to do as they please. Of course God help the person who tries to threaten or get a little over sized for his own pair of shoes.

We reached the garage and yet there was no sign of the driver or the van that had to take the generator to Subramaniya. Swamiji introduced me to His old friend who owned a welding cum cupboard shop. They were really old friends long before Swamiji got initiated by Devi into spirituality and mediumship. For them He was their old Nayak. The same man, who first landed a hard fist and then began to inquire why the fight was going on. The same man, who would do anything for a friend.

"He used to smuggle watches and come over and keep them in my house. I was not even aware what there was and my friend never ever informed me that all the watches were smuggled stuff. Only after He would sell everything and we would be sitting, enjoying a cold beer, that He would oblige me with the details." Then both the old friends began to laugh and we were served with coffee; though good but not a match to the stuff served at the temple.

A young man drove by. Swamiji blessed him and then they spoke for a while in their mother toungue while I observed the huge temple opposite us on the other side of the road. A new car drove up near the temple and then after a while the priest came and began to sprinkle holy water on the Esteem (I assume) and then they broke a coconut and a red *tikka* (mark) of good luck was made on the bonnet. The entire process took not much time but it made me feel proud to be born in a country that has God in its very roots and in every breath. Whatever, the economically advanced countries may think of India, I am of the firm belief that if God were asked to reside in a country it would be ours. He would feel most at home. Everywhere there are temples, churches, mosques and other religious places. You cannot walk through a street without bowing down in obeisance to God in some form or the other. It's good to be born in India, no matter the poverty, the dirt, the corruption and all the other things that makes one want to scream from time to time. Because inspite and despite politicians, India still survives and that is thanks to the common man's faith and prayers.

"Ruzbeh is writing a book on Devi and the miracles that She has been responsible for."

"You must write about how Swamiji could tackle four men at a time, just to help out a friend or the fun He and my father used to have when they were young and dashing."

"Oh, those were the days! Forget them now. Even thinking about them makes one sad. You know, in those days there used to be hardly any traffic on this road. One car would pass every ten minutes and now look at the traffic. Bangalore is not what it used to be. His father used to go every year on a pilgrimage walking more than hundred kilometers to pay his darshan to Devi."

"I remember going on Swamiji's bike. Really great, those days were?" They spoke for a while and the young man left in his swanky car. Swamiji contacted His home and was told that there was no sign of the drivers. Swamiji abused them and we all started laughing. There is something innocent about the way He throws out swear words.

"Come, let us go. They don't understand that by doing this they are going to get into trouble." Saying this, He wished His friend a good bye and we drove back to the mandir. On the way, we saw the van going by and Swamiji sighed. "The stupid bastard is going to give me excuses that will make interesting listening. They don't realise what they are doing by trying to fool me and abscond from their duty."

I did not understand what Swamiji meant by saying that the driver and his colleague didn't understand that they were getting themselves into trouble. I did not have to wait long. The very next day, they left for Subramaniya and then due to some problem with the traffic department had to wait for virtually twelve hours on the road without basic necessities and comfort. When Swamiji heard of their problem, He made a few calls and sorted out the mess but the fact is that often I have seen that those who land Him in grief or discomfort have to go through the same sort of discomfort but many times more intense. And this give and take occurs virtually within a few days. If the person is smart enough he puts two and two together. We had our meal and then sat down to discuss the agenda for the next day. By the time, I slept it was half-way into the night.

The next morning, I woke up on my own. That silly sparrow was nowhere to be seen. To tell you the truth, I sort of missed the damn winged gramaphone. I paid my obeisance to Lord Krishna, Ma Radha and Lord Hanuman, washed up and went to the mandir. Said a Namaste from outside to Ma Mookambika and touched Swamiji's feet for blessings. As usual, the scene was ecstatic and real sublime. Amma was already up and about, saying her prayers and decking Ma Mookambika with lovely flowers. Swamiji was giving instructions to the driver and his colleague. They were oblivious of the day's proceedings. Swamiji was giving them a paternal admonition. One of them had caught hold of Swamiji's feet and the other stood with a sombre face but it was obvious that Swamiji's reprimanding them was nothing new and they were very much at home with it.

"Bloody chaps will never learn. I was telling him to drive slowly. He drives like a man possessed and people have to actually jump out of his way. The traffic police and the cops do not treat him very roughly knowing he works for me but I am scared someday he will kill some poor person and get himself into an ugly mess. Bloody fools will never learn. Come, let us go for some coffee."

The law of immunisation had begun to work. No longer did the numerous plates of south Indian dishes make me want to wince with pain. I ate whatever was kept in front of me as though having three dishes at six thirty in the morning was something I had done from the dashed cradle.

"Lalit is coming today. "

"That's great. We might leave together. '

"Yes."

"Swamiji, why don't you speak to Lalit about the hospital?"

"You see, if I tell Lalit that I want something to be done, I am certain he will move heaven and earth to get it done. But the fact is that he is not very keen to see Me get involved in the hospital project."

"Why?"

"Because, he thinks that once the hospital project will start, all the headache and the hard work in seeing that the project gets completed will come on my shoulders and that will affect my health. He does not want me to get involved as he fears for my health and welfare, otherwise for him my word is the law. He will do anything for me." That is the truth. A number of devotees have put aside their personal egos and grievances and admitted, that though they might not agree with Lalit's possessive tendencies, where Swamiji is concerned, but the fact remains that if Lord Rama has Hanuman, similarly Swamiji has Lalit.

The morning passed the usual way. Swamiji answering phone calls and solving problems of His devotees and Amma busy with the temple prayers and work. The pujari had come in today. Yesterday, he had for some reason phoned up and said he would not be coming over. That had made Swamiji hit the roof but Amma had calmed down Swamiji and told Him not to get so excited or else they would lose this help also.

"If you want to remove somebody you must ask Swamiji to do it. He is an expert. He will take him back also as quickly as He dismisses them but He does not know how to handle things diplomatically." She had confessed.

After bath and another breakfast (yes it is common to have around two to three breakfasts when with Swamiji) I was introduced to one of the oldest devotees of Swamiji.

"They have seen me through my worst times. In fact very often, they used to send me rice, so that I could feed my family. Come, you talk to them. He is Vasantrao Birju and she is his wife Suman Birju." Introducing us, He went down to take care of other pending matters.

DEVI ACCEPTS HUMBLE GIFTS

"We met Swamiji in 1975 and we were directed to Him by our priests. In those days there were just ten to fifteen devotees. Those days He was facing a lot of financial problems and He was really in a very bad financial state. In fact, so many times Devi would speak through Him and say that 'tell my *patri* (messenger) not to worry. I will take care of Him and His family. I will give Him so much money that He has never dreamt of. Tell Him to have faith in His Mother'. That is exactly what has happened. Now, Swamiji and His family are so well taken care of, that nobody can believe that, once upon a time He was in such a financial mess." Informed Vasantrao.

"For how long did His financial problems last?"

"I think minimum five years. Yes, more but not less. He did not have money to buy even oil for the lamp or flowers for the pooja. I cannot tell you the type of trouble and hardship He has endured. What you now see and what we have seen are two different things. I think, from 1978 onwards things began to improve for Him and His family. But, from 1970 uptill that period, He really lived hand to mouth. His children were small and even they really went through a hard time. In those days we used to charge just one rupee and twenty-five paisa, for predictions...any number of questions and He used to get so tired by the end of the day." All this was narrated jointly by husband and wife. Both speaking but complimenting each other. Simple devoted people who while talking had tears in their eyes.

Often, the tears could not be contained in the small womb of the eye and would make the journey down their cheeks. Nice, respectable people who were contented with their lot and grateful that Devi had allowed them to serve Her and Her messenger in their own humble way. They spoke softly, haltingly as English was not their mother tongue and I did not understand Kannada. Really humble folks, the salt of the earth, people who make certain that the earth moves on its orbit without a fuss.

"One day, we bought some bangles and then some artificial flowers and saree for Devi. As we did not know whether She would like artificial flowers we left the packet near Her feet and waited outside the temple as Swamiji was not around. Those days, there were hardly any visitors and we could relax and talk with Devi and Swamiji. We waited outside and when Swamiji still had not arrived we went inside to pay our respects and go home. We got a shock of our lives as we saw the packet had been opened, and all that we had bought was decorated on Devi. Flowers and bangles and saree all were on Ma. One thing we were certain of and that is nobody had entered the temple within. Also those days there was nothing here. Just a small room for Devi and a kitchen few meters away. Those days this was a secluded place so nobody could have come in." Tears began to roll down the wife's face.

"We were not sure whether Ma would like the small things we had got for Her so, She wore it Herself. Don't ask us how. It happened. After that, very often, devotees narrated similar incidents. In fact even now when we go to pray to Her, prasad just drops in front of us. Lime will fall from the trishul or the flower will fall down or something or the other will happen, to tell us that She is with us and happy with our devotion. In fact last month itself, our son was to give a very important exam and I told Ma that only You can take care of him. Immediately a flower dropped down near us. She listens to everything. She is really the Mother of the Universe."

Flowers falling down is not a regular feature. The flowers are in a garland and they on their own accord never fall off. If and when they do, you can rest assured that it is more of an exception than the rule. Where limes rolling towards the devotee is concerned, I have seen it happening with my own eyes. I will narrate it at the right sequence, but as an author, I have seen all this happening so have no reason to doubt these good people. I have seen limes roll down and stop near the devotee and I have seen all of a sudden the garland fall off at the precise time, when the devotee has bowed down or thanked the Goddess or asked for an answer.

"The same way, She used to write on the wall to explain to Swamiji so many things He was not aware of. He would go to sleep and in the morning the entire wall would be covered with instructions. Once, we asked how She wrote on the wall and a few days later we found in our house chalk pieces. In our house we got the answer of how she writes on the mandir wall. None of us had bought those chalk pieces so we understood that it was Devi's way of telling us how She wrote messages for Swamiji. You know, whenever we prepare food, first we offer it to Her. Whether in our house or in our mandir, She is there too. So we offer the food first to Her. Every time after offering Her the food when we return to eat the prasad, there is a mark on the food...some distinct mark on the food, that shows, She has accepted the offering. If you leave the food, just like that, no mark appears but whenever we have offered Her food, She has accepted it. Either a trishul mark, or some finger mark appears.

"Also if I ask a question to Her at home and then come to Swamiji, She will give me the answer immediately through

Swamiji without us telling Swamiji that we have come for such and such reason. I ask Her a question and She answers through Swamiji. So many times I have told Her something at home and then over here through Swamiji, She will repeat the same things; just to make us aware that She is everywhere and hearing us speak to Her. Once I was preparing a sweet dish, which both Devi and Swamiji like a lot. I wanted to offer it to both but could not come here. Immediately, His phone call came. He said 'what are you preparing?' Can you imagine? Not even a few minutes had passed when I expressed my desire to offer these sweets to Them, that a call comes through."

"Swamiji informed that you were not getting children..."

"Yes and Devi made sure we got children. She would keep promising us that we would become parents and we became parents. In fact, once in the hospital I was about to deliver my son and I was in tremendous pain. I remembered Her a lot and suddenly Swamiji came into the hospital and blessed me and went away. Immediately the pain disappeared and I was all right.

"You know, Devi likes *bhajans* (religious songs set to music) a lot. In fact, first whenever Swamiji would go in a trance after predictions He would dance when bhajans were being sung. Actually Devi used to dance through Swamiji. Once, we stopped the music and She said 'don't stop I like these songs a lot and want to dance'. Marathi, Hindi, Kannada, any good bhajans. But when She talks in Kannada it is very ancient Kannada. So many times even we don't understand the language. It is ancient Kannada rarely spoken nowadays.

"We have seen so many miracles take place and diseases cured. In fact, just ten days back I could not get out of bed as my bones were paining very much. We went to the doctor who told me that my bones had become weak and they would with little exertion break. He really scared me and really I was in great pain. I came here immediately and did not say anything to *Patri* (Swamiji...messenger). I just asked for the Blessed Lime. He prayed and gave me two limes. I made juice out of them and drank it with water. Within a few hours the pain had gone and here I am. Or else, I would not have come here, as the pain was really killing me. I have not taken any medicine. Nothing. Just Ma's blessings and the Blessed Limes. I could not stand a few days ago. Ma has removed so many evil spirits. So many people have been saved. Even those suffering from white patches that the doctors could not cure have returned to normal health. Lime, blessed water and the kumkum and the disease is cured."

THE GOLDEN COBRA

While chatting about miracles and faith, Swamiji entered the room and we received His blessings. It was obvious that He held this couple in high esteem. It was apparent from the love He had in His eyes when He spoke to them.

"They have really been with me through thick and thin." He turned towards them. "Do you remember that snake incident?"

"You must tell him about that golden cobra, Swamiji!" Gushed Suman.

"You know Ruzbeh, on one of the auspicious days when the *Nag Dev* is worshipped, a real cobra entered our place and with its hood held high stared at all of us. In those days, all this was open and there was a small group of devotees of Ma, gathered to sing bhajans and spend the day in prayer. The devotees got scared because, for the first time, we were seeing this cobra, that was completely golden in colour. A number of devotees were frightened and in spite of all their efforts, the cobra would not move. In the end, Ma told me to light camphor and then I told the cobra that it was most welcome to stay but as a friend. All of a sudden, it lowered it's hood and curled itself up and sat as though waiting for us to worship it. All day through, devotees poured milk on this cobra and worshipped it and it did not once move or object.

"So that day, instead of pouring milk on a statue of a cobra, that day we all poured milk on a living snake. Then, when we sat for evening devotional songs, it just disappeared. The important point to be noted was not that the snake spent the entire day at the temple and allowed people to pour milk on it, but the fact that all those who were present on that day, had all their problems sorted out. That was the important thing. And one thing I can tell you for sure, all those who have come here and who have faith in Devi, always have their problems sorted out. And if the problem persists, then the devotees are given strength to face their problems. Goddess never ever allows Her devotees to suffer. She will either solve the problem or really help them to face the issue.

"You saw the people who had come over here sometime earlier. Yes, the group I was speaking to...well they must have killed at least two dozen snakes...cobras included. They are facing so many problems, that it is unimaginable. They have lost everything. They were once filthy rich, now they have trouble seeing the month through. Their factories, bungalows, everything is gone. The pooja going on in the mandir is being performed for them. Now only Goddess can save them. They too have understood this, for everybody has turned their backs on them. If their problems persist, they will be on the street within a short time. But once a person has faith in Goddess, then in no way She will allow Her children to go through such misery."

A number of devotees walked in and they kept insisting that Swamiji should visit their new bungalow and Swamiji nodded and said that after the *Chandi Havan,* as and when Devi wished, He would pay them a visit. He made sure everybody was served with snacks and coffee and then got busy on the phone. I could hear snatches of the conversation, as a few of His devotees had cornered me and were inquiring about my journey into such an esoteric topic. One of the devotees, taking a good look at my faded jeans and loose denim shirt, informed me that initially he had assumed that I was one of those hippies, come in for 'instant enlightenment' rather than a devotee and an author writing on such a divine subject. What I could read in their eyes, was that though all of them agreed that a book on Ma Mookambika Devi and Swamiji was long overdue, they were not certain, if it could be written by somebody who had not spent more than seven full days with their Master. It did not make things easier for them, when I informed that I had absolutely no notion about how the book would be written. My first book *The Last Marathon,* was written in the same manner. Sat down and the book formed on its own. I knew for certain that this book too would follow its predecessor. This has nothing to being either disorganised or plain laid back (I have both the qualities in abundance), but the fact is, that paranormal topics cannot be handled the normal way. You have to be slightly off the head, not only to track, but even enjoy the hike in such metaphysical arena.

A lady approached Swamiji and touched His feet. Swamiji blessed her, inquired about her well-being and then introduced her to me. Uma Madan was a close friend of Mrs. Nagrajan's, and the latter had informed her regarding the book being written about Ma Mookambika and Swamiji. Thus she had come over to narrate her experience.

ALL QUERIES ANSWERED

"Six years ago, I met Dayani (Mrs. Nagrajan). She kept talking about Devi and I kept talking about Shirdi's Sai Baba. I am His devotee and I was very possessive about my Baba. She told me that He communicates through you. You are very very fortunate."

"No doubts."

"Anyway, six months after meeting Dayani, she informed me that there was going to be a Chandi Homa. Till then I had sort of kept away from Devi as I was most comfortable with my Baba. When I was told to attend the Chandi Homa, I prayed to Baba, that if He wanted me to attend the ceremony, I would most certainly go. But, if He felt for some reason, I should avoid going, then He should create a situation that leaves me in no two doubts about His intentions. Very often, He has made His intentions clear, through messages and creating certain circumstances. Any way I attended the Homa. The first thing Ma told me, through Swamiji, was that, 'you are doing service...serving humanity and you should continue doing that'. I was working with people with disabilities. Nobody had told this to Swamiji and that day the crowd was immense, but still She spoke to me. What really stunned me, was that very moment, I was very confused regarding my future. I was not certain whether I should continue working with people with disabilities or move on to other things. Devi on Her own cleared the path. She said 'this service is the way to your salvation. You must continue'. At that time, I needed this guidance and it came actually like a God-sent.

"My daughter's marriage was not materialising. Though she was in love with a very nice man, due to some reason or the other, the marriage date was not getting finalised. Some well wishers told me to do Devi pooja and that She would make certain that all would go well. Initially I refrained from the pooja only because I am not much of a ritualistic person. But then, for the child, I agreed and got immersed in the pooja. One day whilst doing the pooja, I felt some strange energy filling me up. I knew it was the presence of Devi. I immediately told Her that I don't want to go in a trance. I told her I am very happy with my Shirdi Sai Baba's way of experiencing God; calmly and soberly. So Devi complied and the trance sensation left. Then a day before my daughter's wedding, Dayani attended the function and she went into a trance and then Devi came through her and told me that 'I am coming for the wedding'. I was very happy but moments before I could perform another pooja, this time I went into a trance and this trance was very powerful. I was actually gasping and tears were running down my face. I wondered how Swamiji handled such a powerful energy and that too for such a long time. My aunt realised what was happening to me and she began to sing a devotional song and the moment she began to sing the song, I could feel that powerful energy leaving me. Trust me I still wonder how Swamiji handles Her energy and Her vibrations. I had Devi for a few seconds and I was sapped and He goes in a trance for hours, so often. Anyway, the wedding went very well. Thanks to Baba, Devi and Swamiji.

"Devi did come for the wedding and I got to know about this, a month after the ceremony. You see, there is this lady who is running a home for the physically disabled. We, on and off, do our bit and when we met after a month of my daughter's wedding, we got to talk about the event. I thanked her for coming for both the morning and evening functions. She looked much surprised and told me that she had not come in the morning but just in the evening. I insisted that she had come in the morning too and she emphatically refused saying that she could not leave her wards, as their meal time coincided with the morning function. My mother-in-law also insisted that this friend had only come in the evening for the reception. I was really shocked as I was certain that I had seen her in the morning. You see, that morning, I was seeing off somebody and I saw her for a split second and I smiled at her but did not get the usual wave and smile that I am accustomed too. I even thought it strange, that the response was so different. Then somebody called me and after a few seconds when I turned, this friend was gone. I looked for her everywhere and she had disappeared. That day, I did not read into the incident that Devi had kept Her word. You see, this lady is a very great devotee of Raja Rajeshwari Devi. Ma always tells us that She is the Universal Mother and can use any form and anybody to fulfil Her objective."

MATRICULATION PROBLEMS

"The second incident that has left a great mark on my consciousness is regarding my son. He was really going lower and lower where his educational performance was concerned. He was in his matriculation and his mark sheet was not very encouraging. So I went to Swamiji and He agreed that there was no way he would pass his matriculation, as my son's educational line was not very powerful. But I insisted and pleaded with Devi and Swamiji to somehow get him to just scrape through his tenth standard. So Swamiji told me to perform a Ganesh Pooja, five times; once every week. He told me that the day and the time should be the same every time I performed the pooja and it should take place every week without a break. Now to conduct a Ganesh Pooja for five succeeding weeks was not an easy task but I was determined to get him to pass. His exam was to begin with the onset of the second pooja and the month was also very powerful; it was the month of Ma Durga. I finished the five poojas and the next day the results came through...he had passed, that too with a first class. Amazing isn't it? When you have Sai Baba of Shirdi, Ma Mookambika and Swamiji with you, then there is no place for fear or doubt. They are there, holding us all through the ups and downs that are written in our destiny."

Dr. Sonal Chayya's mother-in-law bowed down and took the blessings of Swamiji. She was a firm devotee of Sai Baba of Shirdi. In fact, what amazed me, was that there were innumerable devotees of Sai Baba of Shirdi who believed that Ma

Swamiji in the year 1972, Bangalore

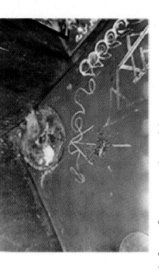

Earlier, Devi used to guide Swamiji through automatic writing.

Devi revealed Her form to Swamiji, by directing Him to burn camphor on the floor

Swamiji in front of Devi,
Bangalore

Swamiji feeding devotees,
Dandeli

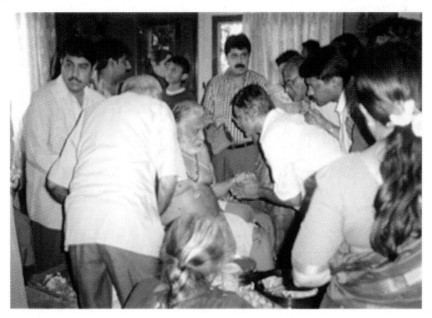

Devi giving predictions through Swamiji,
Bangalore

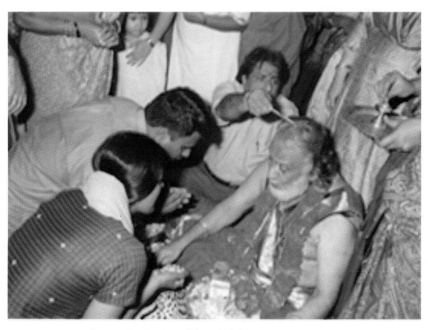

Swamiji during Chandi Havan in a trance,
Bangalore

MA MOOKAMBIKA DEVI

Gurur-Brahma Gurur-Vishnu, Gurur-Devo Mahesvarah,
Guruh Saksat Parabrahma, Tasmai Sri-Gurave namah.

Swamiji resembling Sai Baba of Shirdi

Swamiji at Sahasra Chandi Homa, Mumbai

Swamiji in a trance during Havan, Bangalore

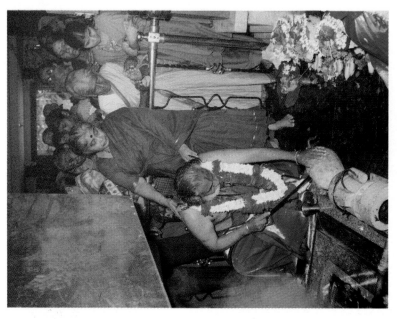

*Swamiji performing a symbolic sacrifice,
Bangalore*

*Swamiji on his divan,
Bangalore*

Swamiji being led towards Ma Mookambika while in a trance,

Mookambika, Swamiji and Baba were all one and worked in perfect unison. Often Devi *bhakts* were drawn to Sainath and so many times Baba Himself sent His devotees to Ma Mookambika and Swamiji.

SACRED COBRAS

"Ruzbeh when the Chayya family came to me they were in a bad shape..."

"We were ruined and our house was like a volcano. Tempers flared every second. Now it has become like an ice-cream parlour."

"They had killed a cobra in their bungalow compound. From that day problems began. I asked them to do various poojas and gradually one by one their problems got sorted out. Of course, whatever Devi told them to do, they have done with full faith and love and their problems have all got sorted out and they are living a peaceful, prosperous life. Faith is most important. How their problems got sorted out is something I don't know. I will certainly not say that I have sorted out their problems. It is only Devi who has performed miracles and sorted out the mess they were in. Devi has blessed them in all aspects. And the best part is that after they began to perform the poojas and believe and worship Devi, cobras were seen and this time they came to bless the house and family and not curse them for killing one of them. They had been completely destroyed. Family conflicts, ill health, financial problems all of a sudden descended on them just because of one mistake and it was through their faith and Devi's grace that they bounced back."

"It is so dangerous to kill a cobra?"

"Very dangerous and this is one act that will follow you through your incarnations. So many people come and tell me that they have not killed any snakes or cobras but they seem to have conveniently forgotten that this is not their first life over here and certainly for most not their last life. They have committed acts for which they have to pay. If they have killed a cobra then they have to pay. Not only they, but the entire family. Sometimes they even forget they have killed a cobra in this life time. I have to remind them and then they remember..."

"But Swamiji the whole family gets affected?"

"Yes. Wherever a drop of blood has been spilled of a cobra the entire family gets affected. They might forget the act of killing but the snake will never forget."

"But it will follow you from lifetime to lifetime?"

"Yes. Take for example all the devotees who come here. Some come from Maharashtra, some from Gujarat, some from even abroad. Why do you think all of us have met here. Why should all of you come here? There must be some reason...some force that brings you all here to get your problems sorted out. We have a saying which when translated means 'you die to be born again'. A man dies but is born again to fulfil his desires and ambitions that he could not complete or experience in his past incarnation. Also to settle his account with all those he has interacted with in his past incarnations. A man has to have some give or take to interact intimately or even remotely with another individual. In fact according to me, without a past life association a man will not even come to a place of worship or temple to ask for blessings or pray that his or her problems get sorted out. Like there is a story where there is a stone statue of a woman and Lord Rama was passing by that place when his fingers touch the statue and that statue comes to life. Actually there was a curse on this woman who had been turned into a statue and Lord Vishnu had promised her that whenever He came back to earth He would liberate her from this stone bondage. So when Lord Vishnu came down as Lord Rama He liberated the woman.

"A man comes down to purify his problems and he has to wait for the call. When the call comes automatically problems are sorted out. But remember a problem that is sorted out is finished forever and not just for this incarnation. So when you have a particular problem solved you should remember it will never come back again in future incarnations unless you repeat the same mistake. For instance, if a person is suffering from *Nag Dosh* (the snake curse) and Devi solves the person's problem by liberating the person from the curse. It means that the curse will not follow this person from incarnation to incarnation. It has been got rid for eternity. But if you go ahead and kill another cobra obviously you are going to be responsible for that act and the cycle will resume itself."

"But to get rid of the problems we have to go through the grind. It takes time. I believe that with prayers and sincere faith, one can make God...Devi, to take the initiative to bring the person to the place where the problem can be solved. But once you have the opportunity then you should not miss it. For instance, whatever is suggested by Devi or if I suggest something it should be implemented. If you have faith and do as told then you are taking the opportunity to solve your problems...caused either in this life or some past life. Whatever is suggested should be implemented as those are means of purification to get out of the nagging problem. Implement the suggestion and see your life turn around. I can say safely that one cannot just come here without the call. Everybody cannot come here. It is Mother, Ma, Goddess that brings them all over here....have the coffee." We took the small steel glasses and for a few seconds only slurps and sighs could be heard.

"The fact is that a mother never forgets her children. However far the children may go, most mothers keep them in their hearts forever. Over here we are talking about the Universal Mother. In which ever incarnation you may be and what ever your new form or avtar, Goddess who is the Universal Mother always beckons and brings Her children back to the fold. For instance take the case of dogs. The mother will give birth to so many puppies. She will feed them and all the time be with them. The puppies will run away and the mother will bring them back. Likewise, you cannot underestimate the love of the mother. There is a small story that shows the love of the mother. There was this small child, about just six or seven months and the mother had to work in the fields. The mother puts the child to sleep under a shady tree and goes to work. She works far away in the field. The child gets up and cries for milk. Nobody can hear the cries of the child. But, the mother comes to know within seconds. That is because, the moment the child begins to cry due to hunger, milk begins to gush out from the mother's breast. Like that when we cry due to our problems and when the cry comes from the depth of the heart, She will definitely come and give us food...food in the form that will dry our eyes and remove the cause for our tears. That is the love of the mother and our Mother, Ma Mookambika is the Mother of all mothers. She will not let Her children keep crying; She will always come to help. You can measure the whole world. You can measure the depths of the sea. You can measure the height of the sky but you cannot measure the love of the Mother. She will solve the problems of those who have love, faith and total surrender. If at all there is anybody who can solve the problems of ours it is the Goddess. In fact even Brahma, Vishnu and Mahesh (the holy trinity...Creator, Preserver and Destroyer...three aspects of God) who are supposed to be Gods, when problems came to Them, They also ran to Devi. Even Their problems could be sorted out only by Devi. That is how it is. People come and their problems are taken care of. Sometimes immediately...sometimes it may take time...however She deems best, but one thing is certain and that is everybody has been taken care of. Devi fulfils all desires that are made with total faith, love and surrender."

"So we were talking about these *doshas* (curses). They continue from generation to generation. Relations that we have with each other continue."

"The relationship between the Mother and us children continue. We forget it from incarnation to incarnation but She never forgets and She brings all Her children together. There is a karmic bond, called *runanubandha*, and that pulls people together and She holds the reigns. We do not know when and why and how things move but the fact remains and that is Goddess never allows Her children to drift away from Her....", suddenly the phone rang and Swamiji listened for a while and then told the other person to keep Him posted. He then switched off the phone and looked at me. "Sandeep Vasani's father. That day he nearly became unconscious and fell down in the bathroom. They immediately called me and asked what should they do. I think they suspected heart attack or something like that. I told them nothing was wrong, it was just a case of low blood pressure. Told them to make him drink some salt water and then advised them to take him to the hospital for a general check-up. Hospital staff did his check-up and concluded it was a case of low blood pressure but for some reason or the other admitted him. He called me up the other day from the bed and told Me that he was fed up and what should he do? So I told him to get up and get out of the hospital bloody fast. Told him to just remove all the tubes and wires they had inserted in him and return home. He did just that and called me from his place."

BUSINESS AND SUCCESS

"That is a common practice of Swamiji." Informed Pawan Kumar. "I have heard Him tell countless of devotees who have been admitted to the hospital. He will tell them, 'just remove all those tubes and walk out of the hospital' and the best part is most of the devotees within five minutes are doing just that. They all of a sudden get so much energy that they get the tubes removed and get their bags packed and off they go home. You see I met Swamiji in the mid 80's. At that time I was in a miserable condition. My aim was to be an industrialist but I had reached a level where I was on the verge of selling my factory. So, a friend of mine told me about Swamiji. We must have come to the gate of the mandir around five times, but for some reason or the other I could not enter within. On the sixth occasion the car tyre burst. It was as though something did not want me to enter. But, my friend and I were adamant and we entered the mandir. Swamiji in the first meeting itself told me to do *pranam* to Ma Mookambika and offer Her a coconut. He told me that there were snakes visiting my factory and I agreed. I used to pay my workers the best salaries going around but yet very often they would pack their bags and run away. Snakes used to come in the factory and move about on the machines. Very often, they would sit with their hoods up and emit those hissing sounds. Swamiji advised us to do a pooja and then from that day onwards there was a phenomenal turn around. I started the company with just twenty thousand rupees and we have reached a turnover of eighty lakh rupees. I am not a very big industrialist but I know that with the grace of God, Goddess and the advice and blessings of Swamiji my life has turned around for the better. I can tell you something for certain and that is there is a great power residing in this temple. Now you see a very well structured temple and building but I have come here when there was just a small temple and a small tent like structure. That Devi resides here there is no doubt. The power is immense and exists very much over here. The moment you stand in front of Mother and see Her face and though initially you may have had ten thousand questions in your mind, Her love and presence make you forget all the cares and worries of the world. I believe firmly that if you have lost confidence in your life and in yourself, just come over here, sit down for a while in front of Mother and that is enough to fill you up with strength and confidence to walk and face the world. That is my firm belief."

Swamiji introduced me to Mr. P.S.K. Shetty and his wife. The wife insisted that she had enough material to fill up a separate volume on the miracles that they had personally experienced with the grace of Ma Mookambika and Swamiji. I accepted another glass of coffee and Swamiji informed that He was going to take another bath as within a short time He would be sitting down for predictions. Mr. Shetty informed that he was a distributor for a multinational company.

"I have been coming here for the last so many years..."

"Twenty years." Informed his wife.

"Since coming into the fold of Goddess and Swamiji we have grown and grown financially and the remaining experiences my wife will tell you."

"See we are devotees for the last twenty years..."

"What is your name?"

"Laxmi. My husband had just a few expectations in life. He wanted to take his family abroad. Second, to start his own business and the third was to have a completely furnished house. With the grace of Ma Mookambika and Swamiji all the desires have been fulfilled. We first lived along with my husband's brother and his family. Swamiji's son used to conduct some business transaction with my brother-in-law and one day even Swamiji came over with His son. I think He was passing by and His son wanted to briefly meet up with my brother-in-law. There were a few people in the office and Swamiji and His son were offered chairs. The moment Swamiji was introduced to my brother-in-law, He pulled His chair backwards and sat at a distance. After the other people left Swamiji told my brother-in-law that he had pulled back His chair for a purpose. Swamiji told my brother-in-law that whenever He looked at him, Swamiji saw a snake instead of my brother-in-law's face. Then Swamiji told my brother-in-law that there was a cobra in our house and if he had not yet seen the cobra then within a few days he would certainly see it. He also told my stunned brother-in-law that in the house there were six statues of Lord Ganesh and two *Yantras* (spiritually charged designs) in the house. My brother-in-law was stunned. Just a few days back he had seen a cobra in the house and he knew that there were a number of Lord Ganesh's statues at home though about the *Yantras* he knew nothing about.

"Swamiji then told him that my brother-in-law was still able to eat food and could feed his family because his parents and grand-parents were very devoted worshipers of God and Goddess. Otherwise, the *Nag Dosh* (serpent curse) was so strong that it would have wiped him and his family and would have ruined them long ago. It was the blessing procured due to the prayers and *seva* (devotion and service) to God and Goddess by his forefathers that had still kept him alive. Swamiji then revealed that in my brother-in-law's native village near his ancestral house there was a Devi Mandir...the temple was attached to the house. This, was also later confirmed, by the family elders. My husband was not there at that time but he did not believe in astrology and God men. When my husband was informed first and foremost he counted the Ganesha Statues and yes there were six of them. But, we were certain that there were no *Yantras*. What we were not aware of was that just one day before the prediction my husband's sister and even our children had gone to a fair and from there they had bought two *Yantras*. Just one day prior these *Yantras* had entered our home. We were very impressed."

"On Sundays, we all came here including my husband for Devi's darshan and prediction. We were made to wait for half an hour then informed that there would be no prediction on that day. I looked at Devi and told her in front of my husband that if your power is really there and you want us to keep coming here then let us get a prediction today or else we would never return. Those days there was hardly any crowd and even Amma used to live elsewhere. She used to come latest by noon and leave in the evening. Swamiji told us to eat the prasad and He went into the mandir. Some time later somebody told us that Swamiji had called us in the mandir for prediction. That day he gave us an hour long prediction where Devi through Him told us all about our past and predicted our future. All very accurate and all has come true too. There was a property where we were associated with. He told us to get out of that property as nobody could thrive in that property. We left and even today after twenty years it is true. Who ever is associated with that property never prospers.

"Sometime ago, my husband at work was associated with two products and he was conducting lot of field drives etc and we came to meet Swamiji and my husband casually mentioned about his work and the two products. Swamiji very coolly told my husband that he should concentrate on Pardhan while the other product Demlin is useless you don't work for that product. Then Swamiji inquired what the products were all about as He did not even know what their functions were. He just told us what Devi wanted Him to convey. Just as He had predicted Pardhan sold very good quantities but the other product was a real failure."

"Then my uncle called us to visit him in America. In those days we did not have money to travel though the ticket to America was just 18,000 rupees. But Swamiji told us that we would go. Within nine months we left for a visit to America..."

"You see," her husband informed softly, "the uncle wanted to sell his bungalow and shift someplace else, but he was not getting the right price and nobody was interested in that property. Swamiji gave us a Lime and told us to hang it outside the front door. He told us that the property was constructed on a burial ground and thus there was so much trouble. He also

200

predicted that not only will the bungalow be sold but for a much higher price than expected. We took the blessed Lime and just as Swamiji had predicted the bungalow was sold very soon and at a price much beyond expectations...."

"You know, there was a time we thought we would have to shut down our business and my husband would have to begin working at a regular job. Swamiji refused. He said that within no time we would prosper beyond our dreams. Now our turnover... I think he will be able to tell you better about the balance sheet."

"When we wanted to start a business we had seen a particular place. We both had liked it and I was about to give an advance..."

"Then I told him that first let us ask Swamiji and then only give the advance."

"Yes. Swamiji told us that the place we had seen had a Shiv temple opposite it. I agreed. He then told us that nobody had ever prospered in that place and that we would get a place..."

"Within fifteen days, Devi will get you a good place you don't worry. And can you believe it within fifteen days we got a better place...."

"We immediately bought it and He visited the place and blessed it. In 1992 when we started our business the turnover was nine lakhs and now we have crossed 50.5 crores. In fact we have bought a building..."

"Costing 50 lakhs. Swamiji Himself came and also made sure the right Ganesh and Naga poojas were performed. In fact some time back we wanted to buy a place. Everything was appropriate..."

"But I insisted that we come and ask for Devi's and Swamiji's approval." Informed Laxmi.

"Yes. Swamiji told us not to have anything to do with that property as a murder had taken place there...."

"When we inquired form private sources then we were informed that yes a murder had taken place. In fact the owner's son had been murdered there..."

"We got another offer to become partners with a friend of ours. There was a property and we were to start some work on

201

it. Swamiji told us that even if somebody were to give Him that property free of cost He would not buy it. So immediately I went and told my friend not to buy that property. He did not listen. Within three months he lost his job of seventeen years and now he is in such a bad condition that we all feel sorry for him. Also now he can't sell it as it is of no value and he is facing so many problems that it is very sad...."

"My son-in-law last year was to go to Dubai for a job. We told Swamiji this and He said that within fifteen days my son-in-law would be back as the person who was supposed to help him was of no use. Everything was already done and my son-in-law insisted on going. On the fifteenth day, he was back over here. Then Swamiji told us that he would go this year to USA. That prediction he made last year. This August 9th, my son-in-law and daughter are going to USA as they have got a job. We had a theft where we lost some twenty pairs of expensive earrings. Swamiji told us that within seven days we would get the things back but we would get only eighteen pairs and not the twenty stolen. Within seven days we got them back but as predicted we got eighteen and not the twenty pairs. As I told you, there is so much that can be said that one volume will not suffice. In the temple, Ma Mookambika and Swamiji have helped thousands of devotees. Saved them and made their lives steady and firm."

Lalit entered with Swamiji and we met warmly. As mentioned before Swamiji is very fond of Lalit. Whenever there has been some sort of financial problem, as Swamiji often begins projects with faith in Devi and absolutely nil bank balance. In spite of such rich devotees Swamiji has virtually nothing on His name and has never asked anybody for a single rupee. So often, He starts projects for the welfare of people and is promised by certain devotees to go ahead and they are backing Him. When He goes ahead and turns around usually He sees nobody behind Him to back Him. That is the time Lalit enters and bails the project out. Lalit calls a spade a spade. Diplomacy is not his style. But nobody ever doubts the fact that if there is a person who Swamiji can turn to for any assistance (though He never does) then it is Lalit. As I have said often...Shri Ram has Hanumanji's never failing devotion and Swamiji has Lalit Nagpal's.

I had met Lalit and his wife at their lovely home in Chembur months ago. I had met him at around seven in the morning and he had spoken briefly about his relationship with Swamiji and his eternal indebtedness. Both Lalit and his wife, Ranjana, are staunch believers of Sai Baba of Shirdi and that got us closer. The fact that Sai Baba communicated His messages and helped number of people was something that fascinated them and that morning we had chatted for a few hours intimately. Of course, we all knew that we would have to meet again for more details and also because I wanted to record their experiences as Lalit has a very expressive flow of words and I felt that it would liven the pages. But for some reason or the other the meeting kept getting postponed.

"So Ruzbeh, how are you? I am sorry we just can't meet up."

"No problem, at least now that you are here we might be able to get a few minutes to our selves. Of course, you go ahead and get the prediction done and then we can chat."

"When are you leaving for Mumbai?"

"Today, by the evening flight..."

"Good, so am I and we can chat up then."

"Lalit, Swamiji is very keen on the hospital project. Why are you not getting involved in it."

Lalit sat down and for a while said nothing. He refused the coffee and waited till I had finished placing the dicta-phone back in its cover.

"Ruzbeh, you know that money is not the issue. What I am worried about is that, as usual, Swamiji will be left all alone and will have to do all the running about. The hospital is to be made in Subramaniya. It is a virtual seven hour drive from here. He will have to keep shuttling and you know He likes to drive the car Himself. Swamiji is seventy-two years old. He cannot handle everything but I can give you a guarantee that in the end He will be doing all the work Himself. If the project was in Mumbai I would have not been worried, assured that, we all

203

would have managed the show, but so far away I know he will have to bear all the responsibility and I don't want to tax His health. That is why I am not entering the picture."

"But you know Swamiji depends upon you a lot."

"I know and even He knows that in the end He has Lalit Nagpal. I am nobody. All my wealth and everything belongs to Devi and Swamiji. When I first met Him I was a nobody who hardly had five hundred rupees in his account. Okay, now I have everything and Swamiji knows that it all belongs to Devi and Him. Come let us go down I need to sit with Devi and Swamiji. Ma has to answer a few questions and solve a few of my problems." The fact that there was some serious issue bothering Lalit was palpable. He was tensed and the fact that he had flown for just a prediction itself spoke volumes about the sensitivity of the issue. Otherwise all predictions are done on the phone itself. Most of Swamiji's devotees in Mumbai get their problems solved and queries answered by speaking to Swamiji on the telephone. So we went to the temple and within a few minutes Swamiji sat down for predictions. Lalit entered in Ma's abode and the door was shut.

PROBLEMS BANISHED

Swamiji minutes before had asked me to meet a young Christian couple, who sat near the temple's door with a small infant in a cradle. I climbed up to the third floor and after a wash and making certain that I had enough cassettes on hand went down to meet and record the experience of the Christian couple. I introduced myself.

"Hi! I am Clement and this is my wife Linda. We have been coming here since the past two years. Let my wife tell you all about our experiences. "

"Two years back we were in a terrible mess. I mean we had actually lost everything and there was no light at the end of the tunnel. One night a friend of ours told us about Devi and Swamiji and the next morning we were here. Actually, we were told about this phenomenal place at eleven in the night and the next morning at four we were knocking at the gates. You can imagine our state of plight and mind that we did not think it strange to knock at a temple gate so early in the morning. Poor Swamiji came down, opened the gates and I am sure must have wondered whether we were out of our minds. But He told us very politely and tenderly that we should come back at nine the same morning as He could not possibly sit down for predictions at so early an hour. At nine we both sat in front of Him and we both were in tears. In fact I could not stop the flow of tears because believe me we were in a terrible mess; financially and emotionally we were bankrupt. Goddess through Swamiji guided us beautifully. He told us exactly what to do and what not to do. In fact during those days we needed this kind of guidance as we could not think straight and were bowed down by pressures of all kinds." Divulged Linda.

"In fact, after everything was predicted He told us that we had come here and were now under the protection of Goddess and She would make sure that we would not come to any harm...something we both were worried about." Informed Clement.

"We had not done anything wrong. Harmed nobody. Wished no one ill but yet we were really suffering but all through He kept reassuring us that nothing ill would happen to us..."

"He also emphasised that in fact these troubles were a blessing in disguise as the problems would make us better people and also make us recognise who are our own and who are not. Also if these troubles had not come later on we would have been in a far worse situation. Also I had lost my job...though I was on the rolls I had to leave the company, but Swamiji kept reassuring that I would not lose the job and that we would get everything back." Added Clement. "All came true. Not only did we get everything back but much more as if we had not gone through those horrid days we would not have met Devi and Swamiji. So we feel we have got much much more than we have lost out on. And no decision henceforth was made without Swamiji's approval. Once we were on the verge of allowing a friend of ours to stay with us for a few days. But, Swamiji told us to refuse. We then did not understand but complied. After sometime we found out that this friend was very badly addicted to drugs and she would have caused us grave trouble had we kept her. So now without Devi's and Swamiji's blessings we take no decision. Sometimes logic does not apply but faith is most important. Very recently I got a great offer from another company. Swamiji told me to refuse the offer. I did so. In a short while that organisation closed down. Thus though logically I should have taken the job our faith in Them has saved us from so much trouble."

"In fact, this child of ours is called Devi's child. We have named her after one of the name's of Devi. We call her Shivani...one of the names of Devi," said Linda.

"One thing I am certain of and that is if you have faith then you can ask for no more. We were supposed to move into our new house but kept postponing it as moving in the house meant added expense in refurbishing and taxes etc. But Swamiji told us that only if we moved into the new house would our remaining financial problems be taken care of. Now we thank our stars we listened to Swamiji as really now we are so much better off. Also He had told us that after the birth of our daughter things will get much better and so is true. Also now at the moment I am working outside Bangalore. I visit every Sunday and try to come here at least twice a month though my wife nearly makes it every Sunday. I am working out of Bangalore due to Devi's and Swamiji's instructions. He has told me that till He does not give me an approval I should keep working out of Bangalore and very soon the time would come when I can shift back. You know, we had to pay a huge monthly instalment, huge, almost twice what was coming in. He told us, not to worry Devi would take care. Believe me all the instalments were taken care of. Don't ask me how, but, at the end of the month, we had money to pay off our loans. We have never defaulted. In fact, we even stopped worrying. Devi and Swamiji have helped us so much that we will be forever indebted to Them," informed Clement.

Lalit was still in the mandir. It was obvious that he had made this whistle stop to Bangalore for just a few hours, as he needed guidance from Devi and Swamiji for something really important. This is the type of faith that most people have in Devi and Swamiji. They do not mind going through any expense and trouble just to be able to spend some time being guided by Her through Her messenger.

I saw Sunil sitting with his entire family and decided that it was best that I heard his experiences too as in Bangalore Sunil assisted Swamiji in a number of important as well as mundane matters. Swamiji relied on Sunil and was obviously fond of him. That was obvious from the way it was Swamiji who had insisted the day before that Sunil should come into the temple for a healing session. Within a few minutes Swamiji had healed Sunil and had taken the severe cramp in the leg onto Himself. This had happened before my very eyes and thus there was no question of being informed by a third party.

"I am Sunil G. Patel and met Swamiji in the year 1997. Ironically I used to pass through this road since the year 1990. I used to bow down to Ma from outside but never ever entered the temple complex. Then in the year 1997, Swamiji came over to my office to purchase some cleaning acid. My father was alive then. He wanted to pay for the stuff He had taken but we told Him that as whatever He had purchased was for the temple we did not want any money. Though He insisted I told Him that we do not charge anybody if they are purchasing something for a religious or a noble cause. He was pleased with such an attitude and before leaving He told me, that I was suffering from Nag Dosh, (the Serpent Curse) and that it would be best if I went to Subramaniya and performed the required poojas. He even offered to guide me and told me to come to the temple so that He could tell me exactly what was required to be done.

"Those days we were flying really high. My parents were healthy, my wife and children were all right, my business was doing really well and to top it all I had a factory some forty odd kilometers from here that was also doing very well. We had our own bungalow and though I had invested around forty lakh rupees on the factory it was doing very well and there was nothing to worry about. I still remember Swamiji before leaving the shop turned back and told me not to take His advice lightly as once disaster struck it would be irreparable.

"When Swamiji told me that I had Nag Dosh it did not occur to me, that just a few months back I was responsible for killing a cobra. You see before meeting Swamiji, a few months I had entered my house when I saw this cobra in our compound. Nobody but I noticed it and committed a grave mistake, by telling the watchman to have the cobra killed. He did so and that was the end to that matter. I had clean forgotten about this incident. Anyway a few months after Swamiji's visit my problems began. My father who had always been hail and hearty first got a severe heart attack, he had to undergo surgery and then he died soon thereafter. My factory that had been running smoothly began to face all sorts of unexpected problems. My business that had been doing really well began to suffer. In fact, within months our entire life turned upside down. It was as though which ever way I turned there were only problems of varying degrees. It came to a stage that I wanted to sell my factory but could not though there were buyers willing to purchase it. It felt like holding a plate of food and still not be able to eat the meal.

"Months after that one day sitting with a numerologist friend, he recommended that I should visit Kuke Subramaniya. The moment this friend recommended Subramaniya, a familiar bell began to ring in my subconscious. I was certain that somebody else too had recommended this same pilgrim spot. In the end, I remembered Swamiji and decided to go and meet Him immediately. But even after many attempts I could not arrange a meeting with Him. In the end I decided to visit Subramaniya, perform the necessary poojas and then meet Swamiji. I was supposed to leave the next day when I decided to take a chance and meet Swamiji. To my luck, He was there. That day, He hardly spoke to me. He just made sure that I had made the right arrangements but even then He did not tell me that He had a guest-house and that I should stay there.

"We reached Subramaniya and within half an hour were out of the lodge where we had previously booked. We wanted something better and landed up at *Ashraya*, Swamiji's lodge. I saw

Devi's photograph at the entrance and met an acquaintance, who informed that this lodge belonged to Swamiji. You will not believe it, but fifteen days after the pooja, everything began to fall in place. We had been trying to sell the factory for months without success, virtually it immediately got sold. My business that was doing badly began to do well. My mother who was keeping bad health, began to recover and get back to normal. Problems that we were facing all of a sudden began to ease. I mean it was as though a miracle was taking place. Slowly I began to visit Devi and Swamiji daily. Then one day, during prediction Devi told me that She had given me an opportunity to prevent all the misfortune that we underwent but we had ignored the warning, henceforth never to take Her words lightly. Now whether it is a small issue or a major step to be undertaken, nothing is done without Devi's and Swamiji's consultation."

Suddenly the door opened and Lalit came out of the mandir. He looked like another man. When he had entered for the prediction he was tensed and edgy. Now he was relaxed, beaming and the happy-go-lucky person one is so used to interacting with.

DEVI AND SWAMIJI

After a short while, the prediction session was concluded. We all were seated next to the silver temple that is situated in the middle of Devi's mandir and the Ganesha and Nag idols that are nearest to the main gate. We all stood up when Swamiji walked towards us and after he was seated the usual warm and humorous chatter broke forth from all sides. There was a mention in the newspaper about a lady monk who had fasted for a few weeks and now lay in a critical condition suffering from various health problems.

"I do not believe in fasting to come closer to God. I believe that one should not be greedy but food is important for the functioning of the body and the mind. If these two are in proper condition automatically one can concentrate on the demands of the soul.

"I always tell Ma that tell me to do anything but all this

fasting-basting is beyond me. And if you still insist that I should fast then do me one favour, all those years when I did not have money to eat food and had to fast compulsorily, you adjust those days with the days you want me to fast and then let us talk after that. But, She is a very hard taskmaster. Yes, She is full of love but She wants everything to happen Her way. She used to virtually hit me and wake me up at two in the morning. She would tell me 'go have a bath and begin worshipping Me'. So I would open my eyes and tell Her 'Ma you are My Mother. But You have a terrible sense of timing and humour. You want me to have a bath at two in the night in this cold Bangalore winter. No way.' You see in those days, I had barely enough money to feed my family. Possessing a hot water gyser or a heater was out of question. Those days winters in Bangalore were chilling cold. That too I lived all alone here and this was a jungle. So I would once again go back to sleep. Then after sometime my blanket would slide of my body. She would once again wake me up and tell me to go have the bath in hot water. I would get up and go to the bathroom and there would be hot water in the bucket.

"I was not at all interested in how poojas are performed and all these ceremonies. She taught me everything on Her own. Those mornings were like my training ground. My schooling. She has taught me around more than hundred ways of performing the Havan Kund. And the fire used to be lit on its own. You know I don't think there is anybody living at the moment in this world, who can claim that He has spent days and nights experiencing virtually the physical presence of God. I can claim that forget the physical presence I have been slapped virtually every morning by God/Goddess so that They could teach me a few things about religion and spirituality. Believe me, I have been hit by Her very often. She has a strong hand, My Goddess. Solid thrashing I have received. Trust me Goddesses, are no laughing matter. Not to be taken lightly. Till everything is all right She will do everything for you but you start disobeying Her and God help you. In fact, where Devi is concerned even God will not be able to help you as Gods are known to approach Devi when They are in trouble. Goddesses are dangerous. Take me for example. I was not interested in becoming a Swamiji. I was a carefree and happy-go-lucky man. She actually forced me to get into this field of service. So often even now I tell Her that now I am tired of all these predictions and seva to everybody. But does She listen or even bother? No! She wants me to serve people and She will make sure that I follow exactly what She wants out of me. Once when I was very adamant of leaving all this, She told me one thing that really made sense. She said ' do you think you will ever get an opportunity like this to serve mankind. Do you think you will ever get another birth like this to help people and thereby help yourself also. I have given you an opportunity make the best use of it.

"You know when my mother expired, I did not have money to even buy the wood to perform the last rites. Somebody gave me some two hundred odd rupees. After all the last rites were performed I sat in the mandir and told Ma that 'now I am all alone. My mother, my father and my sister all are dead and gone. I am alone in this world. Yes, I have a wife and children but they have come later on but the bond with my parents and sister is so strong that now they are no more I really feel all alone in this world. So who should I call out when I want some solace and love. My mother too is dead and gone. Who do I call out to?' Then Devi said just one sentence 'you stay with me....I will take care of you'. And to tell you the truth, now if there is somebody for me, then it is Devi. I am living in Her protection and comfort. I do not depend upon anybody but Devi."

"But, Swamiji we are also with You. We are part of the same family."

"Yes, Lalit that is true. You know everybody is of the opinion that Devi has hundred hands and hundred heads. I don't think that is the case. According to me all our hands are Her hands. Everybody's hand is Her hand. Now can you imagine how many hands Devi must be having. Similarly She has innumerable eyes and innumerable heads. Thus though She has just two hands and two eyes but when all Her devotees come together to serve Her can you imagine what a force, She becomes. Do you know the power She has got. You ask for a prediction. You ask about something in America and within two seconds She will give you the complete description and scenario of that place and situation. Ask Her about anything happening anywhere in the universe and She will be able to give you the answer in a second. That is how I can answer any sort of question for She shows me the entire universe. I sit in the mandir and describe your cestral house thousands of miles away. I do it all the time. How is that possible? I do it for She shows me like a movie the entire place and scenario. That is why we can answer questions pertaining to past, present and the future. We can answer about unseen people, dead people, living people...what they have done and what they should be doing...everything comes in front of me like a movie...and all this is possible because of Ma Mookambika. Nothing can be hidden from God. It is not possible for God really is everywhere. Only when you understand this most of your troubles will be wiped out. You will never think you are ever alone. You will always be careful before cheating or hurting somebody. You will not want to deceive anybody and you will not get scared of anybody knowing that there is a Power that is seeing and protecting you through out."

SPINNING BLESSINGS

While Swamiji began the usual predictions, Mr. B. K. Goyal, introduced himself to me and began to narrate his fascinating story of his interaction with Swamiji.

"When I went to meet Swamiji with a close friend of mine, we were apprehensive that we would not get an audience for a prediction. But Devi was so kind that virtually immediately we were taken into the temple and Swamiji sat down for predictions. He asked me what I wanted. I told Him that I had come for blessings and not really a prediction but for some odd reason on that day I kept speaking aloud the fact that I knew the Chairman of KSFC. This stands for Karnataka State Finance Corporation. I myself did not understand why I kept telling Him of my links with KSFC as Swamiji is a spiritual personality and what possible interest would such a Chairman have for Him. Anyway, I once again visited the temple the next Sunday and was fortunate to have darshan and once again I blurted out that I knew Maheshan, the Chairman of KSFC. When I reached home I was really upset with myself. I mean where was the need to talk about a financial corporation to Swamiji that too in a temple. A few days later Swamiji telephoned and told me that He wanted to meet Maheshan, the chairman of KSFC as He wanted to start a guesthouse in Kuke Subramaniya and He needed a loan to complete the project. It seems Swamiji was trying to get in touch with Maheshan but for some reason the meeting was not taking place and that is why Devi forced me to time and again blurt out my connections with the chairman.

"I thanked Devi for allowing me to be of some use to Her and Swamiji as after the meeting took place the funding was allotted and the guest-house project started. This incident itself took place in the early eighties. Since then Swamiji has been my father-mother; brother and guide; friend and confidant. He is everything rolled into one for me and I am blessed to have Devi and His blessings on me and my family every moment of the day and night. I must tell you an interesting incident that took place years ago. You see I wanted to make a silver *Kalash* (cask) for Devi. I am a business-man dealing in pump sets and generators but those days I was going through a tough time. I inquired how much a silver cask would cost and was told around 6000 rupees. Those days, 6000 rupees was a big amount and I did not have so much money so I inquired how much a smaller version would cost and half the price was quoted. I did not have that much money too either. So eventually, I said I shall make for Devi a copper cask. Then I conveniently forgot about my promise. Now whenever there is a *Chandi Homa*, I stand by Swamiji and hold Him as when in a trance and with the crowd one has to manage Swamiji. Now during *Chandi Homa* hundreds of devotees gather and in this temple there isn't even space for a fly to move about freely. Anyway a few of us were with Swamiji, and the bells were tolling and drums were beating and it was really very charged when suddenly I saw some white flash of light pass by me on the left side. It was a dazzling flash of light and I was surprised that nobody had noticed something so spectacular. When I looked around to my surprise I saw this copper cask spinning like a top very close to me. It kept spinning for a while and then it stopped very close to me. I inquired from a few people close to me but they were deaf and blind to my existence. I picked up the cask and saw it had a dent on it. I looked around but nobody was bothered about me or the cask. Eventually, I asked Swamiji, as to what was I supposed to do with the cask and He began to laugh very loudly. It was a real loud laugh and I found the whole incident rather strange. You understand my situation don't you?"

"Of course, flying casks and laughing Swamijis make a strange combination."

"Exactly. Anyway the havan got over and I placed the cask in the mandir and went home. There at home I picked up a cask, I had at home and tried to make it spin like a top. I tried and tried but to no avail. The cask would fall flat and rattle for sometime and that was it. There was certainly no spinning and flashes of light around. In the end, I telephoned Swamiji and He told me to come over and we would ask Devi. When I asked Devi, She came through Swamiji and laughed the same kind of laugh that I had heard yesterday. Then it struck me, that when I had asked Swamiji about the cask, He had not laughed but it had been Devi who had laughed. Then Devi said that 'I have given him the prasad'. Then when the prediction was over and I told Swamiji what Devi had spoken through Him, He told me 'salla, Devi gives you prasad and you leave it lying around. Go get your cask'. There were around fifty casks but only one with a dent. I still have the cask at home. It protects me and my family all the time."

FROM THE JAWS OF DEATH

"But one incident I shall never forget is how Swamiji through His prayers and beseeching to Devi saved the life of my son. One day before my son really fell ill, I landed up at the mandir, though I had not planned it and for the first time Devi made Swamiji give me a coconut that was blessed by Devi and Swamiji. He told me, to immediately install it in the prayer room at my house. I did so though I was also surprised as to how I landed up at the mandir and why Swamiji was so insistent that the coconut be installed immediately in the prayer room. All day through I had this strange feeling that something was going to go wrong. It was a gut feeling. Anyway in the morning at around six I went to wake up my son for his exams and the door would not open. We knocked and knocked but to no avail and only after saying a prayer to Devi and Swamiji that the door opened and we were shocked to see our son all white and almost death-like. Trust me, it was the prayer and the power generating from the blessed Coconut and Lime that gave my son the strength to walk up to the door and open it. Because, according to the doctors they could not believe that in so critical a state and virtually unconscious my son could have walked and opened the door.

"My son suffered from some acute food poisoning. It was so acute that when we rushed him to the hospital the doctor was certain that my son would not survive. He was frothing from his mouth and it was a lost cause. Before rushing him to the hospital I had telephoned Swamiji and He had told me that He would make sure that by 4 o'clock that afternoon my son would be out of danger. The doctor spoke a different language but I had full faith in my Mother and my Guru. So much faith that I left the hospital and went about my work. I attended a court case and then went about my business. Exactly at 4.05 in the afternoon the doctor tapped my wife and told her that a miracle had taken place and that my son's toe had moved which itself was a sure sign that he was on the way to recovery. Unknown to me, Swamiji in the temple was lighting an oil lamp every half an hour and praying for my son's health and long life. So many of my friends told me that Swamiji was tensed all day through and every half an hour He would go to Devi and light a lamp in front of Her statue and pray for my son's health." He stopped speaking as tears began to flow down his cheeks. It was obvious that the incident had left a deep gnash on his sub-conscious.

"I shall never ever forget what Swamiji did for my son, for I know for sure, that if He had not intervened on behalf of us, we would have lost our son. But, when He told me that my son would be out of danger at 4 o'clock, I knew He would stick to His word. That is why though everybody thought me mad I went about my work just to show Devi and Him that their word was law to me." Believe me, I don't know how many of us would show such faith at similar times of crisis. Believe me, you do not meet heroes only in the battlefield. They are all around us going about silently with their lives."

"In fact, let me narrate to you a very recent incident. On 7th July I had an angina problem. Today is 15th July. A few of my friend's telephoned Him and He said that I had two blocks and I would have to go in for angioplasty and all would be well and I had nothing to worry about. Exactly as He had predicted, I had two blocks and doctors advised angioplasty. I was advised a week's stay in the hospital and from the hospital I am coming here directly. I have not gone home or any other place. He told me that now I had nothing to worry about and that He wanted me to meet you and speak to you about my experiences. So here I am straight from the hospital. He is everything for me. When I need to talk about my problems He becomes my father and mother but there are times we spend hours together cracking jokes one after the other, those times He is my best friend."

To talk to such devotees makes you feel very humble. Their devotion and love and dependence is so great and palpable that you can actually feel it when one is in the same room with them. This is not an exaggeration. I am not prone to either rhetorical overstatements or wanting to sprinkle a dash of poetic mysticism in the life of this amazing Sage who is guided by the Supreme Force, Ma Mookambika. You have to be physically present to feel the vibrations and the love and the faith and most of all the love that devotees especially in Bangalore have for Devi and Swamiji.

As mentioned before, devotees all over love Devi and Swamiji but in Mumbai the love has traces of the present year's balance sheet and the stuck up projects or a non-profitable project. In Bangalore and other places, there is love and regard that transcends the stock market and the debit and credit accounts and moves closer to a spiritual realm. I do not wish to be condescending or judgemental. Just stating an observation. Of course without an iota of doubt, whenever the need for funding of a social project is concerned, the major chunk of financial assistance has poured through from Mumbai. Very often, the finance has come through liberally and whole-heartedly, albeit only when the realisation has dawned that the project, very close to the heart of Swamiji would be postponed indefinitely.

Swamiji was still in the prediction room. Cups of coffee and plates of fried potatoes were being passed around. I settled for the coffee and avoided the tempting potatoes. Though of course, after being fed those heavy meals by Swamiji a few fried potatoes would hardly matter to the increasing weight count.

MIRACLES GALORE

"Hello, I am Narayan Shanbaug. I know Swamiji, since twenty-five years. With the grace of Ma and Swamiji we have been taken care of always. In late 80s, we got a very good proposal for my sister's marriage. The only problem was that we did not have the money to hold the wedding in a big way. We needed a minimum of fifty thousand rupees and we did not have so much money. Those days, fifty thousand was a large amount. Anyway, we came here and Ma through Swamiji said that we must go ahead with the marriage and that I should not worry as She and Swamiji would take care of all the expense. Will you believe it, actually well wishers and those who owed us money but had refused to pay us, they on their own accord came and gave us money. The wedding took place with such pomp and grandeur that even if we had spent ten lakh rupees we could not have managed such pomp and show. Even now people talk about the wedding. When you have Ma and Swamiji on your side you really don't have to worry at all."

I have not mentioned a number of cases where childless couples have become proud parents of mischievous children or those being admitted to hospitals have been told to pull out the tubes, shove the medical rules under the carpet and walk out of the medical institution expeditiously. Neither have I gone into details regarding the number of cases where trained engineers have given instructions to dig bore wells in a particular place and the tenant on the advice of Swamiji digs exactly opposite on the other side of the plot. Of course what further stuns the engineer is that the advice given by Swamiji was through the phone and to add further insult to injury it is not only accurate but the water gushes out as though there is no tomorrow. I have also not gone into details regarding those cases where dry wells have all of a sudden become pregnant with water (all the year through) just because Swamiji took one round of the well and left behind a Blessed Lime near the entrance of the well.

All this may defy one's sense of logic or scientific ground rules but then we are dealing with a totally different dimension where such metaphysical happenings are viewed as normal day to day events, more of a rule than an exception. In such a play, ground laws of physics and natural rules do not apply. We Indians take it all in our stride. We are exposed to the spiritual, paranormal, metaphysical side of nature and to the Spirit world. At times of difficulty or strife, we are surprised when the Heavens do not collaborate with us and throw in a miracle or two for good measure. Miracles for us are a part of life. We are stunned when the heavens play dumb and deaf. But for people from the West, they might find many things that I have penned hard to accept and digest and it really is not their fault. They have been conditioned to believe, since they could first burp and gurgle, that logic and hard cash rule the roost. All of a sudden to acknowledge that in the world of faith and surrender there is no place for logic is itself a bolt out of the blue. Accepting the philosophy, that, each one of us is looked after, only if we allow Them to do Their job, itself requires a certain bent of mind.

The Bible so clearly states that none is as blind as the person who refuses to see. In fact, that is solely why on the back cover of my previous book *The Last Marathon*, I have not published the synopsis of what the book contains or the silly mug of my face grinning from ear to ear. Instead, I allowed to be printed only a simple quote I found in one of our Avesta prayer books. It says...

> *For those who believe in God, no explanation is necessary.*
> *For those who do not believe in God, no explanation is possible.*

Murli and I reached the airport, as usual, hours before the flight. Murli has something about arriving at the airport long before the pilot has even woken up. So we sat, our mouths stuffed with tobacco, watching people from different parts of the country and the globe, in different states of temperament. Journeys usually bring out the worst or the best in most of us.

"I am so happy that the meeting regarding the hospital is going to take place. Swamiji is really very keen on getting it up and about soon. You awake or what?"

"Vijay is coming along with us specifically for this work. He will return with us too. Tell me, have you ever seen Swamiji go in a trance? "

"No."

"This is the biggest *havan* that takes place. Tomorrow is not only His birthday but also the day when Ma Mookambika first appeared before Swamiji about thirty years ago. Though Swamiji goes in a trance like this four times in a year, this day is very special. Hundreds of devotees will gather and it is really an experience."

"When will Lalit and Samir and the remaining gang arrive..."

"Tomorrow. So today is important. Lot of doctors and surgeons shall be meeting Swamiji and us today..."

"Why doctors..."

"According to Swamiji, He wants the medical fraternity to take an active part even in the conceptualisation process, as He feels that their suggestions will be so much more constructive and practical then all of ours put together. They will also give suggestions from the viewpoint of helping the maximum number of patients..."

"That's Vijay."

Vijay shook hands with both of us and got his bag tagged in and then took us to the first class passenger cabin, where he ordered coffee and got down to work immediately.

"I have got my architects to draw up a beautiful first draft. I hope Swamiji likes it but Murlibhai, I have drawn up a state of the art hospital and not just a few bed-nursing-home like area..."

"Let's see what Swamiji and Ma Mookambika have to say about it..."

"From my side, Swamiji knows He has full co-operation. I have promised to put money mentioned for this project plus I shall be visiting the site of construction once every fortnight. I shall stay at Subramaniya for two days and see that the project is completed in the shortest period of time."

"Samir has also promised an equal amount..."

"That is very good but Murli I still think we should hold a meeting and get other devotees to contribute towards this noble cause."

Murli gave his reasons for not wanting to hold the meeting, fearing that the Mumbai crowd would not respond with the same enthusiasm, where coughing up cash was concerned.

"I don't believe this Murlibhai. Why would our people not wholeheartedly support this venture when they know it is for such a noble cause and especially when they know how dear this hospital is to Swamiji's heart. I mean after what Ma Mookambika and Swamiji have done for them, why would they not co-operate..."

"I agree with Murli. I mean forget coughing up money, most of the devotees, the so called inner group do not have the inclination to give me the time of the day to be interviewed for the book. How many times have they been reminded and how many co-operated? If they can't cough up time and their contact list, you really think they are going to cough up hard cash. Forget it..."

"No Ruzbeh, I really feel if we..."

"Compared to Swamiji's devotees in Bangalore, the devotees in Mumbai are only interested in their balance sheet. That is my opinion and this is horrible coffee." Giving my two bit opinion, I opened my novel and got absorbed in the story.

At the security, our bags were once again checked just before boarding the plane. My bag was filled with mini recording cassettes, a dictaphone, a walkman, books, clothes and sandal wood for the Havan.

"Why so many cassettes?" Inquired the security.

"See those guys I am travelling with. They are scientists and bore the hell out of me with their constant blabber of gravity and cavity. I need as much diversion as possible." The security eyed Murli and Vijay, nodded sympathetically at me and let me pass through.

In the plane, after the air-hostess once again performed gymnastics regarding basic security measures, we sat down, chatting about how the hospital should look and how soon it should be got on its feet, so that the maximum number of needy people can avail of its benefits.

"So Vijay, tell me how you met Swamiji?"

Vijay handed me the tray of breakfast and informed the airhostess that he would refrain from any meal or drink.

"As you must be knowing Ruzbeh, I am into the construction business. My father expired in 1995 and after his death, unfortunately there was a family dispute and you know how all this upsets your state of well-being. Around that time I had constructed a very prestigious club known as 'Club Aquaria' and I had really invested lot of funds in it. Unfortunately, there was a general recession in the market and the club got a poor response and because of so much money locked into it, I was going through great financial strain.

"Murlibhai and Samir are my Chartered Accountants but they are more than just professional acquaintances. In fact they are like my brothers. They realised that my position was not very strong and I was really going through a hard period, so they informed me about Swamiji. In fact it was July 1998 and they told me that Swamiji was coming from Bangalore and He would be staying over at either of their houses. So they told me to just come and take His blessings. Frankly, I agreed and even went to meet Swamiji as a formality. I did not want to hurt their sentiments. Also, when a person is going through a rough period, he does not mind trying to knock at different places and hope that God will have mercy on him. I went all alone. Usually, I involve my family...wife and daughter...in all that I do but I was worried that they would laugh at me or think I have gone mad by going and meeting Swamiji.

"The moment I met Swamiji, He began telling me things that I had not told anybody and also telling me things that I myself was not aware of. He told me all about my father and about my family that I had no inkling of. So, I went home and narrated all this to my mother, brother, wife and daughter. Now even my mother was not aware of certain things that Swamiji had narrated, so we telephoned my father's eldest sister and narrated to her all that Swamiji had informed me. To our surprise and shock, she informed, that whatever Swamiji had told us was cent per cent accurate."

"Then, I remembered that Swamiji had even told me that there was a broken Ganesh idol in our pooja room. I had disagreed but asked my wife to go and check whether there was a broken Ganesh idol in the prayer room. My wife went and checked and to our greater surprise she consented that one Ganesh idol indeed was broken. So the next morning with my entire family, I once again met up with Swamiji. He then divulged so many things about our past and predicted our future that we had no other option but realise that we were in the midst of a towering personality.

"Swamiji told us that my family suffered from *Nag Dosh* (curse of the Serpent) and then very casually told us that my father had made a wish to visit Vaishno Devi and that the commitment was still pending. My mother agreed that my father had desired to visit Vaishno Devi. He asked us to go to Subramniya for *Nag Dosh* and then visit Ma Mookambika's temple."

I returned my break-fast tray and then looked outside the window. It was a nice clear sky and the pilot announced that we were flying some twenty thousand odd feet high and that it was minus fifteen degrees and implied that he was doing us a major favour by making certain the airplane maintained earthly temperature.

"Swamiji, later visited the Club and told me that there existed a very old temple at a particular spot, which was even visited by Shivaji Maharaj, and asked me to reconstruct a small temple and give respect to the Power that existed there. Soon after the construction of the temple the Club began to do reasonably well."

MARITAL PROBLEMS AND MIRACLE CURES

"One day, I took my sister to meet Swamiji. He looked at her and said that she had a daughter living in America. My sister agreed that her daughter was married and living there. Then Swamiji told her something that shook her very roots. He told her that her daughter's marriage was facing severe problems and that there was no chance of the marriage coming out intact through the rough weather. This came as a rude surprise to us all, as we were not aware that something was wrong with her marriage. Upon inquiry, she agreed. My sister and brother-in-law tried very hard to make the marriage work but to no avail. When she met Him again, Swamiji informed her that if she would send her daughter back to her husband, she would commit suicide. So in the end we got mentally prepared for her to divorce her husband.

"Now in my community, it is very difficult for a divorcee woman to remarry but Swamiji assured us that we will get a good boy, who will be like a son to the family. In no time, just as Swamiji had predicted, we got a very good proposal for my niece. Swamiji asked us to get her married on August 25th. But the problem was that we had just applied for a divorce and the date fixed by Swamiji was just round the corner. But by now, our faith in Swamiji and Ma Mookambika was so well rooted that we went ahead and began to make plans for the marriage. Everyday we made the rounds of the court to get the divorce passed but for some reason or the other the date would keep getting postponed. Wedding cards were printed and even distributed and still no divorce. We were all apprehensive. Till August 20th the divorce was not sanctioned but Swamiji was firm and told us to go ahead with the preparations and not to doubt Ma Mookambika. On

August 22nd, the divorce proceedings were postponed to August 24th. You can imagine our state...then Swamiji told me to take a Lime and throw it in the court room, and on August 24th, at 4.10 p.m. just sometime before closing, we received the divorce papers and the next day the wedding took place as per schedule."

"Really amazing."

"And the most amazing thing is that not once did Swamiji waver or change His mind. He was certain, that Ma Mookambika would see through the matter. Another important thing is that Swamiji never has asked for money for Himself. He always insists on feeding the poor and the needy and serving them. He is always there for everybody, rich or the poor. You can call Him up at the oddest hours and He is there. He is really amazing."

The air-hostess announced that the plane was about to land and hinted that those who did not have their seat belts around their waist would either be flung out of the plane or get a nasty creak in the neck.

It felt good to be so near Ma Mookambika and Swamiji.

I woke up to find Murli fast asleep. We had gone to sleep rather late, around two-thirty, discussing various issues ranging from Sai Baba of Shirdi and Swamiji to Laloo Prasad Yadav and other amazing Indian politicians. The sky still had a darkish silver tinge to it and the wind that waltzed through, caressed my face with her cold fingers. Paid my obeisance to Lord Krishna, Ma Radha and Lord Hanuman and then looked down to see tents erected for the *Chandi Havan*. Today was Swamiji's birthday and after fifteen minutes, I went down and saw the boys busy at work.

Chandi Havan is a big day at Ma Mookambika temple and when it falls on August 2nd, it takes on mammoth proportions what with it coinciding with Swamiji's birthday. In 1970 or there about, it was on this day that Ma Mookambika revealed Herself to Swamiji in all Her glory. I bowed down to Ma and then took Swamiji's blessings.

"Happy Birthday, Swamiji!"

"Ahhh Ruzbeh." He was visibly embarrassed and accepted the parcel of sandal wood with a smile." Come let us go for our coffee. Where is Murli?"

"Sleeping like a log and snoring like a flute." He laughed uproariously and after giving instructions to the boys busy at work we left for our usual Café. As usual, we had our three-course meal and finished it with piping hot coffee. It felt nice to be with Swamiji and in the familiar routine. Whilst walking back, we saw posters of various Sages proclaiming to dish out, from instant kundalini awakening to instant God realisation.

"Temples and Swamijis should not be publicised and marketed. We are not filmstars like Raj Kapoor or Raj Kumar. In fact, most Swamijis are products of good marketing. To become a Swamiji or a Sage you need to be blessed from the Great Power, what ever you may call that Power. Blessings are given to those who are destined. If you are destined to meet your Guru, you will meet Him or Her. You don't need to publicise God. That is why I have never marketed Ma Mookambika. She gave you the permission to write the book only because there are so many people going through hard times that they can be really helped.

I can easily make tons of money by just hiring a good PR firm and within a month amass lots of wealth. You know I can..."

"No doubts Swamiji." In fact, our Swamiji has often got offers from big industrial houses to help them increase their market stakes through the grace of Ma Mookambika and be a partner in the spoils.

"Now, you see the temple and the building and feel that Swamiji is rich and well off. What most people do not see is the years and years of sacrifice and abject poverty that Swamiji and His family have undergone to reach this stage of comfort. For nine years I lived all alone in this place. There was just a temple and a small kitchen. Nothing else. I used to sleep in the night in front of the temple. During rains, the roof used to make sure that every drop of rain was invited to enter and drop within. So, I used to often sleep with an umbrella in my hand and lie down on a jute sleeping bag. I used to be often drenched but I will tell you something...those were the best days of my life. Though those days were really hard they were the best. Just the Goddess and Me. I used to get sleep immediately and whatever little I earned through predictions was spent on Goddess, family and then if left, on myself. Of course those days even one rupee or fifty-paisa was important. Hard days but I was never alone. She was always with Me and My family. People now only see the big temple and the big house. Nobody knows the struggle that we have gone through. But as I said, that is all okay as Goddess was always with Me." We reached the temple gate and Swamiji got busy with directing one and all about the preparation.

When I reached the guest-room, Murli was awake, bathed and ready as punch. We spoke about the plans for the day and he insisted that he was not going to eat a morsel of food for the rest of the day. I nodded my head and said if wishes were horses and then went in for bath. By the time I got ready, Vishnu, a hard working lad who constantly greeted you with a smile, announced that breakfast was ready and that I was called down to eat grub. When I reached the hall, I saw Murli sitting in front of a plate spilling over with dosas and idlis and whatnot. He stared at his food sullenly and I could not avoid grinning.

"I thought somebody was not going to touch a single morsel today." He pretended not to hear me and with an audible sigh began to eat the laid out tiffin. "Thank your silly stars you woke up late as I have already eaten the same thing an hour earlier." He groaned out loud and shoved another morsel in his mouth.

"You have enough cassettes ready, for today."

"Yeah. By the way is India playing today or what?"

"Yes and we are going to be beaten today also..."

"Nobody can touch us today. Swamiji's birthday, *Chandi Havan*, I mean if we can't win on this day we should stick to marbles."

"How is Swamiji feeling today?"

"It's a miracle He is completely alright, for yesterday He was really down and out."

We concluded our tiffin in silence and drank the coffee. After that we went down and met Swamiji.

"Oh good-morning! What happened about meditating whole night. You boys were snoring..."

"That was Murlin snoring, Swamiji. He snores loud enough for two people..."

"I thought I would have to wake you up and that is why I did not come down for meditation." Murli said it with a straight face. In reality, the bugger was flat on his back, oblivious to the dashed word.

The morning passed in meeting the same people I had interviewed last time and they greeted me warmly. They all inquired as to the progress of the book and whether it would be completed within a few days.

"With Ruzbeh, nothing gets completed in a few days. He takes a month to write just a letter." Murli spoke in all seriousness. We were standing near the gate of the mandir when we heard a loud crash. We saw a car and an auto that had collided with each other. Suddenly from nowhere, Swamiji came out and walked briskly to the scene of the accident. There was a crowd already gathered. An aged man had been injured and was screaming at the top of his voice, saying rather unpleasant things in a language I could not understand a word of. I assume that the general gist of the conversation was that each one involved tried to doubt the parentage of the other and spoke things that would be censored even by a liberal censor board.

Swamiji took hold of the aged man and very coolly put him in the same car that was involved in the collision. He assured the screaming man that nothing had cracked and that he was going to be all right and that it would be best to get an x-ray just to be on the safe side. After the car zoomed off, He walked back to the mandir.

"It was the old man's fault, but there is no sense in wasting time blaming each other. We most often waste precious time in just accusing each other than in getting the job done. Come, let us go up and have some snacks." I looked at Murli, who had this resigned look on his face but his eyes twinkled.

"Swamiji, Murli says he is on a diet and might not join us." I spoke this with a straight face. An Oscar deserving performance.

"What nonsense. Come on Murli, you too must eat with us."

"I keep telling him, that without petrol the car cannot move." I winked at Murli who sighed loudly.

"No, he shall eat with us. Right Murli."

"As you say, Swamiji."

We climbed to the first floor. Both Murli and I were rather tired with this constant climbing of the stairs. But Swamiji who was twice our age and more, never once seemed to tire of the constant exertion. In fact, in a day He might easily be climbing twenty to thirty times the two-floor staircase.

There were a number of people who had assembled to partake of food, a sweet dish, steaming coffee and (for those who desired) there was even hot milk. When I entered the dinning room I saw Murli with a laden tray speaking to a few friends. Murli introduced me to them and informed them that I was a medium of Sai Baba of Shirdi and had been instructed to write this book on Devi and Swamiji. By now a number of Swamiji's devotees were aware of me being a medium, all thanks to Murli.

He has no ego and unlike many devotees, who feel threatened or insecure, when their Guru spends time with other devotees, Murli is an exception. So very often Swamiji forces Murli to accompany Him for a meal or a walk. Murli does not like to impose his presence when Swamiji is in company. Little wonder that a number of friends called him *Chote Swamiji* (Swamiji Junior).

"I thought somebody is too full to even think of food."

"Very funny. Try refusing Him and see." He had not even completed the sentence when Swamiji instructed Vishnu to hand me a plate stuffed with food.

"Eat, Ruzbeh!"

"Yes, Swamiji." I sighed and shoved a morsel in my mouth. Murli in the background had a smile stretching from ear to ear. I drifted towards, Swamiji who was speaking to a few of the devotees.

"One should not do evil things and especially for something so trivial as money. What is the sense. You steal hundred rupees and eventually the law of karma will force you to pay the person double or more, either in this lifetime or the next. Nobody can escape the laws of destiny. Sometimes, if you are lucky, you have to finish your account in this life itself or else imagine, you have to come down here just to repay this petty amount with interest. When you come down again, you accumulate more karma and the cycle again continues. Where we are concerned, that is Swamijis, we may be aware that a devotee has committed a heinous crime, but still we protect that person. The reason is that you can get a diamond only from coal. That is the law of nature.

"You want to appreciate the colour white, then you have to accept the colour black. Only when you have the colour black, you will appreciate its contrast colour. Yes, even your Zarathushtra talks about God and the devil. To appreciate something noble, you have to experience something evil. To appreciate happiness, you have to experience sadness. Black and white. In the same way, we all have God and the devil in us. It depends on the individual, where he wants to dwell and what he wants to choose. But I cannot forsake my devotees just because they have sinned or are doing wrong. My work is to get them on the right track. Just like you have past life connections with Sai Baba of Shirdi, you all also have past life connections with me. With most of the devotees the connection is of lifetimes. I cannot forsake these children just because now they have taken a wrong path. My job is to slowly bring them back on the right path and make them walk along with Devi and Me. They are my children. Does a father forsake his children? Never. Very often good people create trouble for themselves, by either associating with crooks or allowing people to take advantage of their goodness. They create sufferings for themselves. Partly karmic-partly over goodness. Very dangerous combination."

"Swamiji what is the most important thing between a devotee and the Guru?" inquired a gentleman, after he had accidentally tripped another devotee who flew across the room with a muffled yelp.

"You must have faith. Total faith, love and surrender. Immense faith and patience is what is needed. You should not have any expectations. Just have faith in God and your Guru and They will never let you down. People want instant results. That is where their fault lies. You have to put all your faith in God, Goddess, Guru, whosoever, and then calmly live your life. You will then never be let down. They will never let Their children down. Even if there is pain and suffering in the devotee's karma, Providence will see that the child gets enough strength and wisdom to accept the situation calmly. Of course, very often, after people are helped through their crisis and their work is done, then Devi and Swamiji are forgotten. Crores of rupees are made and saved but once the work is done nobody bothers to put aside some of the money to help the needy and the poor. That is their misfortune because it is only by helping the poor and the needy does one really create positive karma. Feed the hungry; clothe the naked; shelter the homeless; take care of the sick and the ailing. That is how one serves God, Goddess and Guru."

It was now nearing mid-afternoon and Swamiji was once again in prime health. It was difficult to believe that this was the same man who just the day before needed immediate medical and herbal treatment. But then Swamiji himself had mentioned that by the day of the *Chandi Homa* He would be back on His feet and raring to go. According to Him and a number of His close devotees, every time *Chandi Homa* was to take place, a day prior, Swamiji was always very ill, needing all sorts of medical assistance. But, invariably on the D-Day, He was back on His feet, able to stand hours of trance, the heat, the smoke of the sacred fire and the surging crowd of devotees, all intent on seeking blessings of Ma Mookambika;, a prediction, a word of advice or just a glance.

I need to mention once again that sitting in a state of trance is extremely nerve wrecking and exhausting. When full possession takes place i.e. when the medium gets totally enveloped by the Spirit who is taking control, then the after-math is all the more intense. You feel as though somebody has sucked the marrow out of your bones and your blood out of your veins. It is a state of intoxication merged with exhaustion. That, is my experience and believe me, this is felt after being in a state of trance for not more than ten to fifteen minutes. Swamiji is totally possessed (where He remembers absolutely nothing) and He is in such a state for hours on end. At the age of seventy-two (2001-2002), to be able to withstand such extreme pressure, is something out of the scope of a normal human being. To add to His discomfort, the fact that a day or two before the state of trance, He is always very ill, does not help Him in any way. It is little wonder that Swamiji goes on consuming, on and off, either food or coffee, as His body is put through the grind and it needs the strength and stamina to withstand the power of Devi.

THE ONLY DOCTOR YOU NEED

The Indian Cricket team is getting a thrashing of their lives. Murli still insists that I change my mind about our team winning today. But I stick to my stand. If we lose on such an auspicious day then God help us all. Then Swamiji approached me and introduced one of His oldest devotees, B.L. Gandhi. Till now

I had met a number of people who worshipped Ma Mookambika and treated Swamiji as their Guru. B.L. Gandhi was one of those few people who not only worshipped Ma Mookambika but also worshipped Swamiji. In the sense, this thin gentleman never sat down in the presence of Swamiji. I have observed him. He remained constantly standing if Swamiji was in the same room. The only exception being, when we all sat down to eat our lunch. Even here, this man sat far away from Swamiji out of respect.

"I have been worshipping Swamiji since the past twenty-two years. I remember, it was an auspicious *Poornima* (full moon). It was my good fortune that Swamiji was there in the mandir and my turn for prediction came that very day. Ma Mookambika through Swamiji only told me one thing: 'You will have to do *seva*'. I will tell you something. I was going to die. I was going through such a bad period that it was having a severe affect on my health. Even my life line on my palm showed a short life and I will honestly tell you that my constitution and health had reached a stage, where even doctors kept telling me, that if I continued the way I was going, I would not live long. But see the grace of Ma and Swamiji. Not once did They tell me anything. I was told to come as often as I could and do *seva*...that meant I should come and spend time in the mandir and be surrounded by the healing vibrations. Swamiji would tell me to have the holy water and *prasad* (blessed food) and I followed Their directions. Trust me, I cannot tell you what I was going, through but believe me, if I did not have Mother and Swamiji, not only I but I fear even my family would not have survived the ordeal. Days turned into weeks and weeks into years and gradually we got out of that impossible situation. But through it all, Ma and Swamiji have been with me. When you go to meet Mother and Swamiji, you should go as though you are a child. Your attitude should be, 'I am your child so forgive me if I have committed a blunder or sinned. If I have sinned, forgive me Mother'.

"Trust me, since years, so many impossible things have been made possible and I know it is because of Mother and Swamiji. Yes, we have faith and have totally surrendered. They keep telling us to just have faith and totally surrender everything to Them. That is all that is asked. Never once has Swamiji asked even for a rupee. Never hinted, forget asked. It is selfless service. I mean, I am not a rich man. What benefit will Swamiji get through me. But He has never made me feel any different from any other devotee who comes to Mother and Him. That is His love for us all.

"Do you know, I have not visited a doctor since I entered Ma's abode. I mean, though I was so ill and was told I would not survive yet I have never ever gone to a doctor. Ma and Swamiji are my doctors. Can there be better doctors than Them? Never! For me the Lime, *kumkum,* the blessed water and the *Chandi Havan's* ash are the only medicines I need. I was suffering from a disease that is so rare, that doctors told me that it comes to one in a million people. Death is a certainty. But Ma Mookambika and Swamiji made sure that even death was kept at bay. I believe that whosoever comes here with total faith and surrender, they have no longer to worry about themselves or their family. I am of the firm belief that all your wishes get granted here. Nobody can give you life but with total surrender here, you might be even granted life. Remember, we all have to go through our destiny. But when you have Ma and Swamiji by your side, the journey becomes easier and the task ahead becomes lighter.

"I will give you an example of my daughter. When she first became pregnant with a child, after the delivery, the doctors told us that she should not get pregnant again. After sometime, she once again got pregnant and complications were seen at the ending stage. This time the doctor told us that they would either be able to save the child or the mother. Mangala (Swamiji's daughter), was also with us. Swamiji was in Mumbai. Amma telephoned Swamiji at around one o'clock in the morning. Swamiji told Amma to make certain that my daughter's delivery is done at Dr. Sudhir Vinekar's clinic. He telephoned them to keep everything ready. Remember, all this is happening at around one o'clock in the morning and that too when He is in Mumbai. The earlier doctor had told us that either the child or the mother would survive. With Mother's and Swamiji's grace, not only did both of them survive but a few years later, my daughter for the first time gave birth to a baby boy. Then Swamiji told her to get operated and to make certain that she did not deliver again. When the entire medical fraternity put their hands up, Ma and Swamiji very easily made the impossible take place. This is Their grace. They defy all medical and logical opinions."

Swamiji by this time was standing close to us and listening. When I looked at Him, He smiled. He made certain that another cup of coffee was put into our hands.

"Ruzbeh, everything works on faith. If you have unconditional faith in God, Goddess, Guru then nothing is impossible, but if you put conditions or try to make a business out of your faith, then it is wrong. Ten days earlier a very rich man came to me and gave me a blank cheque. He had signed it and told me to fill in whatever amount I so desired but his son was dying of cancer and he wanted Ma and me to save his son. I refused. I told him only one thing, 'if you want to make this a business deal, then I am not interested. But yes, if you have faith and trust in Devi then go put your head on Her feet and pray to Her. Who knows She might take pity on you and save your son.'

"Nobody can buy Devi and Me. We are not for sale. I was telling you just yesterday, that if I want, I can get the money for the hospital within twenty-four hours. It is not at all difficult. If Devi can make paupers into millionaires, why can't She make certain that Her own hospital gets financed without any outside help. But that is not the way She works. I mean I could easily have taken the cheque, filled in the amount I needed for the hospital and worse comes to worse, if the boy died, I could have named the hospital after the boy. You think this is how we function? So I told him only one more thing. I told him 'I will give you a Blessed Lime, costing only one rupee and your boy will be cured but please take this cheque away and never ever make the same mistake of offering a bribe to Devi or me'.

"Ruzbeh, I can tell you very honestly. There is not a man on this planet who can buy me with money. Nobody can bribe me into doing anything. For love and devotion We can move mountains but for money, I will not even move my own one hand. Money comes and goes but what is more important is humanity and one's word."

There were a number of His devotees and most of them were simple folks who could not comprehend the rich man's actions. They could understand the man's dilemma and a father's agony and frustration, for they too were parents but they could not understand how anybody could even think of offering Swamiji money to get some work done. The opinion about the rich person was divided. Some said he was a damn fool and lucky that Swamiji did not chuck him out of the mandir. Some said he was rather brave, to even have the guts and the gall to make such a ridiculous offer, to a man known never to mince words and known, never to bow down to anybody but the Supreme Power.

Murli strolled in. He entered with a friend of his, from Mumbai. He inquired if I needed anything and asked with a straight face if I wanted to have our fourth breakfast. He did not understand the smile on my face but soon comprehended when Swamiji placed a cup of coffee in his hand and asked him to eat the sweetmeat somebody had got from Mysore.

"Swamiji, Murli is not eating anything for he fears he will put on weight."

"What nonsense Murli. If the car does not have petrol how will it move."

"Yes Swamiji." I turned and faced Murli's friend. We had been introduced yesterday but I had not got his name.

BLESSED BY DEVI

"My name is Mrityu Jai Panday and I too am from Mumbai. I was introduced to Swamiji in June 1997. I also have a house in Bangalore. So, one day I got my wife and child and we sat for a prediction. The first day itself, I was smashed out of my wits. First of all, He began to tell me things about myself that I was not aware of myself. He also told me that I had a mole on my right chest and a cross on the mount of my palm, which was very auspicious. Both were very true. He also mentioned that my name and what my name should be according to astrological and *kundli* forecast were different. I said it was impossible but He

235

coolly told me to go and get it checked by my elders. I did that and He was hundred percent accurate. I was completely floored. He told me then that I should always be present during the *Chandi Homas* that take place thrice a year. Since then I have only missed one Homa."

"In the beginning of 1998, my wife and I wanted to be parents again but due to some reason or the other, she was not conceiving. I came here to Swamiji and He told me not to worry and that everything would be all right and that 'she would come'. He also told me she would be from my family itself and she was going to take a reincarnation. Fourteen days after He told me this, my wife conceived and with my daughter's birth a lot has changed in our lives. My daughter was born one day before Diwali *(Dhanteras)*. He had told us that after her birth things would change in our lives and it is true. In fact, even the naming of our daughter was done here. She is named Vaishnavi, and even the name has been given to her by Devi Hersef, through Swamiji. In fact, what happened was that Devi had told us not to name her till She did not give the name. My daughter was born on 14th October and till mid January we did not give her a name. Then during the *Chandi Homa*, when Swamiji went in a trance, and though there were hundreds of devotees, Devi walked towards my wife and child, placed Swamiji's hand on my daughter's head, blessed her and named her Vaishnauvi. The fact that there were so many people and still She remembered a small child is really amazing.

"I can only tell you one thing and that is Devi is the epitome of Courage and Bravery. You remember Her and you yourself are filled with the same sterling qualities, that are enough to take you through the river of life. I have always been a believer of righteousness and have stood for what is right. So naturally, I am surrounded by lots of detractors. As long as She and Swamiji are on my side I fear nothing and no one. I was going through crazy problems but slowly and surely I am getting back to normalcy and that is because of Her grace and Swamiji's guidance and blessings."

Swamiji once again joined us and for a while spoke to a few of His devotees. The talk once again drifted to the to-be-built hospital. It was obvious that this hospital was very close to Swamiji's heart. In fact, a number of devotees even wondered whether this hospital would be Swamiji's swan song. Very often Swamiji had mentioned to me, that He had told Ma Mookambika, that He wanted to go *home* and be with Her for eternity. He said that He had seen it all and done it all and that now it was time to move on. He has time and again hinted that He was over here in the physical plane only for one particular reason; most of us think the reason could be the successful completion and working of the hospital. Subramaniya is very close to Swamiji and He is aware that if a person even requires to be injected then the patient has to be driven miles and miles away. And God forbid, if it is a serious case then in all probability the chances of survival were rather dim.

HOSPITAL IN SUBRAMANIYA

"This hospital that we are planning to build is not being constructed by us. It is not as though I or you or he is doing anything to construct this hospital. We are not doing anything. We are making this hospital and giving Her name to the hospital because we all are Her children. We are building this hospital for the public. To help the common man. To help the poor and needy person. Ma Mookambika will make certain that this will truly be a hospital for the poor in Subramaniya. And I will tell you something that I have told nobody. Subramaniya is the most sacred place on the face of this earth. A day will come when there will not be even an inch of spare land in that holy place. You are witness from the beginning and you will bear witness when my words will come true, that there will not be one inch spare land in Subramaniya. Of course even now the Subramaniya temple (run by the Government) has a fund of twenty crore rupees. But the irony is that they are not able to build the hospital but we will succeed and who do you think will make us succeed? Ma Mookambika. They have twenty crores but they themselves told me that they cannot even think of making a hospital in such an offbeat area. They are telling me to build the hospital. Why? Because they too are aware that this is not the job of a normal

237

human being. I or you or they can do nothing. It needs divine intervention. The place has nothing. No infrastructure, no working force, no proper electrical facilities but they know that through the grace of Ma we will succeed in building this hospital.

"Why do you think all these people come right from Mumbai over here to do *seva?* Murli comes here so often. Why? Not for anything but to do *seva.* Now Vijay Wadhva and Murli will have to spend so much of their time travelling from Mumbai to Subramaniya and back but they will. Why? Just to do *seva* and who makes them do this work? Ma Mookambika. You know when I wanted to build the guest-house in Subramaniya, I wanted to construct it because all my devotees were going through inconvenience, as there was no proper accommodation. I told Ma only one thing. 'You are directing Your children to Subramaniya, so there must be some place that feels like home'. I did not have a rupee when I was told to make this guest-house. I knew Ma was with me. I went ahead and even loans were sanctioned and everything fell into place. Now the guest-house is as good as any accommodation you might get, even in the city. How did all this get accomplished? Only through Her grace. So I am not worried about the hospital too? She is with me and all will be taken care of. Yes, we have to do our work and leave all to Her.

"You remember (referring to one of the devotees), when we went to see the site to make the guest-house, first the car broke down. Then a big stone hit the windshield. We came back, got the windshield fixed and then we went again. On the way the car caught fire. In the end we reached at mid-night. There were difficulties but we did not get scared or deflated. We went about our job and then, She did Her job to make certain that the project got completed.

"Even now, I sometimes wonder why I should bother about building this hospital. I am getting on with age. I have so much responsibility over here itself. I have my devotees to take care of. Predictions to do. Temple to run. Poor to feed. From morning to night telephone calls from those in need. Why do I need to take on added responsibility of building a hospital that too in Subramaniya, which is so far from Bangalore. It takes me half a day of driving to the place and that too, the roads are not very good. Why bother? But then I know that Ma Mookambika is with Me and She wants this hospital to be made for the poor and the needy. See the irony. You know who is Nagraja? He is the commander in chief of Devi's army. This venture is Devi's venture. And what is the name of the person who is going to be in charge of constructing the hospital? Nagraja. So I always tell everybody to remember that we are doing nothing. She is doing everything. If you believe that everything is being done by God/Goddess/Guru, and you are only an instrument then there is no job, no work, no mission that cannot be handled and completed successfully. That is my firm belief. Have faith and totally surrender to your God/Goddess/Guru, do your *dharma* (duty) and leave the rest to Them. They know what is best and They will never ever let you down. That is my firm belief and promise." Saying this, He left once again to comfort and guide a devotee who had telephoned.

"So you are the Sai devotee. Hello, I am Nitya Murti. Kavita Vishwanth's friend. I was introduced to Swamiji around eight years ago. I used to always come here every week and take the blessings of Devi and Swamiji. I never asked for any sort of prediction, but would just come here for Their blessings. One night I got a very severe heart attack. It was October 16th, and exactly one year earlier I had visited Shirdi to take Sai Baba's blessings. In fact, that day the priest had singled me out and allowed me to stand in front of Baba's statue for as long as I had wished. (Usually the priests do not allow anybody to stand for more than a few seconds.) When I got the heart attack, Swamiji had been informed and He had predicted that if I survived till mid-afternoon then I would live but my state was very critical and till mid-afternoon anything could happen. Ironically, our doctor mentioned exactly the same thing to my husband. He too said that if I survived till twelve in the afternoon I would be out of danger. Anyway thanks to Ma, Baba and Swamiji as well as Kavita and her mother, I lived through the ordeal.

GOD SENT DIAGNOSIS

A few months later, we went to Madras and due to the insistence of my mother and daughter, I allowed myself to be put under observation. The doctors found two blocks and insisted on a bypass surgery. That shocked me no end. But they were insistent and this hospital is one of the best in Madras. So we booked the day of the operation and came to Bangalore to arrange for the finance. But from the station I came directly to Swamiji. He took one look at me and asked me to sit with Him for a prediction. There, He told me that I need not to go in for a bypass. In fact, He insisted that Devi would not allow a knife to touch me. He said that there was no need for a bypass and I should go for a second opinion. I did, as advised and the doctors agreed that there was no need for a bypass operation. A simple angioplasty was done and I am hale and hearty, even after seven years thanks to Ma, Baba and Swamiji."

(This is a common phenomenon. I must have met more than twenty such devotees, who have been saved from the surgical knife. In fact, so often devotees first go to Swamiji, get a diagnosis from Ma and then approach the doctor, aware well in advance, what really is wrong with them. In fact, very recently when Swamiji had come to Mumbai, he was staying at Samir Sanghvi's house. Samir's wife and he, had asked me to come over to meet Swamiji and spend some time with them in the evening. Their lovely nine-year old daughter and I share the same date of birth, and we chatted, like true Scorpios, about this and that. That evening, a family had come over. Swamiji was absolutely exhausted with the predictions he had been subjected to, for two days, at the homes of other intimate devotees. Thus Murli and Samir had made certain that till Swamiji was with them, He would not be allowed to exert Himself.

Swamiji was suffering from a nasty pain in the neck. He informed me, with a twinkle in the eyes, that the pain had got worse, thanks to the massage done by one and sundry on the previous day. When I met Him, He was exhausted and sat on the big sofa, looking like an ageing lion, who still maintained His kingly demeanour. We spoke regarding the book and He mentioned that I need not take everybody's experience as that would make the book too bulky to handle.

He asked me to keep some information for the second volume. A family arrived and Samir informed, that Swamiji would no longer be giving predictions that day. They had no problems and insisted that they had come for blessings. Swamiji sat and observed the man.

"Why are you looking so scared?"

"Swamiji the doctors are insisting that he should go in for a bypass or else he will not survive." Informed Samir.

Swamiji took the man's wrist and seemed to check the man's pulse. He shut His eyes for a few seconds and then sighed.

"No need. Some of these doctors will do anything to earn an extra rupee. You have two blocks..."

"Yes Swamiji..."

"But they are minor. They do not need to be operated. You are feeling very exhausted and breathless..."

"Yes Swamiji..."

"That is not because of the blocks in the heart. Tell your doctor to check your lungs. You have a problem in your lungs. That is making you breathless. Not the heart."

"Swamiji I am thinking of shifting to another city..."

"Don't. If you do, you will be back in Mumbai in four months. Don't go for any heart operation but yes, get your lungs checked and don't shift your base. You will begin to do well in a few months. These doctors are really very funny creatures. You know, this big doctor was advising me to go in for bypass surgery. He said if I did not, there would be nothing that would save me. I just nodded and asked him the meaning of bypass surgery. So he began to explain to me how they took some nerve or vein from the leg etc and then I stopped him, and told him, *My* meaning of bypass. Basically your money from your own account is bypassed to the doctor's bank account. I am not saying it is not necessary but most doctors will cut up a person for any reason. That is wrong. They don't know how they are harming their own karma and future. Of course, let me make one thing clear and that is that all doctors are not knife happy. My doctors in Bangalore try their best to lower the cost and the agony of their patients but sadly they are an exception and not the rule.")

HAND IN HAND WITH MEDICAL TECHNOLOGY

One thing needs to be kept in mind and that is, Swamiji is not against modern medical facilities or technology. In fact, often He Himself suggests to the devotee to get admitted in the hospital and get proper medical treatment. Lets go back to the day at Bangalore, a few hours before *Chandi Havan*. Earlier I was speaking to Nitya Murti who had suffered from the severe heart attack and was advised against a bypass surgery. Her husband shook hands with me and narrated an incident that collaborates with the above fact that different health issues require different measures.

"I won't take his name but a famous Karnataka film actor was very badly injured during a film shoot. The film actor was being treated at Putur, where they treat the patients by applying herbal medicine and leaves, to heal the wounds etc. Anyway fifteen days later this actor got severe pain and he came for the first time to Swamiji. You see in my wife's case, Swamiji said 'no knife will touch you' but in the actor's case, Swamiji insisted that the film actor forget all the herbal medicines and treatment he was undergoing and get himself admitted to a proper hospital to treat his leg. He insisted that the film actor be admitted immediately. In fact, Swamiji said that the actor should waste no time and get admitted that very day within a few hours or he would regret it for his life. The actor had enough faith and common sense to do as he was told. He got admitted in a hospital. The doctor after examining the injured leg said that if the actor had come one day later, they would have had to amputate his leg. The doctor insisted that now his leg would be cured but a day later and he would have had to live with one limb amputated. For a famous film star that would have meant the end of his successful career."

The room was choc 'o' blocked with devotees. A number of them assured me that the work I had undertaken would really help a number of people, who till now did not know of Ma Mookambika and Swamiji. They were aware that with the publishing of the book, Swamiji would be assailed by new devotees and people seeking guidance and comfort. This in turn translated to the fact that they would get to spend less time with Swamiji, but it would help humanity at large and that was what really mattered. They insisted that when they were down and out, Ma and Swamiji were like pillars to them and it would be really selfish if they would grudge others from getting such comfort and often life-saving help and guidance.

I sat down to take a breather. Lalit, Samir, GD, Vijay Wadhwa and Murli all were near by, chatting with Swamiji and His family members. Murli informed me that our Indian team was getting a hiding of their lives and did I want to change my stance of winning at all costs. I insisted that there was no way we could lose and we would for sure win today. He chuckled and then introduced me to Prakash Khilnani, a devotee of Ma Mookambika and Swamiji since 1996.

OMNISCIENT SEER

"I think one of the outstanding aspects of Swamiji is the way Devi gives predictions through Him. If you go to any astrologer or those, who prepare the horoscope and *kundli* (an in-depth birth-chart/ birth-document that in detail outlines the person's future and star position), they require certain details. The astrologer preparing the birth-chart and the horoscope of the person requires the exact time and date of birth, but where Swamiji is concerned, He requires nothing. He sits in the temple, lights a ball of camphor and then looks into the camphor and Devi begins Her predictions. Most often you don't even have to ask any question. This manner of giving prediction by Devi and Him is the most amazing.

"Another thing is that you can telephone Him and ask Him the most intricate question and He will give you an answer that always comes true. Even here He does not ask any question regarding date of birth or star sign or *kundli* or any thing. I doubt if there are many people, who function on similar lines. I have visited so many astrologers but none are as accurate as Him and that too without any papers or information. Of course, the most difficult part of the prediction is to be able to get time from Swamiji for a future reading session, as He is really so busy whole day helping those in need. It took me months before Swamiji sat down to predict my future. But I will never forget that day. We sat down and I asked him a question regarding my business and He immediately said that the person who I have entrusted the day to day running of my business, as well as its financial matters is cheating me. He predicted that the man was sucking me dry on the sly. Frankly, I did not believe Swamiji. That man was very close to me and I really trusted him with my life. I told

Swamiji that I really trusted him and He told me that within ten days, I would come to know, that this man was a cheat and fraud. Exactly as He predicted, within ten days we found out that this man was a cheat and he had really been cheating me. After that, time and again He has predicted so many accurate things that we don't take an important step without His permission."

Murli came over and introduced me to one of the oldest devotees of Ma Mookambika and Swamiji. Mr. K. Vasudev Shaney, popularly known as the *agarbati-wala* (the incense man). He is extremely popular among the devotees, as he is the man who usually navigates Swamiji from the second floor during the *Chandi Havan*. Swamiji enters into the state of trance and Vasudev holds Him and makes sure that the throng of devotees do not, due to their enthusiasm or devotion hurt Swamiji or that He does not fall when coming down the staircase. One should remember that while in a state of trance, Swamiji's body sways. He also steps on burning camphor and this journey begins from the second floor. He, then is led through the long temple corridor, bursting to its seams with devotees. Then He is taken into the womb of the mandir, where Devi's statue is placed and then He walks out and sits in front of the raging holy fire, where devotees throng for blessings and a word or two from Ma Mookambika.

All the while, devotees are seeking blessings and throwing themselves in front of Swamiji, in the hope, that Ma Mookambika will bless them and spare a moment to guide and help them through their daily lives. Through this entire paranormal journey, Vasudev and a few old devotees and friends, are like pillars, making sure that the pilgrimage goes smoothly but respecting the sentiments of the devotees. So they have to use their discretion and allow the devotees to show their devotion but also keep in mind, that Swamiji is in no way hurt or taxed or put to any sort of discomfort. It is not an easy job and what with the rush of devotees, the camphor, the smoke from the holy Fire and then general excitement all around, the spiritual task gets only more difficult.

UNBELIEVING BELIEVERS

"My name is K. Vasudev and I am actually related to Swamiji. To tell you the truth when He first became a Swamiji I really did not have faith in Him as we have known and heard about Him from childhood. As you know, He was anything but a Saint in those days. Around 1970, when we heard that He had become a Swamiji, at least I had my reservations. Then it so happened that my daughter fell ill. She began to have severe pain in the stomach and in spite of medicines she got no relief and also for days, she could barely take a sip of water. Eating food was out of question. With doctors and medicines not giving any relief, in the end, I had no option but to go and visit Swamiji. I paid my respects to Ma Mookambika and then, Swamiji gave me a Blessed Lime and He told me to go home, remove the juice out of the Lime and make my daughter drink the juice slowly. I took the Lime and frankly wondered, that if medicines were not giving any relief to my daughter, how a simple Lime would be effective. But my daughter was in such pain, that I had no choice but to make her have this strange spiritual medicine. She had a few sips and to my shock and surprise the pain subsided and within hours, she was eating food as though nothing was wrong with her. I was really stumped. I mean just a few sips had stopped the pain and by the time she finished the entire glass, she was up and about. I then admitted that there was some power in Him and that Devi really existed in the small shed like mandir.

"I began to spend time with Him and doing whatever *seva* (service) I could do for Devi. Those days there were not many devotees and we used to spend a lot of time talking to each other. Those days, the charge for one prediction was just one rupee and twenty-five paisa. In that, the cost of oil, flowers, incense, camphor and to top it all, even a meal was provided. So one thing is certain and that is, no matter the hard life Swamiji and His family have gone through, they have never allowed money to come before the welfare of the devotees. Devi would speak to us for hours and often told us such beautiful stories, which I feel really sad we have not recorded. I must admit, that on and off, I used to have my doubts regarding Swamiji but then thrice Devi showed Herself to me in different forms....Ma Mookambika, Ma Kali and Adi Shakti...and slowly I became one of the firmest devotees to visit this spiritual powerhouse.

"Before I started the business of incense, around five years back, I incurred a loss of around fifteen lakh rupees. I was in real bad shape. Then Ma, through Swamiji, guided me to start this business of selling incense of and even drew for me a trademark. She told me to put this trademark. The trademark is that of Subramaniya, Ma's son, and after I put this trademark my business sales shot up tremendously. Now my business has a turnover of about five to six lakh rupees a month. I own a three-floor building and am doing really very well, all thanks to Ma Mookambika and Swamiji. In fact, my son is exploring the possibility of exporting the incense sticks all over the world. I named the *agarbati* (incense sticks) after Ma. They are called Ma Mookambika Agarbati. All my success is due to Her thus the name.

"But I must tell you that Swamiji really went through a lot of hardship. There was a time, they did not have food to eat. In fact, there were certain occasions when there was no lime to give devotees, but Ma would make sure that everything was provided. Before He became a Swamiji He was doing well for Himself and His family. But this man never once hungered for money. He left everything to be with Ma. Yes, in the beginning He did not understand what was happening, but once He accepted Her wholeheartedly, He never left Her. He has never ever hungered for money. Never taken advantage of the fact that He has such power with Him. Somebody else in His place would have amassed crores of rupees. Had many bungalows and lived in style. But He is not like that. He had a big shop in Bangalore but He gave it all to His brother. He comes from a rich family but not once did He ever stake a claim for even a rupee. He just left everything and embraced Devi. It takes really a strong and a good man to do so.

"Even the language that Devi used to speak or write on the walls was such ancient Kanada, that very often we could not understand the meaning. I am so blessed that since the beginning,

Ma has insisted that I be present, whenever the *Chandi Homa* takes place. She insists that I sit along with Swamiji. She does not allow anybody to accompany Her and Swamiji. I remember during one such Homa, a young man had been brought here. He could not walk. You must have met Nagrajan, who was suffering from stomach cancer. Just like him, there was this young man who could not even walk due to some ill health. Ma through Swamiji just held him and picked him up and then after a few moments told him that now he was cured. That very instant he began to walk. We all were shocked to see this man able to walk. She told him not to bother about medicine. She gave him a Blessed Lime and he was all right. I was suffering from so many health problems. Blood pressure fluctuations and very high sugar levels were constantly troubling me, but She and He have taken care of everything. Yes, you have to ask Ma to help you. You have to get down on your knees and tell Her, that you need Her help and She will be there to help you. You have to throw your ego out and approach Her as a child. First I used to doubt, but now there is no question of doubt. I leave all my problems at Her feet. I do my best and tell Her to take care of the rest. And She always has taken care of my family and me. There are thousands who have benefited by coming here and asking for Her blessings. You have to ask Her as She is our Mother. How can Mother see Her children suffer? It is not possible. But yes, the moment a person thinks he is very smart or tries to show his wealth or power or attitude, the person is in trouble. She will give you a warning, but if you don't listen, then I have seen people really pay a heavy price.

DOWNFALL OF THE EGOISTIC

"I will give you an example. There was this bank manager and I had gone for a loan of five thousand rupees. This happened many many years ago. This man wanted to be a father and he had taken the help of doctors, as well astrologers, but to no avail. Even *poojas* and *havans* did not help him so I recommended that he come to Ma Mookambika and take Her blessings and sit down for predictions with Swamiji. He came over and Ma told him that within ten months he would be a father. Within ten months, he became a father and on and off he used to come over here, to sit for predictions or even do *seva*. He began to grow further in his career. But his attitude I think began to change and he began to think that he really had become a big man. One day, he did not sit on the ground, as we all do, in front of Ma, but sat on a chair. A big chair and he became even higher than the pedestal on which Ma was placed. Swamiji and we disciples were seated on the floor. But this man did not get down from the chair. Within a few minutes, the chair broke and he actually fell down. After that his downfall started. He even lost his job. When you are in front of Ma, you have to become a child. Not out of fear but out of love and respect. She has made bankrupt people become very rich industrialists but if you come here with pride or ego, then God help you! She is the Universal Mother, full of love and care and all she wants is love and respect from Her children.

"But when we used to meet Ma on normal days and when nobody was around for predictions, Ma used to tell us really funny stories. I remember one story that She had told us."

The story goes somewhat as follows. One day there was this very rich man who had this burning desire to see God. He was very rich and he had everything but all he wanted was to see the good Lord. He met many sages and many astrologers and so called God men, but nobody could fulfill his desire. Then, somebody out of sheer frustration, told our man that there was this forest and it was rumoured that for some odd reason, that only God could answer, the Heavenly Father patronised this jungle and paid daily visits.

Our man that very instant left for the forest. He met a few sages who were meditating. I assume our man disturbed them to and got them out of their bliss. Some sage, with an unusual sense of humour, agreed that though they had not had the fortune of meeting God in person, but maybe if he travelled further into the forest, who knows, he might just get truly lucky. So our man walked deeper into the dense forest and met a band of bandits. Instead of getting scared of them, he posed his question of whether they had chatted with God. Now the bandits realised that they would not have to exert themselves in order to rob this chap. They all nodded that they had seen God but would only reveal the exact location that God patronised, if he gave them all the gold and jewelry he carried upon himself. According to them, God did not like meeting rich people. So the next moment, our man removed all the precious jewelry and money he carried with him and gave it to the bandits. The band of thugs then took our simpleton to a deep well and gave him a gentle nudge. Our man justified the law of gravity and fell head long into the dry well. On making contact with the dry land, he justified further natural laws and died instantly. But lo! there stood God in front of him. God was very pleased, that during times of such materialism and debasing of ethics, there was somebody on earth, who had such a craving to see Him in person that he had in the end paid with his life. So God embraced this man and said that He was rather tickled with his devotion and was there anything he wanted further? The man was ecstatic on seeing God and said that he did not want anything more, but on an afterthought, told God, that it did not seem right that he had God's vision and his masters (the band of bandits) were denied of His presence. 'I don't want anything, but I would like to have my gurus here too so that they too can see your heavenly form.' Next moment, on Mother Earth, the band of thugs got struck by a thunder bolt and with differing yelps and curses, left their physical body and stood next to our man in stark spirit form.

"You know our Maharaj, this Swamiji is like those people, who would go out of their way to serve and never bother about money. Even before He became a Swamiji, He was never bothered about making money or saving anything for Himself. If somebody came crying to Him, He would remove whatever He had and give it to the person. Earlier, He was like Valmiki, tough and did not tolerate fools. In an argument, He spoke later but first gave the chap a hard whack on the face. He loved to drink beer and eat fish and lived life to the fullest. He has really lived life to the hilt. But even in those days, He never craved for money. Whatever was earned He spent lavishly on family and friends and those in need. You know, He was an electrical engineer. He owned this small shop, where He repaired radios. So many times somebody would come to Him and tell Him that he did not have money to buy a radio, our Swamiji would give that person a radio free of cost. He was supposed to be doing business but His heart is so big that very often, He had to spend money from His own pocket, just to keep the shop afloat...all due to His large heartedness. So many times He would give a poor chap a rich man's radio and then rotate different radios to different people. He was really one of the worst businessman around. Another thing was that He refused to possess a driving license. He would drive his big Motorbike, Royal Enfield, without a license and we had to convince the RTO, that He had either forgotten it or lost it or something or the other. In the end even they got used to Swamiji not possessing a license. That is why, whenever He would tell me to accompany Him on the bike, I used to fold my hands and refuse. Sitting with Him and then dealing with RTOs and the speed with which He rode the bike was frightening."

The match was on full flow. Shewag seemed to have been possessed by the spirit of Tendulkar, for not only did the man look and walk like Sachin, but also batted like the maestro. The boundaries just did not cease and one by one everybody began to conclude that just maybe, a miracle was in the offing and the Indian cricket team would win this match. Saurav too was batting well and that came as a breath of fresh air. He had been suffering from a lean patch and I assume the nation released a collective sigh of relief to see the Bengal Tiger roaring and all raring to go. Swamiji came out of the bathroom and that was a signal, that it was time for the Chandi Havan to commence. The television set was switched off and all of a sudden, all of us became silent. Swamiji was already getting slowly detached and more inward and within moments it was obvious that He would go into a trance.

THE DAY OF THE CHANDI HOMA

Swamiji's family and most of us from Mumbai were in the room. Also present, was the old gang of faithful devotees cum friends like Vasudev (the incense man), Guptaji and a few others. Murli told me that he would be going to Ma's mandir and that I should make my way there, the moment Swamiji gets out of this room. I nodded. Swamiji was being draped in a saree. The saree is worn by women, but as Devi enters His body, Swamiji loses consciousness and Ma Mookambika predominates. Her tastes, desires and actions prevail. The room began to get more crowded and I thought it would be best if I stood outside. So I touched Swamiji's feet and left the room. Outside, in the main drawing room, a huge gathering of devotees awaited the arrival of Ma Mookambika. A few of them asked me the progress within the room and one smart ass asked me the cricket score. Suddenly the door was opened and Lalit peered through and called on to me. He held my arm and pulled me within the room.

"What are you doing outside? See how Devi enters and take Her blessings. Once Swamiji leaves the room it will be a free for all."

"Thanks Lalit..."

"Don't be stupid. This is a sight of a lifetime. Don't miss it for the world. That is why I made sure they too are in here." Lalit was referring to his daughter-in-law, his daughter and her friend who too were present and looked on with awe. He looked on at Swamiji and there was obvious love and veneration pouring through.

Swamiji was all adorned and then the musicians began to play the hand drums and the shehnai (a wind instrument). Suddenly, I observed a tremor surge through Swamiji's body. It was as though somebody had switched on a current and energy in torrents gushed through His body, starting from the head, moving through the shoulders and culminating at the feet. His entire body swayed, as though live energy surged up and down, as well as danced side to side, jolting His body in a strange rhythm. Everybody began to touch His feet aware that now Ma Mookambika had taken over Swamiji's body. The energy within the room and around Swamiji was palpable. Swamiji's eyes become large and spoke volumes of emotions hard to describe. In a trance, His expressions change from person to person, every second there is a new depth to the intensity in the eyes and face. How does one explain such a phenomenon in words? Like trying to explain a blind man the magnificence of a rainbow. Like trying to explain the beauty of a Chopin recital to somebody born deaf. It is a sight to be seen and the vibrations need to be felt and experienced. The room was choc'o' blocked with devotees and after I took blessings of Ma Mookambika and Swamiji, I left the room. Swamiji had begun to take steps and every time somebody would light a ball of camphor and Ma Mookambika would step on the burning fire. All through Her journey from this room on the second floor right up to the mandir and then outside where the Havan Fire raged through, She would walk on burning camphor. I waited outside and then realised that if I wanted a message from Ma Mookambika I would have to be near Murli, as He understood the Kannada language and Ma only spoke in that language. So I made my way to the ground floor and it was jammed to the gills. Fortunately for me, a number of devotees managing the crowd knew me by sight and allowed me to enter within the main temple where Murli, Samir and GD with a number of other devotees waited.

"I was wondering where you had disappeared? "

"Got Ma's blessings!"

"Good. Now you stand near me okay as I am certain She will tell you something regarding the book."

"How do I know you will be translate it accurately and honestly..."

"Ruzbeh, where is Lalit?" Inquired Samir.

"He is with Swamiji..."

"I hope Swamiji does not fall ill after this session, as last night He was really down..." Suddenly all eyes turned towards the staircase. The rhythm of drums and the invocative tune of the wind instruments got louder. Devi was on Her way. By the time Swamiji reached where we were standing, another fifteen minutes had elapsed. A number of devotees were scrambling for Devi's blessings and She through Swamiji was speaking to a few of them. To manage the scene is a difficult task. Those in charge of protecting and maneuvering Swamiji have to walk a tight-rope;

they cannot be rude and cold but at the same time, they have to make certain that Swamiji is not hurt or His movement does not come to a standstill. One must realise that He is in motion and all this while, He is in a state of trance. The state of trance as mentioned above sucks the very life force out of you and thus each minute that Swamiji is in this paranormal state takes a further toll on his health.

Eventually the musicians too got into the main mandir and then Swamiji got in. His eyes were both tender and flaming at the same time and His movements and actions were so unlike Him. Usually He is full of humour but at the moment there was a state of difference that was palpable. His eyes mainly made all the difference. Devi stared through. Devi addressed a few of the devotees and then flashed Her eyes at Murli and me. She then spoke to Murli for sometime and then looked at me. She through Swamiji spoke to me for sometime. I could not understand anything but distinctly the words, *Agni* (fire) and Sai Baba were mentioned more than once. She then blessed me and then Murli suggested that we move out of the room. We once again took Devi's blessings and left the room. It was blazing hot. The smoke and the heat from the Fire, the surging crowds, the thumping of the drums and the blare of the music, as well as the strong vibrations, made a heady combination.

Murli and I got out of the main gate and saw numerous devotees being fed lunch. For a while, we both saw the goings on and I realised that such *Chandi Havans* would not go on for many years. Swamiji had time and again, hinted that He would not be on the physical plane for too long, as His time over here was coming to an end. I wondered how, after He left His physical body, would this special day would ever be celebrated. Certainly never like this, unless Ma Mookambika thought otherwise. Nothing is beyond Her.

"What did Ma say?"

"She said...I am Fire and I am your Agni (Holy Fire that Zoroastrians worship in their fire-temple). I know you worship Sai Baba. I and He are one. You are doing a very noble task of writing this book. Through this book a number of people will be helped. Whenever, you really call out to Me from the depths of your heart, I will come and bless you and help you."

"Have you missed out anything?"

"No!"

"Are you sure or else I can always ask Ma again?. I mean I have my spiritual contacts."

"Very funny."

We both entered and I saw the surge of devotees crowding Swamiji. He was in a trance and He was near the Holy Fire that raged in a huge sanctified chasm. One by one, I saw the faces of the devotees change from apprehension and tension to tranquility and often to sheer euphoria. Vijay met me and said that he was really stumped at the accuracy and force of Devi.

An hour and a half later, Swamiji was still surrounded by desperate devotees wanting a word or a touch from Devi and Him. We took Their blessings and left for Mumbai. It had been an exhausting day for us. I wondered how Swamiji, twice my age and involved with countless responsibilities, apart from the main task of sitting in a trance, managed and that too, with a smile.

A month or so down the line there were a series of poojas to be held at Samir's place. He had invited me to attend the pooja ceremony and have lunch, with Swamiji and the other guests. Sunit, Meena and the kids were to arrive a little time later. Murli and the old gang were already present. The pooja was being performed in the main hall and Swamiji was busy in the other room, as usual caught and bound by devotees, who were keen to know about their future. In Mumbai, usually the devotees wanted to know when they would make their next million. This was an old joke Murli and I shared. I entered the hall where the pooja was being conducted and saw Samir and his wife, through the thick smoke that emanated from the sanctified abyss. I waved out to Samir and he, with one eye shut, managed a weak smile. It was obvious he was fighting a losing battle with the smoke. Murli stood near by and he inquired if I needed anything to drink.

"I think Samir would love to have goggles at the moment."

"Poor guy. The smoke is really thick."

UNFORESEEN PREDICTIONS

Swamiji came out of the room and blessed me. He introduced me to Dr. Krishna Maheshwari, who has a PhD in Chemistry from USA. Swamiji had often spoken about Dr. Maheshwari and it was obvious that Swamiji was fond of the good doctor. Murli helped me locate an empty room in Samir's palatial home. Dr. Maheshwari and I sat in Simran's room. Both Sidhant and Simran, slapped my hand in a warm greeting.

"Ruzbeh, I am downstairs, if you need anything let me know."

"Murli, silence would be appreciated." I spoke with a straight face. He sighed and walked away. After I had the doctor holding the mike and adjusting the dicta-phone, we began the recording.

"I must have met Swamiji in 1988, all thanks to GD Shah. We were involved in some work together and He was our distributor and on and off he mentioned Swamiji. I was the

256

President of RPG Enterprises. Once it so happened that certain goods were not being released by the customs, due to some minor oversight in the documentation. It was not much of a problem and we expected the material to be released soon but GD insisted that the material would be released only in August. I was rather taken aback. It was still April and August was too far away. But GD was very certain, as Swamiji had told him, that the material would only be released in August. Eventually, the material was released only in the month of August, much to the surprise of many of us so called professionals. This incident made me eager to meet Swamiji and fortunately, I met Him at GD's residence. He inquired about my well-being and I was really happy meeting Him. He told me to come to Bangalore and offer prayers to Ma Mookambika. I agreed and the next time when I had to go to Madras, I travelled via Bangalore. I prayed in the temple and He told me to come as often as possible and offer prayers to Ma Mookambika.

"The next three occasions I could not have a sitting with Swamiji. Though I used to offer prayers and He would be standing close to me, for some reason, thrice He told me that the time for predictions, regarding my future, was still not appropriate. On my last trip, He told me to come on such and such day and we would go to Subramaniya. I did not want to disturb Him, so I offered to visit Subramaniya on my own. He told me that I would never be able to visit Subramaniya without Him. At that time, I did not understand what exactly He implied by saying that I could never visit the pilgrim place without Swamiji.

"When I arrived at Bangalore, Swamiji informed me that a number of people were travelling to Subramaniya, along with us, albeit in different cars. He insisted that I should accompany Him in His car. I was more than glad. We left for Subramaniya and just at the outskirts of Bangalore, a huge stone from God-alone-knows where, hit our windscreen and damaged it considerably. Swamiji told the group to continue and insisted that we return to Bangalore get the car repaired and then move on to Subramaniya.

"The mechanics informed us that replacing a new windscreen would take considerable time but Swamiji was adamant that we would only travel to Subramaniya in this car. By the time we left for the place, it was really late and even Swamiji's daughter was apprehensive. But, as you must be aware, once Swamiji makes up His mind, except Devi, nobody and nothing can change His course of action. At around two in the morning, nearing Subramaniya, the engine caught fire. Swamiji got out of the car, opened the bonnet, put His hands in the flame, did something, banged something three or four times and the fire subsided. Then He walked around the car and after sometime once again pulled out a few wires and did something again and the car came back to life and we reached Subramaniya at around three in the morning. It was then that I realised, that if left to my own means, I would really never have reached Subramaniya alone. I remembered Swamiji's prediction, that it was mandatory for Him to accompany me on the pilgrimage. He then asked me to perform certain poojas and now at least once a year, I go there and pay my respects to Devi and Lord Subramaniya.

"Sometime later, the factory in which we had invested around twenty-three crore rupees, would just not function. We had a German Collaborator and they were virtually the leaders in their business and technology. We just could not identify the problem. I approached Devi and Swamiji. She, through Him, told me that there were certain inherent mechanical problems and the fault lay squarely on the shoulders of the German collaborators. He identified the mechanical and technical problem and to our surprise, we realised that all the predictions were cent per cent accurate. Though it seemed impossible, there were many mechanical and technical faults. We began a series of correspondence with our German collaborators and they refused to acknowledge, that the fault lay at their end. So in the end, we thought of approaching the High Court to seek justice. I asked Him whether it was the right move and He approved. He told us not to worry and put the case to the High Court. So we filed a case against the German collaborators and to our horror, we lost the case. That meant we had to pay the money to the collaborator, irrespective of the wrong technology it had passed on to us.

"I rushed to Swamiji and said that everything had gone wrong and that we had lost the case. Swamiji very calmly told me to go in for an appeal and observe how Devi's magic works. He predicted that we would get whatever we so desired. So we went in for an appeal. The court ruled that it was obvious, after going through the entire case and the correspondence between the two companies, that the German collaborators had not provided the technology desired and that both the respective parties should meet and try to sort the matter out cordially. For twenty-five days there was no correspondence or communication from our German collaborators. Then we received a fax, that if we wanted, we could send somebody to attend a meeting scheduled day after tomorrow. So immediately, other company officials and I, left for Germany and after a lot of hard talk the German collaborators, agreed to give us equipment and technology worth two crore rupees free of cost. This was implemented in the plant and the plant is now running at 130% capacity. In fact the problem really was with the place and it was after Swamiji performed a pooja and we built a small temple that things began to move. Every year, we perform the pooja and now things are moving beautifully. Hindus, Christians and Muslims, all come and touch Swamiji's feet as they know that without this Man of God, this place would have been barren.

"I will tell you another incident. I had two very good friends. One day one of them called me up and told me that our friend, Dr. Manmohan, had cancer of the throat. Immediately, though it was around 11 at night, I called up Swamiji and told Him that my friend was suffering from cancer of the throat. Swamiji asked me his name and his height. He then inquired whether this friend of mine had a long nose and I agreed. He revealed to me that my friend did not have cancer of the throat, but actually had cancer of the rectum and the cancer had travelled all the way up to the throat. I asked Him regarding my friend's chances of survival and He said that he would not live beyond March 15th. It was already mid-January. I rushed to Delhi

259

and met him and his family and politely inquired with his wife whether she had all the necessary documents signed and she told me, that the doctors had diagnosed that he would be all right and there was no danger to my friend's life. Two weeks later, my friend was operated upon by a very famous doctor, who informed us later that he had worked on the case and had found nothing fatal. On March 6th my friend died.

"My own daughter's case is very interesting. She wanted to go to the US for further studies and I was not very keen. Swamiji told me to let her go and also predicted that two years later she would send me photograph and proposal of a boy she loves. The boy will not be from my community but I must agree to let my child marry him, for she will not get a better person for her welfare and happiness. Exactly as he predicted, two years later, my daughter sent the proposal and he was not from our community. We gave our blessings and now they are parents of two children and all are doing well."

I went downstairs and the smoke had only increased in intensity. I could no longer see Samir and his wife, Rajul. They were both enveloped in the smoke. Swamiji sat nearby and inquired about my son's health. Pashaan had a miraculous escape. In fact, even the doctors were surprised that Pashaan had lived through the twenty odd minute convulsion and with a viral fever that refused to slide down. In fact, during the fight to revive him, Pashaan had stopped breathing for more than fifteen seconds. We thought we had lost our son, as I could only see the whites of his eyes and there was no movement of the body. Thanks to all our spiritual Masters and Guides, Pashaan returned to Earth Planet. Without him, I doubt, life would be worth living on.

BUSINESS HEALTH

I was introduced to Sandeep Vasani, cousin of Samir Sanghvi, by Murli. Adjusting the dictaphone, we found a comfortable spot, next to the pooja, but away from the smoke.

"I came in touch with Swamiji, about five years ago, at my cousin, Samir's place. Swamiji described our factory layout and surroundings with such great detail that it left me speechless.

I mean, our factory is about three hundred kilometers away from Mumbai, but the way He described it...it was as though He was seeing it on a monitor. He even told me, about the type of manufacturing and quality problems we were facing. He revealed to us, that before He could really do anything for us, at the earliest we should perform the *Sudarshan Havan* at our factory. I know you might not believe this, but the very next day, after performing the *Havan,* we got a major new account that really accelerated our growth."

"We produce chemical powder in our factory. Once we had serious quality problems and in spite of our best efforts, we were not able to locate the reasons for the poor quality. I am a qualified engineer from USA, and my father is a chemical engineer with 40 years of hands down experience, but still we could not locate the crux of the problem. When I telephoned Swamiji, who was in Bangalore, He told me that the problem was in the raw material. I disclosed that we got our raw materials from abroad and that too from one of the most reputed companies in the world. But He maintained that the problem was with the raw material supplied to us. We were in a quandary. We were anticipating processing problems and after checking the raw material, we could locate no problems with it. So I telephoned Swamiji again and He predicted that the problematic raw material was in powder form, which was least expected. So we immediately contacted our chemical powder supplier and in a few days, we got a reply from this reputed company that the raw material they had shipped to us was from a different mine and not suitable for our product. It really surprised us that a problem, which could not be identified by qualified technical experts, was detected by Swamiji, who was hundreds of miles away and who had not even stepped in our factory. In fact, so many times, He has solved technical problems, when we were confused and at sea. Once we had a problem with one of our machines. Swamiji on the phone pinpointed the problem and advised the technical men how to go about solving it. In fact once, he identified a processing problem and told us to reduce the speed of the machine by ten per cent and that really solved the issue.

"Once, He informed us that we should get rid of the Factory Manager, who was irregular and performing below par. On acting on Swamiji's advice, we removed the man and later found out that the Manager was spending company money to support his consumption of liquor. Swamiji has also helped us very often, when ill health has struck family members. The help that Ma and He have given us and the gratitude, we feel towards Ma Mookambika and Him, cannot be expressed in mere words. You know once Swamiji paid a visit to our residence. Immediately after entering the flat, He inquired as to whether any untimely death has taken place in the building. We were certain that no untimely death had taken place but Swamiji kept asking us to think hard and remember. We moved to one of the bedrooms and Swamiji was now very emphatic that somebody had committed suicide by jumping out of the window to her death. Then we remembered that one young girl had committed suicide and she lived just below our flat. Swamiji revealed that the moment He entered our building, this dead girl's spirit accompanied Him and kept crying and requesting Swamiji's assistance for relief. He also mentioned that this was one of the reasons, not only members from my family but from those living in the building were suffering from ill health...which was true. There were lots of people suffering from ill health in the building. Swamiji advised us to perform an *Agor Havan*. After the *havan*, number of those people suffering from ill health recuperated. I am certain that the poor girl's spirit must be at peace. I tell you, He is no ordinary person. So gentle and calm and you can ask Him a question ten times and He does not lose His cool. Meeting Him and through Him having darshan of Ma Mookambika, has been one of the best moments of my life."

After the Havan, I sat down with Samir and his wife, Rajul, in their spacious drawing room. They have treated me as part of their family and always insist that I dine with them, whenever Swamiji stayed over at their flat.

"We met Swamiji through Murli. You know that Murli is not just my partner in business, but also my friend and part of the family. Murli was aware that I was a non-believer, thus he made certain that my first encounter with Swamiji was in the Lion's den...Ma Mookambika temple in Bangalore. It was in the year 1991. Frankly, I was not very keen, but to please my friend, we sat down for the predictions. Our lives changed from that moment onwards. What really stumped me, was that Swamiji gave me predictions, without asking any details or without looking at the palm or the horoscope. My role was limited to saying 'yes', so as to confirm that He was on the right track. He even described, at length, the location and shape of our ancestral property. He also dwelt at length on the physical and health problems of family members with medical analysis. All this, without any hints from our side. Then, He touched upon my education and financial status and some very personal facts of which no one, but I, was aware. He ended the prediction, with my relationship with my grandfather and great-grandfather, including a description of my great-grandfather, and also what clothes he used to wear when alive. Believe me Ruzbeh, that day was the first time in my life, when I bowed down to a human being in the real sense. From that day onwards, I have totally surrendered myself to Ma Mookambika and Swamiji. The perfection, clarity and precision was so good, that I felt I was communicating with GOD directly.

"The best part, about Swamiji, is that He is always frank but caring and affectionate like a father. Always by our side, at the time of crisis. With His support and guidance, I am able to tackle the worst situation smoothly and with ease without much tension.

"I remember, Rajul and I wanted desperately to become parents, but were not having an issue. Swamiji asked us to perform the *Nag Dosh puja,* which we performed in the Subramanyam temple. He told us that we would have to be patient and have complete faith in Devi. He promised us, that we would become parents, but it would take time. Eventually, true to His word, our daughter Simran was born in 1995."

"I think, the most important point I would like to point out, was that He was very positive about us becoming parents." Added Rajul. "He insisted that there was no medical problem with us and He also cautioned us against any medical surgery. One of the leading fertility experts suggested that Samir should go in for surgery for vericosis. But Swamiji asserted that there was no vericosis — so the question of surgery did not arise. Moreover, He insisted there was unnecessary risk involved in the surgery. The very next day, we happened to talk to our friend, who informed us that he had undergone this type of surgery and that his sperm count had reduced to Nil...all due to the surgery. Coincidentally, a day later, Samir met Dr. Indira Hinduja, who suggested that he should take the colour Doplor Test. The test confirmed that there was no symptoms of such physical deficiency in him. Swamiji finally blessed us in December 1994 at Dharangadhra, our native place, saying that I would conceive within three months. He blessed us on 14th January 1995 and the news was confirmed on March the 31st 1995. Another important point is that He even predicted how our daughter would look in the future. He said that our daughter would have long hair and that she would be very slim and have a birth mark. Just take a look at Simran. She is very slim, with long beautiful hair and has the birth mark that Swamiji had predicted even before she was born. Swamiji is really phenomenal" Saying this Rajul stood up to serve the guests.

"You know, Ruzbeh," began Samir, "my cousin sister Purvi within 15 days of her marriage met with an accident, while going with her husband and her in-laws to her native place in Gujarat. The only information we got, was that, she was admitted to the hospital after the car accident. Beyond that there was no more information. We did not even know whether she was alive or not. All the family members were worried, so we called up Swamiji at Bangalore and asked Him about the accident. You must understand that He has never met my cousin sister. He asked me to pause for a minute and then He began a running commentary. He informed me that there were six people travelling in the car. Due to rash driving, there had been a head on collision and the vehicle was travelling at the speed above 140 Km. Out of the six passengers, there were only two survivors. Both the survivors were women. All the men had died in the accident. To my relief, He then mentioned that out of the two survivors, one was my sister, who had been saved by the grace of God. He then sadly informed that the other survivor would also die the next day. Swamiji's clarity was as if he was watching a live telecast of the incident. After He gave us all this information, it took us eight hours to confirm the above facts. Everything had occurred exactly the way He had described the accident, even to the fact, that in the end only my sister survived the tragedy.

"Even the speed mentioned was later confirmed, when we learnt that the speedometer was stuck at 160 km. Purvi, my sister, was able to remember after a year of the tragedy that she had changed the seat just a few minutes before the accident. Swamiji had also predicted then, that Purvi would be bedridden for a year and that later she would once again marry a very nice man. As predicted, and by His grace, my sister is well settled now. Just imagine that the accident took place in Gujarat, Swamiji was narrating to us, how the accident took place, from Bangalore, that too through the telephone.

"In numerous instances, I have sought His advice on the telephone regarding health problems of third parties, who Swamiji has never met or even heard of. But as always, His predictions prove amazingly accurate. So many times, He has just on the telephone, told my friends not to go in for surgery. He has often told them that the by-pass/Angiography was not required. Often, He has insisted that they take a second opinion, and as expected, they are told that no surgery is required. Another amazing thing about Him is how just on the telephone He can predict the number of heart blockages. He gives precise answers. Like, He told a friend of mine that he had three 50% blockages and that he would have to be operated. The Angiography confirmed that there were three 50% blockages. Often, He has told people to immediately get a medical check up, as there was infection after surgery. Always, the patients have returned confirming, that if they would not have gone for the medical check up, they would have been in a further mess. I once remember Rajul was being troubled by nightmares. Every morning she would complain that she was not able to sleep well, as she had nightmares. So we spoke to Swamiji. He gave her a *Nag* pendent to wear and from that night itself, all the nightmares stopped. I mean what more can one reveal about Him? Ma Mookambika and He are one."

"Tell me, about the incident when He saved your life?"

"Oh, how can I forget that incident. One day, Swamiji and I went to visit the house of a close devotee. We all entered the house and Swamiji went in a trance for a moment and held my hand. He did not let go of my hand, till we sat down on the sofa. Later, when He opened His eyes, He looked up at the ceiling. To my horror and surprise, I realised that the ceiling fan was extremely low. So low, that there was no way I could have crossed the room without bending but I was certain that as I had not observed the ceiling fan, I had not bent down. I am very tall. Six feet and more. It then dawned on me, as to why Swamiji went suddenly in a trance. In fact, when I stood up, I realised that my neck was in the same line of the whirling fan and that I had walked through the room, passed through the fan without a scratch on my neck. I am certain that I had not bent at all. When I left the room, I had to really bend low. Obviously, Devi and Swamiji made certain that I lived to tell this tale and that I always keep my head on my shoulders. This is one miracle, I will never forget. Really, I think we all are blessed to have Devi and Him in our lives...by the way, have you met Vijay. Come, even he has experienced amazing stuff." We stood up and walked through the room in search of Vijay. On the way, we were stopped about five times and offered an assorted array of cold juices and snacks. Samir and Rajul take care of their guests extremely well.

Vijay Doshi was only too glad to share information about how Devi and Swamiji have changed his entire life. Making certain, that I was comfortably seated, Samir left to make certain that the lunch was being served and all were comfortable.

"I came in contact with Hon'ble Shri Swamiji in 1991/92, through Samirbhai and Murlibhai. Infact, since the time I have met Swamiji, I have been contesting a court case filed by certain people. Everybody was of the opinion that I would lose the case, within a short period of time. But, Swamiji insisted that nothing was going to happen and till now I have incurred no damage. He predicted that I would not have any problems, exactly a decade earlier, when all were certain that within months I would lose the case.

"Then, in the year 1997/98, I was passing through financial problems and I was in debt, running into crores of rupees. I had borrowed from banks, financial institutions, relatives etc. My flour mill business was running at huge losses. Due to this, I had thought of shifting to Russia and I had planned to put up a flour mill over there. I had visited Russia twice for this project. When I asked Swamiji, He told me to 'cancel the whole project otherwise you will loose more than you are investing there'. Upon His advice, I decided to drop the project and in the next three months, Russia devalued their currency. If I had not listened to Swamiji, I would have gone bankrupt.

"Still my financial position was deteriorating by the day. Samirbhai and Murlibhai told this to Swamiji. I came and met Swamiji at Samirbhai's house on 16th of September'98. I was in tears that day. In fact, that day whatever Swamiji had predicted to me, I wrote it down in my diary. I have carried the diary especially for you. Read this page." Saying this, he handed me the diary.

This is what was written: *Swamiji has said 'not to worry. I foresee very good future. From today, I am taking over the responsibility of both your flour mills'* (He had already decided to close both the factories). *Swamiji said — you wait for 15 days. There will be major change in your Industry. You will come out of all the problems. He gave me two coconuts. One to be kept at home and the other in the factory.*

I handed back the diary to Vijay. He shut the book and placed it in his bag.

"I was not ready to believe this, as there was total darkness. I was not able to see any future for my business. But in less than 14 days, something unbelievable happened. The Government permitted import of wheat for flour mills. This changed the entire situation. I was able to pay off my debts within just one year. This was exactly what Swamiji had predicted.

Then Swamiji visited my factory in the end of October 2001 and He advised me to perform various *Havans*. My wife, my son and I immediately decided to perform the same. My factory used to look like a haunted place before the *Havans*. Today we can all feel the difference. There is a certain vitality that has entered the area and that has made a difference to all those connected with the factory. Even workers have commented that now they feel like working, unlike earlier when they would just long to leave the premises. Believe me, Ma Mookambika and He are a blessing to mankind. I only hope people have the sense to take Their blessings and seek Their help."

I was with Sunit and Meena, when Murli approached and inquired as to how the book was progressing.

"Ruzbeh, have I spoken to you about my mother?"

"No. Getting stuff out of you is serious business." Saying this, I switched on the dictaphone.

"In March, 2000, my grand mother, who is 85 years old, fell very ill, and my mother, her only child, was planning to bring her to Mumbai, from her native place. Meanwhile, I happened to go to Bangalore, for a day, to meet Swamiji. My mother wanted Swamiji to ask Devi about my grandmother's health. In the Mandir, before Goddess, Swamiji told me not to worry about my grandmother but to take care of my mother's health. In fact, he specifically warned, that my mother could have breathing problems and serious chest congestion. On my return, I informed my mother about the prediction, whereupon, she casually dismissed it by saying that she suffered only from arthritis (joint pain), for which she might have to undergo surgery. My grandmother was brought to Mumbai where she recovered. But in April 2000, my mother got an attack of asthma and had severe breathing problems. Doctors opined that she was suffering from pneumonia but the illness was not very serious and she would recover. About a week later, I was in Bangalore with Swamiji, when Daxa, my wife, called me to inform that my mother was being admitted to a nursing home. In the evening, I rushed to the nursing home directly from the airport, whereupon doctors told me that there was no cause of worry, since only fluid had collected in her chest, which could be removed by a simple procedure in the morning (insertion of syringe). Within hours my mother breathed her last. It appears that Swamiji had told my friends who were travelling with me from Bangalore to Mumbai, that my mother would not survive. For obvious reasons He had revealed nothing to me."

A month later, Swamiji once again flew down to Mumbai. This time to organise and attend one of the biggest poojas, organised this side of the country. Normally most people content themselves with the *Chandi Havan.* Lalit decided to hold a *Sat Chandi Havan*...hundred times on a larger scale than the normal *havans* organised all over the country. To give you a brief glimpse, more than ten tonnes of wood are required and around two hundred kilogrammes of rice are needed, just to tend the holy fire. More than twenty priests, pray together and the hall is designed in the shape of a Shri *Yantra.* Before the main *havan,* for a few days, small *havans* are performed through out the day and on the final day Devi is brought from the small *mandap* to the main *mandap* with all the pomp and honour She deserves. In fact elephants walk ahead to honour Devi.

I met Swamiji in the evening, a day before the main pooja was to be performed. He had tied a *kafni* (cloth) on His head and looked very alike Sai Baba of Shirdi. He blessed me and inquired as to the progress of the book. As usual He was in high spirits and joked about with one and sundry. That is the most endearing quality about Swamiji. He does not take Himself seriously. In fact, to an outsider He appears to be a very humourous and well informed person. A gentle lion, but it is only when one has experienced, first hand His powers and the grace of Ma Mookambika that flows through Him, that one realises His greatness and spiritual strength.

UNCONDITIONAL FAITH

I strolled about and met Murli who was glad that I could make it. Yatin Dosa was also with him. I had been wanting to meet Yatin and get his experiences with Devi and Swamiji. We found ourselves a comfortable spot and I switched on the dictaphone.

"You are on, Yatin."

"I can still recall the dark days of 1998. The world around me was crumbling. There was great stress and strain in my life and the mind was utterly disturbed. I was completely lost and carrying the burden of numerous problems. No matter where I looked at, there seemed to be no way out. Hope was an elusive goal.

"It was under these circumstances and background that one day I poured my heart out to my friend Samir Sanghvi, who in turn suggested that I should meet his colleague Murli. I was on the verge of a nervous breakdown and I must confess that I was even contemplating taking my own life. Murli asked me to be patient and not to give up hope. And as a faith-building exercise, he suggested that I meet his Guruji.

"I sensed a powerful current in the air, the very first moment I had my darshan of Guruji. Immediately, I could feel the vibrations of energy transfer between our bodies. And then His holiness began to reveal things about my life that He could never have known. The events and incidents of my past life were like an open book and already known to Guruji and the pin-point accuracy with which He was revealing my past moved me to tears. Next, Guruji gave me some basic talk on philosophy and put life in its correct perspective. He explained to me in great detail what life was all about. And with that Guruji kindly gave me His blessings.

"On returning home, I discussed this whole episode with my wife and urged her to accompany me when I next met Guruji. Here I must say that my wife was never a great believer in religion nor did she visit temples. The next day we went together to meet Guruji and to my utter surprise, my wife was totally capitivated by Guruji and later she confessed that she had similar experiences like mine. Swamiji suggested that we do a few poojas and religious ceremonies. But at no stage did He make any kind of material demands on us. He emphasized that at times, life is like a disease. Some can be remedied immediately and for others you need medicine and doctors.

"Very soon we started visiting Guruji in Bangalore and at the Subramaniya temple near Mangalore. We participated in all the religious ceremonies and the regular rituals of havans. Even when I had a bypass operation in the year 2000, my condition was considered hopeless by most of the medical fraternity. But surprisingly after Guruji's divine intervention, I was on my feet within three days, much to the shock of my doctors and well wishers.

"Once again, in the year 2001, I contracted this rare ailment of pulmonary vein thrombosis and I was 90% dead and gone, because the medical specialists were not able to diagnose my condition. The doctors had given up all hope. But Guruji opined that I will survive this ordeal and advised me to go ahead with certain high risk injections. I must say that the hospital fraternity were very caring, helpful and cooperative but I am convinced that if I am alive and kicking today it is largely due to Guruji, who has given me a second life."

Actually what took place is really fascinating. Yatin was 90% on the other side, with Angels, all ready with harps and horns and he, in all probability rekindling ties with near and dear ones, passed over long time ago. The doctors were all concentrating on his heart and they were on the verge of operating him, when Yatin dialled Swamiji's number, to keep Him updated and seek His blessings before the operation. But Swamiji stunned Yatin when He told him that the real problem was not in the heart but in the lungs. He told Yatin to insist with the doctors that they check his lungs, as He suspected water congestion.

When Yatin spoke to his doctors, that a certain Swamiji, sitting in Bangalore, without any medical knowledge insisted that the real problem was not in the heart but elsewhere, his doctors understandably did not take the advice very sportingly. Apart from hitting the roof with utter shock, they insisted that if Yatin kept believing such advice he would in all probability be rather too dead, to read the morning paper. Yatin stuck to his guns and said that he did not mind wagering his life but he had firm faith in Swamiji. The doctors realised that Yatin could give a mule an inferiority complex where stubbornness was concerned and decided to humour him and then go about cutting his heart and performing their jobs. After the tests they got the results and to their horror Swamiji was bang on dot. The doctors and specialits were so stunned and amazed, that in the end they insisted on speaking to Swamiji on the phone and asked for more details regarding Yatin's health. Swamiji further advised them that a particular medication to thin Yatin's blood was now doing more harm than good, as there was a case of overdose. They checked this claim and realised that Swamiji's prediction on this count was also accurate. Thanks to Him, our friend Yatin still lives to tell the tale. In fact after being given a second life, Yatin has slowly begun to move more into spirituality and to his horror, once in a while, has even begun to predict on and off the future of strangers and friends. Strange are the ways of Ma Mookambika.

Sunit arrived and He fell at Swamiji's feet. Sunit's greatest strength lies in his faith and total surrender to his Gurus. Be it Ma Mookambika, Swamiji or Sai Baba of Shirdi, he has totally left his lot at Their feet. Very often Baba has given him directions, which at first defied logic, but not once has he faltered and the outcome has been astonishingly accurate and favourable. Always Baba has been right, but what looms out is Sunit's total surrender and faith.

After a while, Swamiji told both of us to go and pay our obeisance to Devi. We entered the small mandap and bowed to the Universal Mother, this time in the form of Ma Ambe. Lalit and Ranjana greeted us with a smile and the latter called me over.

"You came in a little late. A miracle took place right in front of our eyes." She spoke with eyes sparkling. Obviously whatever had transpired earlier on had left a lasting impression on Ranjana. "You see, in this havan, to light the holy fire, we are not allowed to take any artificial help. No matches or lighters etc are to be used. The priests have to rub two sticks of wood and from that start the holy fire. The priests had been at it for a long time with no success. In fact, they had really tried hard, but without any result. We thought that all was lost. If the fire cannot be started, obviously there cannot be any *havan*. Swamiji, all this while stood and watched the proceedings. When at last we thought all was lost, Swamiji asked for two fresh sticks of wood and told Lalit to follow Him. Then He came here and prayed to Devi. He told Her that His image and name were at stake and that She should help the fire to be kindled and started. He held the sticks for a short time and then handed them to Lalit. In fact, according to Lalit, the sticks felt hot and as though ready to burst into flames that very moment. Lalit gave the sticks to the priests and they barely rubbed them for a few seconds, when a blazing fire erupted. No smoke or anything. Directly a blazing fire. Everybody was shocked. Really the grace and power of Devi and Swamiji are tremendous. By the way Ruzbeh, doesn't Swamiji remind you of our Sai Baba?" Ranjana inquired. I gazed at Swamiji for a long time.

"Yes. He really resembles Sainath."